W9-AJZ-374

LUCY LAWLESS AND
RENEÉ O'CONNOR:

WARRIOR STARS
OF XENA

Lucy Lawless

WARRIOR STARS OF XENA

Reneé O'Connor

NIKKI STAFFORD

ECW PRESS

Copyright © ECW PRESS, 1998

All rights reserved. No part of this publication may be
reproduced, stored in a retrieval system, or transmitted
in any form by any process — electronic, mechanical,
photocopying, recording, or otherwise — without
the prior written permission of ECW PRESS.

All photographs appearing in this book are the
property of the individual or agency credited,
copyright © 1998, and are reproduced by permission.
The color section photos (*page, Top/Bottom*) are courtesy
MCA TV/ Shooting Star (1, 6, 15, 16T/B), Joan Stanco (2T, 4B, 10T, 12),
Veronica Arreola (2B), Wendy Sparks (3, 10B, 14),
Amy Putnam (4T, 9T/B), Catherine M. Wilson (5, 7T/B, 8, 11T/BL),
Joyce Bezazian (13), and Jennifer Hale (11BR).

CANADIAN CATALOGUING IN PUBLICATION DATA

Stafford, Nikki, 1973–

Lucy Lawless and Reneé O'Connor: warrior stars of Xena

Includes bibliographical references.
ISBN 1-55022-347-X

1. Lawless, Lucy, 1968– . 2. O'Connor, Reneé, 1971– . 3. Xena,
warrior princess (Television program). 4. Television actors and actresses –
New Zealand – Biography. 5. Television actors and actresses –
United States – Biography. I. Title. II. Title: Warrior stars of Xena.

PN3018.L38S72 1998   791.45'029'0922   C98-930252-0

Design and imaging by ECW Type & Art, Oakville, Ontario.
Printed by Printcrafters Inc., Winnipeg, Manitoba.

Distributed in Canada by General Distribution Services,
30 Lesmill Road, Don Mills, Ontario M3B 2T6.
Distributed in the United States by Login Publishers Consortium,
1436 West Randolph Street, Chicago, Illinois, U.S.A. 60607.
Distributed in the United Kingdom by Turnaround
Publisher Services, Unit 3 Olympia Trading Estate,
Coburg Road, Wood Green, London N2Z 6TZ

Published by ECW PRESS,
2120 Queen Street East, Suite 200,
Toronto, Ontario M4E 1E2.

www.ecw.ca/press

PRINTED AND BOUND IN CANADA

TABLE OF CONTENTS

ACKNOWLEDGEMENTS

The Xenaverse is a fascinating place, full of diverse and interesting people who are always willing to talk about the show and to offer a hand to those wishing to know more. I have a lot of people to thank for their enormous efforts in making this a great book, so here goes. I'd like to thank Debbie Cassetta, a.k.a. Mistopholees, for writing the chapter on the Meow Mix nights and for helping out whenever help was needed; Bonnie Fitzpatrick, a.k.a. Dragon Lady, for giving us permission to reprint her *Grease!* Chronicles, which she had originally posted to the mailing lists; Rita Schnepp, who graciously allowed us to reprint parts of the *Encyclopedia Xenaica*; Jeanette Atwood, for illustrating the sampling of terms; Sarah Thompson, a.k.a. LadySpice, who first introduced me to the world of online *Xena* fandom; Garry Davey, who took time from his busy schedule to talk with me about Lucy Lawless; Donald J. Frozina and his helpers, JoJo Brooks and Catherine Sincich, who squinted their way to deciphering the episode credits for me (and worked overtime to meet our deadlines doing so); Alice E. Taylor and Mil Toro, who helped me out on some last-minute chapters; and Kym Masera Taborn, Julie Ruffell, and Michael Martinez, who read the manuscript in its entirety to make this the most accurate book possible.

In Fall 1997 I asked a group of fans to fill out a questionnaire to help me with my research, and I'd like to thank those who obliged: Debbie Born, karguo, Julie McNickle, Jenny Krznarich, MelissaJB, Richard Carter Jr., Michael Martinez, Cleanthes, Jana Peterson, Acean Harty, Greg Peck, LadySpice, James Murga, Rachel Brody, Zeus, Brenda Haugeum, Sekhmet, Geoffrey Hill, Genna Lane, Shary Singer, Kirk Baldridge, JellyStar, Julie Ruffell, Erin Hunt, Rose Marie Rose, Frances, Meredith Tarr, Jo, Sara Sansone, Pam Markle, Veesa Norman, Oshram, Jeroen Niekel, JudyB, Stephanie Gugle, Michael Lynch, Hazel Wheeler, Marc Langsam, deemcee, Kennedy, dagmom, Linda Tucker, Kim R. Koller, Giana Sivertsen, Alexander Buhr, JettX, Rachel Corey, David Riquelmy, Bonnie Fitzpatrick, Cousin Liz, elinor lerner, Michelle, Jessi Albano, Kelanna Zellner, Roni: Aztec Princess, Andrea Gonzalez, Goofyde, YhakaSpinky, Danae Michaud, Johanna Weaver, Christopher M. "Buzz" Tremblay, Deb "Neuf the Goof," Sharon Sherman, Malea Thomas, Lena

Pontes, Tlachtga, John M. Kahane, Giulia96, Jason Kizer, Vrondi, Pat R., Zandis, desnos, Zapper, Ka-Wai Fu, Autolycus, Boeotian "Library Sidekick," R. Martinez, Xandrina, Tricia Moran, Cathy Hoffman, Cleya, Claudia Kortmann, Lizzy, Liz Wilson, Sherry Loeffler, Cree, Heather, Jesse Lynnae Braxton, Laine R. Lawless, BeeDrew, Michael Evans-Layng, Evelyn Varga, alpha, and Xenallison.

The book wouldn't have been the same without the photographs, and I'd like to thank the wonderful photographers who kept me amply supplied with photos: Wendy Sparks, Veronica Arreola, Joel Jackal, Joan Stanco, Cathy Hoffman, Roger Duarte, Catherine M. Wilson, Bonnie Fitzpatrick, Joyce Benzanin, Amy Putnam, and Andy Poon. Thanks, too, to the many people who wrote summaries of their *Xena*-related activities for the fan clubs and web sites chapter: Venator, ROCweb, Debbie K. Mills, Deb "Neuf the Goof" Neufell, Lana Andrews, Mary Draganis, Tom Simpson, Laura Morris, Bret Rudnick, Jan Holbrook, Beth Gern, and Kym Masera Taborn.

I'd like to thank Paul Davies for donating his expertise in Greek mythology by reviewing and supplementing the episode guides, Cary Fagan for doing the initial edit of the manuscript, and Nicola Winstanley for getting me started. A warm thank-you to Mary Draganis, who helped me out with the cover on short notice, and did a beautiful job. A special thank you to Jennifer Hale, without whom this book couldn't have been written (and I mean that!). But the biggest thanks goes to Julie Ruffell, a.k.a. Xena Torres, who taped all the episodes for me, read over the episode guides, answered any questions along the way, compiled the trivia section, and for just being one of the most devoted Xenites I've ever met.

Thanks to everyone who has written to wish me the best of luck while I was working on the book, and to those on the mailing lists, who made writing the book an absolute delight. This book is dedicated to Xenites everywhere.

LUCY
LAWLESS
BIOGRAPHY

LUCY LAWLESS

TIES THAT BIND

Xena may have been "forged in the heat of battle," as the opening of *Xena: Warrior Princess* states, but Lucy Lawless, the woman who plays her, had a very different upbringing. Or did she? Lucy became adept at horseback riding (although not in battle), she was a skilled gymnast (if somersaulting onto her parents' bed counts), and she learned to fight at an early age (although her "enemies" were limited to five brothers).

Born in New Zealand on March 29, 1968, Lucy was the fifth child for her parents, Frank and Julie Ryan, and their first daughter. Commenting on her rambunctious childhood, Lucy later said that she "lived a charmed existence. I have five brothers and one sister [a brother and sister were born after her], and my mom said I didn't know I was a girl until I was eight." Lucy would later joke about her mother's many pregnancies that she and her siblings were "a lot of traffic for one womb."

Lucy was born to a well-known couple in the Mt. Albert, New Zealand community. Her father, Frank, became the mayor of Mt. Albert in 1968 — the year Lucy was born — and remained so until 1990, when Mt. Albert was amalgamated into Auckland. (He is now a councillor for the Mt. Albert ward in Auckland.) Julie was a home-maker — a demanding job with so many children — but she was, and is, also an ardent suffragette. However, according to Lucy, being a suffragette is not the same as being a feminist. As Lucy would later tell interviewers, the equality of men and women and the idea that women could do whatever men could was taken for granted by all in the family and in her community. After all, New Zealand had been the first country in the world to extend the vote to women, in 1893.

Interviewers and fans would later be surprised by Lucy's assertion that *Xena: Warrior Princess* is not a feminist show, but her belief, as she would ardently explain, arose from her upbringing. "I'm not saying that women in New Zealand are treated better than they are anywhere else. But I am saying that we're pretty strong because it was a hard land to colonize. We've retained that get-on-with-it attitude." In other words, being assertive isn't feminist behavior, it's normal. Unlike in America, where staying at home to raise a large family might be deemed decidedly un-feminist, Lucy's mother found absolutely no contradiction in her life. To this day, she remains a very influential person in her community.

Following the tough-minded example of her mother, Lucy learned to hold her own with her older brothers. Her father recalls the play-fights the children would have with grass clippings and rotten fruit as their weapons. He remembers that Lucy "had a great throw — she's got a good strong arm. And being one of only two girls in the family, she learned early on to give as good as she got." Not only could she fight, but she and her brothers and sisters learned to do flips and somersaults that would later aid her stunts on *Xena: Warrior Princess*. "She learned to do all those flips on our bed, you know," Julie reveals. "The children would open the toilet door so they could get a

TRANZ PICTURE LIBRARY / SHOOTING STAR

good run-up, sprint through and tumble on to our bed."
One wonders how dexterous her stunts were, though,
considering her childhood nickname was Unco, short for
uncoordinated (no wonder all the flips on the show are
executed by stunt doubles!).

When Lucy was ten, her godfather gave her a pony. She developed a passion for riding, that, along with the gymnastics and the fighting, would be useful in her later career. The rotten apples she would throw would become a chakram, and the fights would include a sword. Who knew that sibling play fighting would one day pay off so well? A warrior princess was being forged — if not exactly in the heat of battle.

Although the Ryan family was large, it was very close-knit, loving, and supportive. Later, when Lucy would have trouble finding work in acting, she would come to depend on her family's strength and support-structure to get her through. As children, the Ryans would constantly play together in a rough-and-tumble fashion, but they also enjoyed many peaceful times together. Julie Ryan remembers having six or seven children join her and her husband in bed — all at the same time. Unfortunately for them, beds aren't made to hold nine people, and the weight became too much. Julie laughs that "one of the legs broke so we had to prop it up with telephone books."

Growing up in such a large family, even a loving one, life became a Darwinian survival-of-the-fittest. "You had to be pretty wily to survive, or fast," Lucy says. "And I wasn't fast so I had to be wily!" It was Lucy's desire to be noticed — a desire that is more difficult to fulfill in a large family — that first led to Lucy's love of acting. Frank and Julie remember affectionately that Lucy used to be a bit of an exhibitionist. Lucy would perform gymnastic routines, or concerts, or act for her neighbours. She and her friends would devise elaborate little shows and invite the neighbourhood. Around the house, Lucy was always the ham. She would sing, dance, make jokes, and perform all sorts of stunts, setting herself apart from her siblings, while relying on them as her audience and her source of encouragement.

Of course, it was never enough just to sing around the house; Lucy had to create a stage for her performances, and the coffee table quickly served that function. After Lucy had gathered enough people together in the room, she would leap up onto the table and begin to sing, holding a seashell as if it were a microphone. Or she would find her mother's scarves and tuck them in her leotards and transform herself into a great ballet dancer, leaping around the house. Julie remembers with a laugh, "She always wanted to be rich and famous. It was quite a joke in the family." Even at such a young age, Lucy knew she wanted to perform.

The fact that we can now watch Lucy weekly on television is largely due to Julie's cultivation of her interests in the performing arts. She began taking Lucy to plays, operas, and theatres to introduce her to the real world of performing. Lucy sat in the audience, fascinated at what she saw on stage, choosing her favorite performers. All this might seem like any other child going to the theatre with her mother. The difference was that Lucy would choose her favorite character on the stage and then imagine that she was the performer. She didn't have much longer to wait. Soon Lucy would have her chance to be on the stage performing, rather than sitting in the audience and dreaming.

Lucy would later state that growing up Catholic shaped who she became. Catholicism was an important influence in her life, as it had been for her father, who grew up in schools run by the nuns and monseigneurs. Although her father's Catholic upbringing had been a strict one, he did not put the same pressure on his own children.

"My family was pretty liberal, very trusting," Lucy says of her Irish-Catholic parents. "My mother and father knew well enough not to keep us in a stranglehold. It just forces your kids underground with their behaviour." Yet Lucy was still very much affected by Catholicism and attended church at least once a week until she was 18 years old.

Part of her religious obedience lay in her fascination with the theatrical aspects of Catholicism. She went to church and sat in the congregation watching the priest's rituals, the praying, the singing, the communion, much as she had watched plays with her mother. She especially found the "Hail Mary" prayer to be a dramatic experience, one that was all too real to a young girl. She later explained these early emotions to a radio interviewer: "I mean, when you are six and you talk about death, you go, 'Oh my God, I'm gonna die.' You talk about your own death, repeatedly and . . . it made me in a hurry, it made me in an awful hurry . . . to achieve. To soak [up] as much life as I could." Perhaps these early thoughts have led to the lively and vivacious person that Lucy is today.

Except for two years in a public school, Lucy attended Catholic schools until she went to university. When discussing her time in the Catholic school system, Lucy modestly says, "I discovered how cool it was to be a dunce, because you could get away with so much by just pretending to be a dummy." However, her parents tell a very different story. Frank boasts that "she topped her form in her seventh year at Wesley Intermediate. That was the first time we recognized she had the ability to excel in whatever she chose to do." Lucy was also voted the girl "most likely to succeed," a prophetic declaration if ever there was one.

Lucy was a popular girl at school with both boys and girls. Her lively and funny behaviour, which has endeared her to so many fans, drew people even then. It was this same outgoing attitude that got her a part in her first play at about the age of ten. After years of watching plays and wishing she was onstage, Lucy would now be one of the performers.

The role was a small one, but oddly suitable for an actor who would one day play an evil warrior. Based on the Biblical story of the prodigal son, it dramatized the tale of a boy who was loved by all but decided to leave his family for many years. When he finally returned home again, the villagers shunned him until he eventually won them over. "I was the woman who met him on the road and stiffed him out of his coins and clothes," Lucy laughs, adding, "that felt really good."

The part might have been modest, but it was the start of Lucy's acting career. Part way through the performance, she stood in the school hallway and thought, "I really like this." At last she was no longer the spectator; she was the performer.

As Lucy advanced into the Marist Sisters College, she continued to act in plays, taking the lead roles in five productions, which included *South Pacific*, *The Mikado*, and *The Pirates of Penzance*. By appearing in a stage musical and the Gilbert and Sullivan operettas, Lucy was able to develop her skills in her second love, singing. Lucy had always had a good singing voice, but now she had moved beyond standing on coffee tables and singing into seashells. This was the real thing.

At the college, Lucy excelled in every activity. Besides acting and singing regularly, she was made head girl at the college, and she continued to be popular with everyone, especially the boys. Frank remembers, "She'd get all the telephone calls, but I'm happy to say she was always treated with greater respect. There was no nonsense, and we were never let down by her." Perhaps the respect she received from the opposite sex would contribute to her later surprise about *Xena: Warrior Princess* being deemed a feminist show.

Lucy learned to handle herself with grace and intelligence while at the college. Her mother recalls, "I remember one of the mothers saying Lucy was never a child. She was always grown up in her manner." Despite being mature throughout public school, Lucy was like most other children in not knowing what she wanted to be when she really grew up. She considered becoming a marine biologist, because she thought the name was interesting, and she thought about becoming a pathologist because, she now laughs, "Quincy MD was one . . . God knows what a pathologist does." Lucy had many interests and wasn't about to rush into a decision about her future career.

However, when she began appearing in musicals, Lucy's main career interest turned to opera. Again, her mother Julie stepped in to nurture her interests. Lucy says her father was the one who told her that she could do anything she set her mind to, but it was her mother who helped her fulfill her dreams and "fired the creative side" for her. When Lucy was 15, Julie took her daughter on an opera tour of Europe, a very special and rare gift indeed. It awakened within Lucy a true love of the musical genre, as well as the travelling bug, to which she would later succumb.

Lucy began taking singing lessons, specifically training her voice for the demands of opera. Although she enjoyed singing immensely, after a few years she realized that becoming an opera singer was not in her future. After grappling with the idea of quitting, Lucy simply realized one day that she did not have the passion nor the patience that opera singing demanded. She had begun opera lessons because of the "same bug to perform" that had sparked her love of acting. "I had a certain rough talent for it," Lucy says, "but I never developed it because I simply didn't have enough love for music and the kind of boring life that you have to have."

She still loved singing, however, and in 1986 she enrolled in Auckland University, specializing in languages and opera. While at the university, Lucy landed a part in a local television commercial, which helped her to keep alive her acting interest while studying at the university. However, despite her love of opera and new languages — she is fluent in both German and French and can speak Italian — her third great interest took over. Lucy couldn't forget the trip she had taken with her mother only two years earlier. The travelling instinct had taken hold, and Lucy decided to follow it. In 1987, using the money she had made in the commercial, she left for Europe.

THE ROYAL COUPLE
OF GOLDMINERS

Lucy says that her decision to leave for Europe was spurred on by a need to escape her "claustrophobic family," but it appears that she did not mean they were stifling her. With six siblings and two parents to whom she was very close, Lucy found it very difficult to ever have time to herself or to be completely independent. So she set off for Lucerne, Switzerland, only to discover that it didn't quite have what she was looking for.

"When I got to Lucerne," Lucy recalls, "I found out it was a really upstanding, moral place. It's not the sort of place you go to have a cathartic, teenage rebellion at all." She stuck it out for a while, but soon left for Germany to sample the truly Bohemian experience. There Lucy got her first taste of independence, and realized for the first time in her life what it was like to be alone. She began running out of money — "I lived on coffee and cigarettes until I was skeletal" — but being in a strange place, she could not ask for help and she was too proud to ask her parents for more money.

Lucy began going to plays, as she had with her mother, but these were very different from the ones she had seen a couple of years before. Her lack of funds limited her to free plays in the park, and some were pretty awful. Lucy remembers a particularly surreal one in which the actors were "whacking each other over the head with big mutton chops and screaming about the plague. I sat there, watched it a while, and decided that I wasn't as miserable as I thought."

Lucy was not to be alone much longer. She soon met up with Garth Lawless, a New Zealander she had met at a bar called Club Mirage, where she had once waitressed and he had been the bartender. They became a couple and began touring Europe together for almost a year before running out of money. Instead of going home to New Zealand, though, Lucy and Garth stopped at Australia and decided to make enough money there to allow them to return to Europe, or more specifically, Russia. In Kalgoorlie, Australia, they took a job that sets Lucy's background apart from any other actress of her status: she became a gold miner.

Mining in Kalgoorlie was hard work, but even harder was Lucy's growing discomfort with what was happening to the landscape. "They detonate miles of Outback, and we used to run through the Outback, marking it and taking samples," Lucy explains. "These days, they assay gold in parts per billion, so you could take four kilos of dirt and they would find some molecule of gold and say, 'Yeah, that's worth open cast mining.' " In her time spent at Kalgoorlie, Lucy contends, "I never saw any gold in the ground there."

Whenever she is asked about this, Lucy tries to dispel the exciting conception that some people have about mining. "People seem to have some romantic notion of what gold mining is, like you're down there with the seven dwarfs with little lamps on their heads chipping bits of gold out of rock. Reality is drilling a deep hole and pouring

Lucy in New York
AMY PUTNAM

in explosives." Every chance she gets, Lucy still makes a point of letting people know the irreparable environmental damage that mining causes.

Although she was making the money she needed to travel to Russia, Lucy soon found out that being a miner could be as lonely as travelling in Europe alone. She and Garth had to be separated for periods at a time. Lucy laughs, "I was living in the Outback with a cat called Basil, kangaroos, and emus. I wouldn't see anybody for weeks at a time."

Even in Australia, where, as in New Zealand, the difference in status between men and women isn't as pronounced as in North America, the ratio of women to men miners was about 1 to 50. She insists that she never had any trouble at all, mainly because she didn't flirt with any of the men or signal that she wanted anything out of them, and they respected that. "You don't want a pack of randy miners on your tail, believe me," Lucy jokes. And besides, she was pretty quick with her tongue, too: "There's nothing a man could say to me that I wouldn't be able to give back for, I don't think, short of physical violence." It would seem that Lucy was more like Gabrielle than Xena in those days, talking her way out of situations rather than fighting.

As Lucy and Garth continued mining, they earned more and more money until they were ready to head back to Europe. However, just as they were about to buy their plane tickets to Russia, they discovered something that would change both of their lives forever. Lucy was pregnant.

The pregnancy was an absolute surprise to both of them, and the trip to Russia was cancelled. Instead, Garth and Lucy got married. Three months pregnant and only nineteen years old, Lucy Ryan stood in a cold cement building — "I've always hated cement blocks" — in a registry office. No one from her large family was there to see her get married, and none of her friends could attend the "event." Lucy wore her sixth-form ball dress instead of the white satin bridal gown that many girls dream of. To this day Lucy can't remember why she even had that ball dress with her in Europe and Australia, and even though it was the nicest thing she could wear, it didn't fit her properly because of her pregnancy. With screaming children surrounding them and witnesses the couple hardly knew, Lucy pledged her love to Garth. Lucy Ryan became Lucy Lawless as the two began their ill-fated life together. There wasn't even a cake. Even so, Lucy was happy at the prospect of being a mother and the cancelled trip to Russia was quickly forgotten.

Garth and Lucy happily returned to New Zealand and

adjusted to married life together. Garth landed a job as a bartender, and Lucy returned to acting. It was then that she realized that her new married name sounded like an arrogant stage moniker. As she buried her face in her hands, she sobbed that no one would ever take her seriously again. Later she would realize what a perfect name it was for a warrior princess.

Lucy began looking for work but realized that it wasn't her name that was holding her back, it was her look. Lucy was tall — very tall for a woman at 5′10″ — she had a lot of problems obtaining roles. Because she didn't have the look that New Zealand producers wanted, she couldn't get jobs in theatre, film or television, other than in commercials. Lucy's mother recalls, "It was very tough for her trying to get work in New Zealand productions. They seem to have a set group of people they use all the time. And besides, with Lucy's height, she needs a leading man about seven feet tall!" Lucy's father, Frank, also recalls this low point in Lucy's acting career: "I can remember a time when she was crying on my shoulder, sobbing, 'I'm trying so hard but I can't get a break!'"

That break was yet to come, but for now she had to focus on becoming a mother. Later in the year, Lucy and Garth became proud parents of a baby girl, Daisy. To this day Daisy is the most important person in Lucy's life, and while the warrior character she plays on *Xena: Warrior Princess* isn't exactly the maternal type, Lucy is very much a proud and devoted mother. Having Daisy also gave Lucy the confidence that she needed to go out and get a part, and she decided that nothing was going to stop her. She was going to be an actress.

The same week that she had Daisy, Lucy videotaped a group of skits to use as a portfolio. (Anyone who has had children knows what an astonishing feat this was.) She was then able to use the video as a résumé for any potential acting jobs. Although any *Xena* fan would do just about anything to catch a glimpse of the material on these tapes, Lucy says that while the tapes make her proud, they are very private. "They're kind of embarrassing," she admits, "but they are really funny. At least they show somebody who has the guts to get out and do something really hideous just to make it happen!" They also show Lucy's creative side, for she not only acted in the skits and taped them herself, but she also wrote them.

The first acting jobs that Lucy got were in television commercials. Many New Zealanders may remember her as the young mother in commercials for the Auckland Savings Bank. In 1989 she gained some fame that took little acting ability: she was crowned Mrs. New Zealand. However, in 1990, she got her first big break with a television comedy troupe called Funny Business. By acting with this group of people for a couple of seasons (1990 and 1991), Lucy not only got herself noticed, but she also developed her comedic skills — skills which reveal her brilliant comic talents to this day with such characters on *X:WP* as Meg, Leah, and even Xena herself.

While Lucy enjoyed working with the troupe, it wasn't what she wanted to do for the rest of her life. She was developing her comedic skills, but she wasn't able to explore any other sides of her acting. What she needed was proper training, so that she would have the versatility to earn some substantial roles in television and film. Lucy began looking into possibilities and decided to train at a school in Canada which had been mentioned to her by a woman she'd met in Europe. In mid-1991, she picked up her family and left for Vancouver, British Columbia.

At the William Davis Centre for Actors Study in Vancouver, Lucy was able to cultivate her acting skills beyond comedy. The centre first opened its doors in 1989, although William B. Davis (known to *X-Files* fans as Cigarette

Smoking Man) had been training actors such as Donald Sutherland and Blair Brown since the mid-1960s. Davis trains students for television and theatre, but the emphasis of the school isn't on helping students get quick jobs, but to giving them a solid base in acting technique. Full-time students are enrolled into an intense program which focuses on four main themes: working with the physical body and voice, reading texts of plays, scene study, and developing skills for the camera. Shakespeare plays are core texts, but each student must also do a rehearsal project based on modern playwrights such as Chekhov. The William Davis Centre is one of the few acting schools where every student is personally auditioned to judge her or his potential, and the enrollment is kept very small — a maximum of 10 students is enrolled at one time. The program is a demanding eight months, running from September to mid-May, culminating in a large production performed for the public.

Garry Davey at the William Davis Centre for Actors Study

ANDY POON

One of Lucy's teachers at the centre, Garry Davey, has been a teacher there since it opened, and he is now the artistic director of the school. When asked if he can remember her, he says she left quite an impression on him: "She was quite a leader, and she took a lot of initiative in everything she did." He remembers that she had a "big-ness" about her work and that her very presence was always noticed when she was around. When she walked into a room "it would be like, 'I'm here. What's going on? Let's make something happen.' "

Davey taught her scene study and he remembers two particular scenes in which he was directing her. In *Crimes of the Heart* she played a woman whose sister is trying to commit suicide by putting her head in the oven. The scene was so big because Lucy could play comedy and tragedy all at once, which was perfect for this play. He says that he was reminded of her recently while watching a television biography on Jack Lemmon. "They were interviewing Walter Matthau, I think it was, and he said about Jack Lemmon, 'He brings a sense of tragedy to his comic work and a sense of comedy to his tragic work.' Now I think that that should be said of any great actor, but with Lucy it was especially noticeable." His favorite story involves directing Lucy in a scene from Lanford Wilson's *Ludlow Fair*, where she had to play a girl who never gets a date. The one time she does, she becomes sick but is still determined to go through with it. Most actors Davey has directed "would come out sniffling," but Lucy came out looking just awful, with her hair a mess and looking sick, "but she had this stuf-fing between her toes as if she were desperately trying to paint her nails at the same time! She had just gone the dis-tance to create this poor person." He adds that she was a great comic actor and "her sense of humor is always an impor-tant part of her work." He laughs that he can't remember her doing a straight dramatic role while at the school.

Lucy didn't stay at the centre very long — in fact, she only completed six months of the eight because she had to return to New Zealand — but Davey says the centre definitely considers her a graduate because of her fine work while there, and states that she definitely would have graduated with her class had she stayed. Lucy eventually landed the part of Xena soon after William Davis had won his role on *The X-Files*, and the two still remain in touch. Davey muses, "They must share a little bit of wonderment and say to each other, 'Hey, it happened.'" While many of the students who come out of the school are talented, Lucy is the most well known. Davey tells his students that acting jobs don't just come along and that it generally takes five to ten years to make a mark. But with Lucy, "she was just at the right place at the right time."

Davey has seen her on *X:WP* and says he likes watching the show for Lucy's sense of humor, and knowingly adds that "it wouldn't be Xena if it wasn't Lucy." He laughs that she was a blonde when she attended the school, but he likes her dark hair on the show, saying it makes her appear "darker and stronger." Happy that Lucy has become a star, he remembers her distinctly as someone who could make things happen. "She is always enjoying people and loves to be around them."

Lucy would later recall her time in Vancouver fondly, saying that "by the time I came home in 1992, I felt like I had received some very fine training that will always sustain me. It's stuff that works and I don't hesitate passing it on to others." Despite Davey's vivid memories of her comic sensibilities, the training she received garnered her roles that demanded dramatic rather than comedic talent. She appeared in episodes of *Ray Bradbury Theatre*, *The Adventures of the Black Stallion*, and a made-for-television movie, *The Sinking of the Rainbow Warrior*. The wide variety of parts allowed for an extended training period for Lucy, where she could "practise" her newly learned acting skills.

Lucy was appearing in many American television shows because she was told she did not have a "typical New Zealand look," whatever that may be. It was during this time that she perfected her American accent, which she performs so well on *Xena*, although many fans of the show delight in hearing her slip-ups ("Spiduh . . . sand spiduh"). But despite all the American shows she did during this period, it seemed as if she also auditioned for every part that was available in New Zealand, except for *Shortland Street*, a New Zealand soap opera. "[They] wouldn't have me. Which is kind of cool now," Lucy smiles. "*Shortland Street* said that I did not fit sufficiently within the parameters of their show. I'm sure they were quite right, too."

In 1992, however, she won a steady television job that gained her more exposure in her home country than ever before. Co-hosting *Air New Zealand Holiday* allowed her to use some of her acting skills — many more than audiences suspected — while travelling to exotic locations. The show was designed as a visual travel guide to many places around the world, and Lucy would report on the destinations and recommend them to the viewers. Unfortunately — and here's where her acting talents came into play — she wasn't allowed to be completely honest, and if the location was one of the most hideous spots on earth, she was still paid to stand and smile and recommend it to all of her viewers.

"You'd really want to say, 'Wow. Don't go there. It's crappy!'" Lucy remembers with a wince. She sometimes got stuck "with some God-awful Nazi of a guide in some country." And all the travel meant that she was away from her family for periods of time. Although she admits that she had a lot of fun on the show, she realized that the stint wasn't furthering her acting career and she quit. She has no doubt that giving up a secure job was the right decision.

"I was either going to become a big fish in a small pond or risk it all. So I gave it up, even though there was nothing in sight." She left the show in 1993. And right decision it was, for the following year she would get the break of her lifetime. She would be discovered by Sam Raimi and Robert Tapert.

DESTINY

In 1994, fans of Robert Tapert and Sam Raimi's work got their first taste of Lucy Lawless when she appeared as the fierce Amazonian warrior, Lysia, in the television movie *Hercules and the Amazon Women*. Neither her character nor the underlying story of the show — that Amazonian women were created out of a rebellion against being treated like domestic servants — foreshadowed the arrival of a character like Xena, in whose world men and women are more or less equal. In this film, Hercules is a sexist who learns the error of his ways through these women. The character of Lysia was suited to Lucy's tall frame, and although she doesn't have many lines, she does leave a memorable impression on the audience. But, like all one-off parts, the character was soon finished, and Lucy had to find other roles. In 1995, she played a bisexual role in *Peach*, a short film that has been watched and analysed many times by the ardent *Xena* subtext fans. *Peach* is a strange little film that lasts about sixteen minutes and was directed by Christine Parker. Lucy plays a woman of few words, but one whose very presence teaches a young girl to seize the day before it passes. While Lucy's acting isn't up to the standards she possesses today, the visuals in this film are quite beautiful, and the metaphor of a fresh peach is very clever. She also appeared in episodes of the television shows *High Tide* and *Marlin Bay*. It was obvious that Lucy's talents were beginning to show themselves to casting directors, as she had earned several very different roles in the three years since attending the William Davis Centre for Actors Study. Yet the woman who would one day play Xena, the Warrior Princess, left the most lasting impression on the people who had produced *Hercules and the Amazon Women*. Lucy auditioned for a role in their new television series, *Hercules: The Legendary Journeys*, and in the episode "As Darkness Falls," she earned the role of Lyla, a girl who is labelled a tramp and an outcast because she befriends a group of centaurs. Although Lyla isn't a very positive character to begin with — she attempts to seduce Hercules and gives him a drink that causes blindness — eventually she and Deric, a centaur, decide not to kill him, and the two leave the village, to live where their bi-speciel relationship will be accepted. After playing Xena on the show, Lucy would show up again in the second season as Lyla again, and Hercules and Salmoneus would joke that Lyla looked remarkably like Xena. But after she finished filming "As Darkness Falls," Lucy had to hunt once again for her next role.

Meanwhile, the producers of *H:TLJ* decided to introduce a female character for a three-episode arc. She would be Xena, an evil warrior princess who tries to kill Hercules but fails and dies in the third episode of the arc. Rob Tapert, one of the creators of the character, says Xena was based on an evil princess in kung fu movies played by cult film star Lin Ching Hsia. Lucy tried out for the part, but was turned down. Instead, they chose actress Vanessa Angel, who was best known for her work on *Weird Science*. Lucy had been appearing in many shows at this time, and the hectic schedule was taking its toll on her. When she received the rejection call, she decided it was time to get away and arranged a camping trip for her family.

Meanwhile, Angel began her training for the show and had a few difficulties learning the kung fu routines mandatory for Xena's character. The producers were nevertheless convinced that they had chosen the right actress, until Angel suddenly became sick and was unable to film the shows. The other actresses who had initially tried out for the part were called back, but all of them were busy and no longer interested. Even so, when Lucy's name was tossed around as a possibility, the producers were wary.

Lucy was not an American, and Xena *had* to be an American, as far as they were concerned. She had also appeared so recently as Lyla that they worried viewers would recognize her too readily, ruining the credibility of the character. However, everyone agreed that she would nonetheless make a great Xena, and when five actresses turned down the role, the executives had to come up with someone fast. In desperation they tried to call Lucy to offer her the part. But she'd taken their rejection to heart and was incommunicado on her camping trip. No one knew exactly where.

"When the call came I was on holiday, fighting the flu, trying to give my daughter the camping experience," Lucy says. They were in the middle of nowhere, right outside "some Podunk town"; Lucy can't even remember the name. She and Garth were taking one last shot at a marriage that had gradually been deteriorating. Lucy's constant acting roles had given her less time to be at home, and the separations were taking a toll on the marriage. They were also starting to realize that they were never meant to be married. As they were sharing a miserable weekend with their daughter, Lucy's casting agent tracked down Garth's family and was passed on to Lucy's cousin, who knew the area in which she was camping. Meanwhile, Lucy had purchased a copy of the local paper, and laughingly read out her horoscope: "Fame and fortune await you. Overseas

Kevin Sorbo with Lucy Lawless
JOAN STANCO

travel. This could be the big one. You'll get a call from overseas." The next day, a call was passed on to Lucy offering her the part of Xena. As the horoscope said, it was the big one.

As Lucy boarded the plane to return to New Zealand immediately, she had no idea that this part would be any different from the others. She would be appearing in three episodes of the show — until that point the most she'd gotten from one part was two episodes — but after that, as far as she knew, the search for another part would continue.

When she arrived on the set the following day, there was little time to prepare for the part before filming began. The hair and makeup artists immediately came up with a look for Xena. With blonde hair and blue eyes, she would be a menacing little tigress. But Lucy had visions of her hair all falling out from too much peroxide and came up with a better idea: she would have black hair, and would look more Argentinian than Californian. Lucy's light-brown hair was dyed black, and her naturally pale skin was bronzed with paint. Lucy modestly exaggerates that the color of Xena's hair is the only input on the character she has ever given.

Next came the physical training, but unlike her predecessor, Lucy picked up the moves without any problem. Because she had developed her horse-riding and fighting skills as a little girl, Lucy was a natural for the physical aspects of the role. The difficulty was playing someone who was evil as well, but Lucy was about to show the world how wide her range could be.

As said earlier, Xena was supposed to die at the end of the three-episode arc, and had Angel actually been able to play Xena, that would have been the case because Angel had other commitments. When the producers saw Lucy's portrayal of the warrior princess, however, they were so impressed that they immediately started talking about a spinoff. If they rewrote the ending to the final episode of the arc, leaving her alive, they could spin her off onto her own series, using her dark past as the basis for the show. Lucy thought the producers were kidding around when they approached her with the offer of her own series, but when she realized they were serious, she accepted immediately. The other episodes were re-written.

During the week of March 15, 1995, Xena appeared in

the ninth episode of *H:TLJ* in "Warrior Princess," where she tricks Hercules and Iolaus and threatens to break up their relationship. The episode ends with one of those "I'll be back" clichés and the response to the episode was so positive that the producers knew they had made the right decision about the new show. "The Gauntlet," in which Xena's army turns against her, and "Unchained Heart," in which Xena joins forces with Hercules to fight her ex-lieutenant, Darphus, were the twelfth and thirteenth episodes of the season. After the three episodes aired, the staff of *Hercules: The Legendary Journeys* was inundated with letters from fans saying how much they loved this new character. The executives knew they had a possible hit on their hands with the new spinoff. Here, finally, was a strong woman on television who was not ogled or made subservient to anyone. Nor was she perfect. Filming began immediately on the newest syndicated series on television, *Xena: Warrior Princess*. Little did everyone know that this show would surpass *Hercules* — and every other syndicated show — in popularity.

THE WARRIOR PRINCESS

Starring as Xena, the Warrior Princess, Lucy couldn't believe where her life had taken her. "Never in my wildest dreams did I ever think that I'd be female action hero," she says. "I thought I'd be doing Shakespeare." Instead of Elizabethan dresses, Lucy's costume consists of a tight leather outfit with a skirt of little leather straps and is adorned with metal breast-plates. Running around the New Zealand countryside in that outfit would be uncomfortable at the best of times, but many of the days are cold and wet, which makes filming even more arduous.

To prepare for the part, Lucy underwent intense kung fu training in Los Angeles with Doug Wong, the kung-fu master who trained Jason Scott Lee for *The Bruce Lee Story*. As producer Eric Gruendemann said during the first season, "This is the most physically demanding show for any woman on television," and the fact that Lucy was entirely up to the task strengthened the convictions of the casting agents that they had made the right choice in Lucy. Granted, Lucy doesn't do all the stunts. As she openly explains, "If you don't see my face, it's a good chance it's not me, we simply don't have time to use me in every scene. As well, some things are too dangerous." However, Lucy still performs many of the stunts, and is able to accomplish more of them as she progresses. Although at first she was worried that her childhood uncoordination would haunt her into adulthood, she soon became better at the stunts, and stunt doubles were necessary only to accomplish the really dangerous maneuvers and to speed up the filming process. If Xena's face isn't seen, the director can use a stunt double while Lucy films dialogue scenes. Although the stunt people are used to make sure that none of the actors get seriously hurt, they couldn't prevent Lucy from taking a couple of punches in her own scenes. Once she got a black eye, and she later laughed that "the makeup department took a Polaroid in case they ever need to replicate a shiner."

The producers did an excellent job of promoting the new show by having Xena appear on *H:TLJ* and by showing previews of *X:WP* during *Herc* episodes. As a result, *X:WP* was successful from the outset. Almost all the initial viewers were also *Herc* fans and the pilot of *X:WP*, "Sins of the Past," was so well done that the show was destined to hold onto many of those viewers. The cast of the show all agree that Xena had to become good because fans prefer to identify with a hero, yet it was precisely Xena's dark side that excited the fans so much. Besides, if fans demand a heroine with pure morals, they would always have Gabrielle to turn to.

Lucy was — and is — very proud of the character she is playing full-time. Comparing her to the working woman of the 90s, she believes that people easily identify with Xena because she stands up for good. "There are a lot of people out there who have suffered from some kind of abuse — women, gays, kids — and they all relate to Xena." Xena has a universal appeal because she isn't all good or all evil, but human. Lucy puts it best when she sympathetically states that "the devil's in her gut and the angel's in her heart, and her head has to get the two together."

X:WP was becoming a success, and Lucy was becoming a star. However, things were not all rosy in Lucy's life. In June of 1995, right before *X:WP* first aired, Lucy and Garth split up. The couple realized they had gotten married too young, and although they'd been married for almost eight years, they knew it wasn't going to work. The strain on the marriage had become too much.

The most difficult part was having to tell Daisy, who was seven at the time. Because she was so young, Lucy found it difficult to explain to her what was happening. For a long time, Daisy hated her mother's new show because she thought it was the cause of her parents' separation. Considering the show was being filmed at the same time as the separation, Daisy's misunderstanding was hardly a surprising one. However, Lucy and Garth gave her a lot of their time and attention during this difficult period, rather than just focusing on themselves and hurting the child more, which is all too common in divorce. They agreed that Daisy would spend weekdays with her father and weekends with her mother and both parents lived only a few blocks from one another to help her through the transition. Lucy learned to keep her problems to herself, even though going through the divorce while being a working mother was the hardest thing she'd ever done. "You feel like you're losing your kid and can't defend yourself," she says sadly. "Even your kid thinks you don't care. At times I've had to suppress my natural urge to fight back and say my piece." As busy as Lucy is, she, Garth, and Daisy are still in counselling to ensure that their relationship will remain a civil one.

Although Daisy has come to enjoy *X:WP*, at first she was very ambivalent about it. Lucy understood what she was going through, and how Daisy, "a very private little girl," disliked the children at school talking about her mother playing Xena. As with many other children of celebrities, Daisy learned that she had to "share" her mother with fans worldwide and no one who has not had that experience can possibly imagine what it must be like, especially for one so young. Lucy was horrified to discover that as Daisy left the house with her father one day, her photo was taken by a tabloid journalist who stuck his camera into the car. When Garth was offered money by another tabloid to spill the beans on his ex-wife, he flatly refused.

Now Lucy always lets Daisy know how singularly special she is to her. More comfortable with her mother's fame, Daisy occasionally accompanies Lucy to public appearances. Lucy explains, "I try to stick close to her in a crowd, keep a hand on her shoulder, so she knows she's preferred and not usurped. She's happy these days." So happy that she made an appearance on an episode of *H:TLJ* with her mother. It was a special moment for Lucy, who once told an interviewer, "I consider myself a hard-working mother who wishes she could be with her daughter more often." The combination of two understanding and loving parents and a mature little girl allowed the divorce to be as painless as it could have been.

Meanwhile, *X:WP* was on the upswing and Lucy was

quickly becoming a star. The cast and crew got along well and inside jokes began creeping into the episodes. Lucy tells how many of the characters and the things they say are based on people that the writers and the actors actually know. "Every now and then a line that my father recognizes well will come out of Xena's mouth." In fact, she says a lot of Xena's character is based on her older brother, Tim, especially what has come to be known as "the Xena look." "Sometimes when I see her doing that sneer, I see my oldest brother so clearly," Lucy says. "It's just his face when he was an angry young man." Tim had been the brother Lucy had argued with the most when they were young, but he appears to be her closest family tie.

Tim is now a goldminer in Australia. Lucy's other siblings have also found careers that have taken them around the globe. One is a money manager in London, England, two are plumbers in Auckland, and another is a builder. Soon after *X:WP* began airing, Lucy had her house remodelled and her tradesman brothers did the work — Lucy wouldn't have had it any other way. Lucy's only sister went to Amsterdam to study languages and works in Holland as a translator. Back home, Lucy's parents love the show, and her mother — ever the suffragette — likes it because Lucy "gets to give the boys as good as she gets." They are both proud not only of her work but of the way she has handled her ever-growing fame and popularity.

As *X:WP* became more popular, the media started to catch on and began analysing the show — an inevitability for any program that tackles "issues." Writers began calling it revisionist and feminist, labels which confused Lucy, who had been raised to assume that women were supposed to be tough and to hold their own. At the end of the first season, Lucy participated in a now-infamous *Ms.* magazine interview. This feature was the first major piece to refer to the show as feminist and although it contained many errors when referring to specific episodes, it was an interesting exploration of why *X:WP* had become such a popular television show. However, it referred to Lucy as "defensive" when she answered the question asking if she thought *X:WP* was a feminist show, and added numerous exclamation marks to her responses to make them seem as if Lucy didn't know what feminism was: "No, I don't! Well . . . yes, it is. But it is not anti-men!" Lucy went on to reply intelligently that in New Zealand "women are not disadvantaged, except by their own fear." When Lucy told the interviewer that as a child she never felt that a female superhero was missing in her life — perhaps referring to her mother — the interviewer wrote as an aside, "Good thing she's a good actor."

While the article was one of the first to start the trend of seeing *X:WP* as the ultimate feminist television show, it contradicted itself by making Lucy look strange for thinking that women should be strong naturally. Soon after the interview was published, Lucy was quoted in *The Listener* harshly denouncing the article's implications. "I feel that they are objectifying me . . . they think that I'm a counter-Barbie Barbie. Well, f—— you. Don't set me up as television's gladiator Roseanne. . . . I have enough trouble being my daughter's role model." Although Lucy's reaction may seem uncharacteristically harsh, it was given immediately after she had seen the *Ms.* article, and later she gave a more rational explanation to *TotalTV*. She explained that phone interviews are often "unreliable": "When you see it in print, I sound like an iiiiii-diot. When I said I was shocked to be called a feminist, I didn't mean I was shocked and disgusted. I was shocked because it never occurred to me that [*X:WP*] was a political show." She added that although she is proud of being a strong role model for children, it does become a burden in that she must watch her every move. Lucy is actually very modest about the fact that she quit smoking when she began the role, because she didn't want children to think smoking was okay because "Xena" did it — a deed possibly more heroic than anything Xena has accomplished!

With the fame came the fan mail. Lucy was thrilled to see dozens of photos of little girls in homemade Xena outfits and she received many letters from young viewers telling her how much they loved her strong character. However, she soon realized that fan mail could be as upsetting as inspiring. Lucy discovered that some fans identified her far too closely with her character and often called her "Xena" in the letters. This mistake wouldn't have been so bad, except that the letters often were written by parents with children suffering from fatal illnesses asking if Xena could come and help them. On the contrary, Lucy felt utterly helpless and says that "it got to the stage where I was reading things and I would break down and cry." Eventually her fan mail became too disturbing for Lucy to deal with and had to be handled by other people.

Lucy's face was becoming more widely recognized at this time as well. She'd be stopped by women in the street who wanted to tell her how much they loved and appreciated the show. Owing to the show's "tendencies," men never come up to her the way women do. "Men are horrified by me when I bump into them in the street because they confuse me with Xena," she says.

By the time the second season began, *X:WP* was in the top ten syndicated shows on television in North America. Lucy's stunt work had improved and there were no more black eyes. She wasn't injured during sword fights or harmed during brawls. Despite the fancy moves on horses, she was never injured while horseback riding. That is, she was never hurt on the set of *X:WP*. However, in October 1996, while in the United States, Lucy would take a fall that would change the face of *X:WP* forever.

On October 8, Lucy was scheduled to appear on *The Tonight Show with Jay Leno*, which is a sign to any actor that she has finally 'made it.' However, *X:WP* isn't your average show, and the people at *The Tonight Show* didn't want Lucy to be your average guest, so they devised a stunt to give more exposure to both the show and Lucy. Unfortunately, the exposure that it ultimately gave Lucy wasn't exactly what they'd had in mind.

Lucy was asked to ride a horse from the street into *The Tonight Show* studio. Although she was a little wary about the stunt, she didn't think it would be too dangerous. What nobody considered was that the terrain they were dealing with wasn't the fields of New Zealand, but a polished floor. As they went into the third take, Lucy sensed that something was wrong, but before she could say or do anything the horse tripped — "It was as if someone pulled a tablecloth out from under us" — and Lucy was thrown from its back. She was thrown far enough away that the horse didn't land on her, but the fall shattered her pelvis, breaking it in four places. Ironically, Lucy hurt herself in what should have been a very routine skit. It wasn't the first time she'd broken something — she broke her arm doing gymnastics when she was a young girl — but she had never hurt herself quite so seriously.

Lucy was rushed to the hospital (she eventually *would* appear on *The Tonight Show*, carried in by two men) and began the long and painful recuperation. Meanwhile, the unfortunate incident was quickly becoming the best thing that had happened to *X:WP*'s ratings. Not only did everyone who watched *The Tonight Show* that night see the incident, but Lucy's face was in every major newspaper and many magazines the following week. What had been one of the biggest cult shows of all time went mainstream almost overnight. While *X:WP* fans on the Internet discussed the possibilities of Lucy not recovering fully and agonized fans everywhere awaited any news of her condition, people who had never before heard of the show were tuning in.

Xena lookalike Deborah Abbott

CATHERINE M. WILSON

According to the Nielsen ratings for the week of October 7 to October 13, 1996, Xena was ranked in tenth place with 5,170,000 viewers — the following week, it moved up to eighth place with 5,380,000 viewers.

The writers and producers of the show were faced with a serious problem, though. What do you do when your main star — who's supposed to be a kick-boxing, sword fighting, horse-riding warrior — can't even walk? Their solution was brilliant: kill her off . . . temporarily, of course. In the first season alone, fans had seen the apparent deaths of both Xena and Gabrielle, but now Xena was dead for an extended period of time and her personality made to inhabit various bodies. Gabrielle, Autolycus, and Callisto all became channellers of Xena's spirit and it was fun for the fans to see Reneé O'Connor, Bruce Campbell, and Hudson Leick offering their impressions of Xena. As Lucy recovered enough to be able to stand, she returned to the show, her stunt double working overtime. In most of the fight scenes Xena was filmed from behind so that stunt doubles could do the dirty work.

In one of the numerous interviews she gave during this period, Lucy said that she owed the show's continuation to the crew, and that the stunt people and editors made it look as though she could do all the things she couldn't. She took good care of herself, and was careful not to rush her recovery. She swam every day and used weights in the water. She would "run" in the water, using flotation belts to build up her strength. It took a long time for her to walk again, but she later told an interviewer that she never doubted she'd do so: "I've got them good child-bearing hips," she laughed, "and I did drink plenty of milk when I was a kid and that prevented me from snapping anything."

When she returned to the set after two months, she couldn't kick or run. One day she attempted some running on uneven ground, but when she felt a sharp pain she knew that she had to slow down. Not surprisingly, she was wary of getting back on a horse. By late March she finally convinced herself to do so, although she added, "I don't think I'll ever get on a horse again without thinking of Christopher Reeve," referring to the actor, best known for his work in the *Superman* movies, who became a quadriplegic when he broke his neck falling from a horse. Despite her fear, Lucy maintained an optimistic attitude and her recovery is a result of her inner strength. "I've really learned about the indomitable human spirit. Happiness is a choice. You grieve, you stomp your feet, you pick yourself up and choose to be happy." In the wake of the ratings climb and the huge *Xena* phenomenon, Lucy admitted that the accident was a blessing in disguise, though she was quick to add, "It may have been the best thing that happened to Xena, but not to Lucy Lawless."

AN UNNECESSARY EVIL

In the meantime, the show's numbers were growing and now articles in magazines and newspapers began to focus on the show's demographics rather than the show itself. The series had garnered a large lesbian following in the first season and when the writers and producers heard how many fans on the Internet were avidly discussing the subtext of the show — namely that Gabrielle and Xena were more than friends — they began dropping more subtextual inferences into the second season. Liz Friedman, the show's producer and an openly gay woman, began giving interviews where she refused to say whether they "were" or "weren't," and the other actors followed suit. Lucy explains *X:WP* as a "love story between two people. What they do in their own time is none of our business."

Yet she also credits the lesbian and gay bars for helping the show's success by having "*Xena* nights."

The Internet following was also growing at a phenomenal rate, with new *Xena* sites popping up each week. Mailing lists and fan clubs were devoted to all the stars of the show, including Robert Trebor and Hudson Leick. Each week the fans would analyze the latest episodes, discuss Lucy's condition, and arrange get-togethers to watch the show. They also discussed Lucy's new love interest.

For months, Lucy had been admitting to a special man in her life, although she refused to disclose who that person was. By the spring — and after all the support she had received from him during her accident and recovery — it was clear that she was dating Robert Tapert, the show's creator and executive producer. Rob was slightly older than Lucy, and they had developed a close and trusting relationship while working together on the show. Lucy was extremely happy and said so in many interviews, although she joked that their relationship was "a total cliché, the producer and the actress. . . . But I don't think he's ever been out with an actress in his life. We're very happy." Finally, Lucy's personal life was as successful as her professional one.

Lucy began appearing on more and more talk shows, where viewers were given a chance to see that Lucy — Kiwi accent and all — was completely unlike the character she portrayed on television. Unlike Xena, with her nerve-shattering "ALALALALA!" battle cry, Lucy is herself very quiet. "I'm notoriously hard to hear," she admitted. Lucy insisted that she and Xena were nothing alike. "I use just a sliver of myself to play her. She is just so dour and humorless, so ironical." Lucy, on the other hand, is very personable and funny, and fans everywhere loved her. Unlike most American actresses, Lucy's complete indifference to her weight endeared her to many who were sick

Robert Tapert

AMY PUTNAM

of the anorexic-looking actresses who usually grace the talk show circuit. Instead, Lucy said bluntly in one interview that she didn't own a set of scales and that not fitting into her outfit was the only way she had of knowing if she'd gained weight.

On August 16, 1996, Lucy had appeared on *The Rosie O'Donnell Show* where she fulfilled a childhood dream by spontaneously singing on the show. Rosie knew that Lucy had studied opera and she asked if Lucy would sing. Unself-consciously, Lucy broke into "I'm An Old Cowhand," dazzling both the audience and Rosie when they heard her incredible voice. Before starting her own talk show, Rosie had starred as the tough-talking Betty Rizzo in a Broadway revival of *Grease!* When she heard Lucy sing, she knew Lucy could tackle the part as well. By May of the following year, Lucy had signed a contract to appear in *Grease!* on Broadway during her hiatus from filming *X:WP*. Before she would expose her singing voice to thousands of fans in NYC, however, Lucy would unintentionally expose something else in May.

Tapert had always been a huge Detroit Red Wings fan and he quickly got Lucy enthusiastic about the game. She too became a fan of the team, and when the Red Wings made it to the playoffs against the Mighty Ducks of Anaheim, Lucy was invited to snag the opening spot of the game — singing the American national anthem. Wanting to impress the audience, Lucy hired a costumer, though when she saw the costume she was a little doubtful about its size — or lack of it. However, being the trooper she is, she donned the sequined, strapless, star-spangled number and walked out onto the ice. Wearing a big Uncle Sam hat and long, elegant red gloves, she launched into a hearty rendition of the American national anthem. And then it happened.

Now, Lucy had no idea *what* was happening. All she knew was that she wanted to show off her long, red gloves, as she later told Jay Leno. So on the words, "the land of the free," she raised both arms seductively à la Marilyn Monroe, and her breasts peeped out of the outfit. And stayed out. As an arena of fans (and thousands of others at home) looked on, they saw more of the Warrior Princess than ever before and more than she would have liked. Remarkably, and perhaps mercifully, Lucy had no idea that she had just flashed the audience and went on to enjoy the game. The next day, however, she was mortified to learn what had happened from Tapert's sister, and her immediate response was, "My mother will cry." As with her accident, newspapers ran small notices of her embarrassment. Very few were negative, however. No one (except maybe Howard Stern) thought that she had done it on purpose and on the night of the game far more viewers had called in to request a re-broadcast than to complain.

As usual, Lucy took the incident in stride. She stated outright that she knew "the costume was too damn small" and was upset that she had earned the wrong kind of publicity. *Xena* fans everywhere once again banded together, sticking up for Lucy Lawless and denouncing, or even boycotting, any publication that ran a photo. Later that year, in another interview on *The Tonight Show*, Leno jokingly asked if the male fans seemed to be far more patriotic that night than usual. Lucy managed to joke about it, hilariously referring to it as her "out-of-bodice experience." Internet fans immediately dubbed the incident the OBE (not to be mistaken for the Order of the British Empire, of course!).

HERE SHE COMES . . . MS. LAWLESS

In the summer, Lucy was back in New Zealand shooting episodes for the third season of *Xena: Warrior Princess*, even as ads in the New York papers announced Lucy's upcoming *Grease!* stint. However, in July 1997, a misunderstanding involving Lucy's upcoming appearance almost cancelled the show entirely. On July 22, Fran and Barry Weissler, the show's producers, put up a poster announcing the closing of the show after a successful four-year run. After having advertised Lucy's appearance with the motto, "You can't be a warrior princess all your life," the Weisslers were suddenly faced with the Actor's Equity Association's denial of a work permit. As a foreign actress, Lucy could only take the part "away" from an American if she had star status. And Actor's Equity asserted that Lucy was not a star. The Weisslers immediately sent further documentation to prove that Lucy was a star, including in the package her salary, information about *X:WP*, and her TV *Guide* and *People* magazine covers. In the meantime, they put up a closing notice, because Lucy was scheduled to begin rehearsals the following week and they needed to decide immediately to close the show. On July 23, after having seen the documentation, the Actor's Equity Association reversed its initial decision and allowed Lucy into the country for six months.

When *X:WP* fans heard about the slight they were outraged. To say Lucy lacked star status seemed like a blow not only to the actress, but to the show and the multitudes of fans who had made her a star. Internet Xenites chose designated nights to attend the performance as a group to show their support, although after lengthy discussions on various mailing lists and news groups, they opted to wear simple ribbons to signal their fandom, rather than dressing up as Xena and risk embarrassing Lucy.

Lucy's run began September 2 and continued until October 19. Each night fans could see their favorite Warrior Princess in action as the tough-talking Betty Rizzo. Some fans attended numerous *Grease!* performances and those on the listserves and chat groups posted their experiences of the show, so that *X:WP* fans who lived too far away or couldn't afford the tickets could live vicariously through

The Eugene O'Neill Theatre in New York
City, where Lucy appeared in *Grease!*
AMY PUTNAM

their experiences. Fans commented that Lucy's performance improved as time went on, which was to be
expected, and that she began goofing around on stage,
becoming more comfortable with her character. Her two
solo numbers, "Look At Me, I'm Sandra Dee," and "There
Are Worse Things I Could Do," enthralled the audiences.
After the shows, Lucy would appear at the stage doors to
meet with fans and sign autographs. She was seen at many
New York City spots, including the Meow Mix. (Unfortunately, she didn't show up on a *Xena* night, so she missed
many of the Xenite regulars.)

Shortly after Lucy's run had begun, critics began saying
that Lucy was not drawing the crowds she should have.
Reporting that the attendance had dropped since Lucy had
taken over as Rizzo, they implied that perhaps the AEA
had been correct when they denied her star status. However, these critics failed to take into consideration other

factors, such as the fact that people were going back to school and work, and that generally the fall reduced attendance at theatres as the summer tourists stopped coming. A more accurate comparison would be between Lucy's run and the same weeks of the previous year, as one fan pointed out. As a quick analysis shows, Lucy was filling more seats than the Rizzo from a year before (percentages of theatre capacity filled are in brackets; Lucy's run is in bold):

Sept. 2–8, 1996: $182,635 (49%)
Sept. 1–7, 1997: $294,192 (67%)

Sept. 9–15, 1996: $205,217 (58%)
Sept. 8–14, 1997: $311,651 (73%)

Sept. 16–22, 1996: $233,460 (65%)
Sept. 15–21, 1997: $312,664 (72%)

Sept. 23–29, 1996: $238,117 (63%)
Sept. 22–28, 1997: $352,152 (77%)

Sept. 30–Oct. 6, 1996: $255,565 (65%)
Sept. 29–Oct. 5, 1997: $391,125 (87%)

Oct. 7–Oct. 13, 1996: $325,821 (78%)
Oct. 6–Oct. 12, 1997: $411,987 (88%)

Oct. 14–Oct. 20, 1996: $311,307 (79%)
Oct. 13–Oct. 19, 1997: $441,795 (94%)

In her final week, when Lucy Lawless fans flocked to catch a final glimpse of their idol, Lucy packed the house. The following week, as Lucy headed back to New Zealand, Linda Blair of *The Exorcist* fame took over the role and the numbers dropped to an average attendance level, filling the theatre to 81% capacity in her first week and 62% in her second.

Many of Lucy's friends and family attended *Grease!* during her run, including Rob Tapert, Frank and Julie Ryan,

Reneé O'Connor, and of course, Daisy, who accompanied her mother on stage one night during curtain call dressed in a 1950s outfit. While in New York, Lucy filmed a Public Service Announcement for a women's help line, which aired during the third-season premiere of *X:WP*. During her run, Lucy had very few bad experiences with the press — unless one counts her appearance on *The Howard Stern Show*. Stern asked the usual inane questions — what size her bra was, if she left her husband because she was too famous for him — and Lucy handled it very well. When her radio appearance was televised on *E!* a few weeks later, it was very entertaining to see Lucy's facial expressions throughout the interview. She didn't seem offended at all, just bored. She refused to answer any questions about her breakup with Garth, respecting both his privacy and that of her daughter's. After Howard asked her a dozen times if she would sleep with him, the interview ended when Lucy's publicist appeared to take her to the next interview. Stern accused her of chickening out of the interview, despite the fact that she had just answered a bunch of insulting questions without blinking. It seems that after sitting with America's favorite shock jock for over an hour, she was simply surprised to discover that he just wasn't shocking.

Near the end of her run in *Grease!*, Lucy and Tapert announced that they were engaged, leaving some fans ecstatically happy and others happy for the couple, but disappointed (sigh). Announcing the engagement to *People* magazine, Lucy and Robert seemed to be very happy and stated that the ceremony would take place in the spring of 1998.

As Lucy headed back to New Zealand to continue filming *X:WP*, her life was very different from when she had come to New York to appear on Broadway. She had proven to thousands that she was much more than Xena, and probably won over new fans with her irrepressible charm.

For two years she had been Xena, the Warrior Princess, who wowed millions week after week became a role model for so many. When she returned to New Zealand, however, she was Lucy Lawless, a proud mother, a Broadway star, and a happily engaged woman.

TRANZ PICTURE LIBRARY / SHOOTING STAR

No one knows what the future holds for this multi-talented star. She has made it clear that neither she nor Robert wish to continue *X:WP* past the year 2000. Whatever her future holds, we can only hope that she's happy doing it. After all, as the posters said, "you can't be a warrior princess all your life," and Lucy is destined to be much, much more.

LUCY LAWLESS AT THE BURBANK CONVENTION JANUARY 18, 1998

On January 18, 1998, Lucy Lawless appeared in Burbank, at her third Creation *Xena* convention. Fans commented later that although she avoided personal questions, her breezy presence on the stage was a delight for all the fans, who had shown up to find out about her impending wedding to Robert Tapert, what she thought of the *Xena* rift saga (which was in full swing at this time), and just to hear what she does in her spare time.

Lucy comes out onto the stage amid shouts, loud applause, and flashing camera bulbs. She walks around for a moment, posing for the photographers, and does the Xena yell a few times.

LL: Hello! Tremendous! This is bigger than last year!

AUDIENCE MEMBER: We love you!

LL: Thank you! Man, oh man! I never know what to say when I get up here.

AUDIENCE: Don't say anything! Just stand there!

LL: Don't say anything . . . just stand there. You're so crazy! OK . . . so . . . I'm gonna say nothing for two hours

Lucy Lawless at Burbank: notice
the engagement ring on her left hand.

AMY PUTNAM

and just stand here. Let's have the first question because that always, you know, gets me going.

AUDIENCE MEMBER: When are you getting married?

LL: Are you in the front of that line, lady? It's kind of a state secret, so I'll just tell you guys. *[Laughter.]* I'm sorry, I'm not allowed to tell *[holds up her engagement ring, amid much applause]*. This ring was made by a very fine New Zealand goldsmith, Michael Cooper, and I just love it. It's kind of . . . it's a little bit rough hewn so it looks like something that you can wear on *Xena*, and indeed I did wear it on *Xena* the other day when I was wearing some costume the seamer gave me, some funny ole' "cossie." OK, now, first question.

FAN: Hello Lucy. How are you?

LL: Great, thank you!

FAN: I just wanted to say first of all that I think you did a fantastic job in *Grease!*, and you looked like you were having a great time. I know everybody here will probably agree with that. *[Loud cheers.]* My question is, since you enjoy travelling so much . . .

LL: Enjoy what?

FAN: Travelling . . .

LL: Ohhhh, not as much as I used to . . .

FAN: . . . is there any place you that haven't been yet that you would like to go?

LL: I would like to drive across the States. A lot of New Zealanders do like to do that but it's not their first beck and call so I would sure . . . that's what I'd like to do.

FAN: Hi, how are you?

LL: Great!

FAN: One of the reasons *Xena* is such an enjoyable show is because of the quality of your work. It's instant acting, you have a short time to do it, and you do lovely work. What do you want to do as an artist, as an actor after *Xena*, or if everyone is so dedicated to *Xena* and continuing forever, shall we say, in addition to *Xena*, theatre work, film, or are there any parts you'd like to do?

LL: Umm . . . I'd really like to do film. I doubt that I will do any Broadway any time soon. I really loved it . . . but it really fulfilled that need in me to . . .

FAN: You were on Broadway. . . .

LL: Yeah, I did . . . Broadway! God! What a cool thing for a girl from New Zealand. Um . . . What would I like to do? I'd like to do film. I'd like to do . . . you know, certain people do two films a year and spend the rest of the time with the kids, and seeing the world. And . . . I guess you try and do something good with your celebrity. Something useful. Because in itself, it's not very useful.

FAN: I'm Michelle . . . this is Marilyn. And we're in the Flawless mailing list and the Lucy Lawless fan club, and all the Lucy fans here would like to thank you for being you, and for not dodging the hard questions, and for embracing *all* your fandom, and since you couldn't sign autographs, we decided to give you ours *[they hold up a huge banner filled with signatures]*.

LL: Aw. That's great, thank you! Aw, thank you so much! *[Applause.]* Hello little one! *[Tries to read her name tag.]* Alexena? What a cool hat! It's very much like mine, actually. What's your name?

YOUNG FAN: Samantha.

LL: Samantha.

YOUNG FAN: I heard you like to catch fish. I like to catch, um, bass. What kind of fish do you like to catch?

LL: I've never caught bass, because they don't live where I live. I quite like fly cargo fishing. In Mexico you can catch big red cargo which are bigger than you are. Much bigger than you . . . you just catch them on a hand line. And I like trout fishing because it's a good way to . . . it's meditative. It's easy to calm you down when you do it, and you don't think of anything else but presenting that fly to the fish, and I like that . . . to be out with nature. Thank you.

FAN: Um . . . yesterday when Hudson Leick came up, she attempted the Xena yell, and she said that you would have to do a Callisto scream. *[Laughter.]*

LL: All right. You're going to find out that I can't scream. I couldn't scream . . . but I'm gonna do it for you, because that woman peer pressured me 'cause she said that I don't dodge hard questions, so . . . *[Laughter.]* The least dignified thing I'm going to do today, I know. Everybody turn off your cameras. What does she do? She screams with some sort of rage, and it's so violent. *[Prepares to scream, but stops.]* All right, if I was pumping 40 arrows out of my chest, this is how I would sound . . . *[She screams. Lots of cheering.]* You made me do it! Thank you.

FAN *[wearing a Xena costume]*: I just wanted to know, after going through making this outfit and wearing it a couple times, I'm wondering what modifications . . . name the two best modifications they made to your costume, and why does it help? In other words, this little bitty likes to go like that *[lifts one arm]* I'm just wondering what problems you ran into, and just tell me about the costumes, too.

LL: I think if it gets too long in the body it gets that big old wrinkle, which I know you've all seen because I've seen it in a few photos. And . . . uh . . . pads, pads are a good thing. *[Laughter.]* And mine used to be sort of an all-in-one outfit, like a bathing suit, but I just made it . . . you know, I had to umm . . . have it taken out a little bit. *[Laughter.]* Oh, I mean it's uncomfortable. *[She turns back to the woman in the costume.]* Cool outfit. *Really* cool outfit.

FAN: I tried to see you in New York this year at the end of the show, and got trampled, so now I get to look into those blue eyes now. You have given so much to the character Xena and she keeps growing and growing and growing. I'm very curious about what Xena has taught Lucy Lawless.

AUDIENCE MEMBER: Good question!

LL: Hmm . . . I don't know about Xena the character, but *Xena* the show has taught me surrender. It's taught me . . . there comes a time, I imagine it's like . . . I met a man on the plane the other day, and his wife died of breast cancer. And we talked about the point of surrender, when you know to give over to it, and when do you keep fighting. And I think misery is the point. Abject misery is the point of, is the indicator of when you should surrender, but I have lived to go with the flow a lot more. I can't fight everything every day . . . things that I can't change. Rock on, ya know? Just don't try to change the world.

FAN: Bear with me for this brief expository segueway . . .

LL: I hate expositions, don't you?

FAN: I just need to ask this question. There are others of us who are not performers who work very long hours. When I get home, I don't want to have anything to remind me of work too much. One of the things that I appreciate about *Xena* is that it rekindled my old interest in mythology. So that's something that I can relate to now. Have you had the experience that you want to find out more about mythological figures, or do you just kinda go home and clean out the tub?

LL: I do . . . I do . . . I do have a great need to go clean the tub. *[Laughter.]* I like to put on make-up. Seriously, I do. I don't think about work very much. I come home and my kitchen table is covered with things that I need to attend to, and I really need to get away from it all. *[She pauses to address the people in the back of the auditorium.]* Can you hear me? Down the back? OK? All right. But I did go to Turkey, and went to Ephesus and learned a whole heap of things about how people lived in those days, and all those beautiful marble statues. You know that they painted them gaudy colors? The eyes were . . . there's a very surprising way of life there and we make lots of jokes about it on the set, you know. One of my friends, Nancy, would talk about the need to go to a communal latrine. I have learned one or two things, but mostly I branch out into Titanic and stuff. Mostly I do the dishes 'cause my daughter won't. [Laughter.]

FAN: I wanted to ask you about fan fiction and if you've seen some, and how you feel about your and Reneé's images being used by the fans to sort of . . .

LL: I understand the fan fiction, you're talking about stuff on the Internet? The Barbies type-thing? To me, all that stuff is the fan's world and they are entitled to do whatever they like, and people are very encouraged to, I don't know, I guess, it's their own form of performance, and I think that can only be a good thing. But, no I don't go into it very much . . . the Internet. Cause everything's too much like work, you know. For me to stay fresh, I have to stay out.

FAN: Can I tell you something?

LL: Um . . . yeah.

FAN: I just wanted to . . . when people like Rob [Field] show us the editing and stuff, it really gives a clue about how hard you work. I wanted to do something to show my appreciation if that's okay. [As the woman prepares to sing Lucy a song, the security stops her.]

LL: Well thank you very much, um, Sharon [member of the Creation staff] is shaking her head at me.

YOUNG FAN: Hello. My name's Matt.

LL: What's your name? Matt! Hello, Matt. How are you?

YOUNG FAN: Do you like horses?

LL: I love horses! They are hard-working beasts. They are very individual. Horses have a personality much like people. It took me until just the other day . . . or two weeks ago . . . or not even two weeks ago to realise that my horse Tilly, that I ride on the show, was not the horse that I fell off of, in October, or a while ago. I don't even want to think about it. I like horses a whole lot more now that I realize that. I've always liked horses. Thank you for asking.

FAN: Hi Lucy. I just wanted to let you know that I came all the way from Singapore just to see you.

LL: I'm glad you managed it!

FAN: *[muffled]* So thank you very much for coming. And the second thing I wanted to ask you was actually, you know how Xena has a lot of one-liners . . . so do you have a favorite one?

LL: A favorite what? One-liner? Oh! Ooo . . . *[Looks at the audience.]* Quick! Suggest some to me, and I'll . . .

AUDIENCE: *[Begin shouting all at once.]*

LL: One at a time!

AUDIENCE MEMBER: Kill 'em all!

LL: One at a time! Kill 'em all? You know, when I did that "Kill 'em all," I really had to . . . it happens to Renee and I every now and again, you've gotta go, "OK, I have to stop protecting my character too much," and you have to just go hard with it. And that was one of those go hard or go home moments for me. You can't keep protecting her and keep her nice. Not interesting.

FAN: Can you tell us the story behind that little scar?

LL: My what?

FAN: The little scar that you have on your chest just above the . . . uh . . . bustier costume. Inquiring minds want to know.

LL: Well ya see . . . *[Pauses.]*

FAN: You can make something up that's really dramatic.

LL: It was, um . . . see I don't even want to make bad jokes, because I feel like, you know, I'm going to *[muffled]* Um, actually, it was . . . uh . . . a bee sting! *[Laughter.]* I'm sorry. I can't go into it.

FAN: It's too traumatic?

LL: No it's not too traumatic, but it begs too many questions. Um . . . basically it was a little bit of a botched . . .

I had some stitches and they split which is why I had the scar. Sorry.

YOUNG FAN: How long have you been riding?

LL: Riding? I actually started riding when I was about nine, and I stopped about the time I got interested in boys. That's what usually happens. But . . . if I had to do my time over again . . . I stopped riding about then, but yes, it

CATHY HOFFMAN

didn't last the teenage years, and then I got back on for *Xena*.

FAN: Hi Lucy. I work in a bookstore in Vancouver and I'm always curious as to know what you are reading.

LL: I just finished *The Cure for Death by Lightning* [by Gail Anderson-Dargatz]. Yeah. That was very much like *The Liar's Club* . . .

FAN: That's actually . . . the author of that is from B.C.

LL: I know! I was thinking, 'Is this a place in Utah or something in which they'd know . . . ' Yeah. It would be fun to see Vancouver again . . . I look forward to being in Vancouver again. And now I'm reading *Airframe* by Michael Crichton.

FAN: I just wanted to gush about "The Debt." I thought that was an excellent episode. You really have this amazing acting ability. I think that was definitely Emmy material.

LL: Wouldn't that be great if a syndicated television show got an Emmy? *[Cheering.]* It could happen!

FAN: I wanted to ask you if you liked working with Jacqueline Kim, and if Xena and Lao Ma will be together in future episodes.

LL: I don't know. I loved working with Jacqueline Kim, and um . . . I meant to catch up with her in New York, and things just got crazy. She's a wonderful person, and what a perfect Lao Ma, you know? I would love to work with her again. I don't know. I think that character, perhaps like in the last episode of *Xena* ever.

FAN: That would be a great idea!

LL: I don't know, is the frank answer, but Lao Ma is such a pivotal figure in the making of the character and the character's formation. But who knows, I would . . .

FAN: You really portrayed Xena's many facets in that episode.

LL: Oh thank you. It just about killed me. *[Laughs.]* Thanks.

FAN: Lucy? You have a birthday in a couple of months, and this is my only chance to wish you a happy early birthday.

LL: Thank you very much.

FAN: You are very welcome.

LL: Thanks a lot! God Bless.

FAN: As a fellow hockey fan, I was wondering who you thought would take the Cup this year?

ALL: Red Wings!

LL: Well. The Red Wings! They can't be beat! Well . . . yeah! The Red Wings!

FAN: Thanks.

LL: I'm a blind fan. Thank you.

FAN: Hi Lucy. Congratulations on your engagement.

LL: Thank you very much.

FAN: How's your family and Lucky?

LL: Lucky's been off to good behavior school. *[Laughter.]* Lucky's a good boy, but um . . . What's the story with Lucky? I got Lucky, I got this dog from the SPCA. Daisy picked him. He was a scrawny little dog, and he's grown up to be this most fearsome-looking creature. *[Laughs.]* He's a little terrifying. But he's good! He hasn't bitten anybody yet. My family's great, thank you very much.

FAN: *[She doesn't realize it's her turn and isn't watching the stage.]*

LL: Hello? Hello! Hello, hello! You, Madam! Hey! Hey! Hello! ALALALALA!

FAN: Oh! Um, where did Robert propose to you?

LL: In New York. Somewhere in New York. On his knees! *[Laughs.]* It was a great day, I have to say, no one has ever asked me to marry them before. Thank you for asking.

FAN: Remember last year's? *[Holding up a frisbee that looks like a chakram.]*

LL: That's last year's one, did you say?

FAN: Last year you threw this to the back of the auditorium.

LL: Are you asking me to repeat the feat? You know it's a question of luck with me.

FAN: *[Throws it to her.]*

LL: *[Misses the frisbee and drops it.]* Let's try this! *[She throws it into the audience.]* Next year she's going to be back and she's going to like, dribble off the side of the stage, and I'll be really busted!

FAN: How do you like working with babies and small children on your episodes, and will you be working with many in the future?

LL: Has "The Deliverer" shown over here? Um, I love . . . I think babies bring a really humanizing influence to the workplace, and I'm quite fond of babies, but um . . . they're not a problem, why do you ask? What a funny question!

FAN: Oh, because I have small children and I know how it is dealing with them.

LL: Well, it was a little bit difficult in "The Deliverer," *[note: she means "Gabrielle's Hope"]* because we had this mother of newborns, these *gorgeous* little twins and here I am saying, "I'm gonna kill her!" This mother *hated* me! And I had to go "It's just acting, love. It's in the script. It's written here." And she . . . *[begins talking to Steven L. Sears, who is sitting in the audience.]* Hey! Did you write that episode? Did you write that episode? Who wrote that one? Oh, you wrote "The Deliverer." That R.J. *[R.J. Stewart]*. Anyway, I said, "It's just acting," and she goes "Yeah. Yeah. I understand *[sounding really sarcastic]*. I understand you just fine, you little Xena you!"

FAN: When you were in New York doing *Grease!*, I read a lot of interviews and saw a lot of interviews that you did, where you talked about your personal philosophy on life. You know, like living each day for its importance, and when you're older, when you get on in years you won't have any regrets because . . .

LL: Because I tried everything, yeah. I try to live like that.

FAN: Perhaps you could just reiterate that a little bit to remind us all of the importance of things. [*Some audible groans.*]

LL: Well . . . I hate to . . . I don't like that guru feeling. This is just what I muttered out in my 29 years. I mean 28 years! I'm staving off turning 30! Um . . . I realized at a very young age that I would die, and that scared the hell outta me, but when I grew up it made me take every opportunity. It made me take the scary option, take the risk, sometimes I failed. But that's all right because I don't want to be 80 and be kicking myself. Something else in there I think I left out but I can't remember . . .

FAN: I come from the Czech Republic from Prague, and I would love to know when are you coming back to Prague?

LL: Oh! I went there when I did a travel show, and they had the best-looking human beings you ever saw sitting in the Wenceslas Square in Prague, and . . . when am I coming back? I don't know! I don't know when I'm going to get *here* next. The only thing I'm sure of is that I'm gonna spend nine months a year on the set of *Xena*. I would sure like to come back.

FAN: I have a four-year-old son who loves *Xena*, and I have the animated movie, which I have seen at least five or six times, and I love the song that you sang in that, I thought you did a wonderful job. And I don't know if you recorded the music for *Grease!*, whether you think they are going to release the CD, or are there any more CDs?

LL: Oh no. I don't think so.

FAN: I think they'd love to hear you sing for us. [*Cheering.*]

LL: They didn't think of . . . nobody proposed that idea, because I don't think they'd heard of *Xena*. They work every night in the theatre so they've never seen the show. They didn't know if I was hot spit or nothing! So I had to fill 'em in! [*says this in Meg voice*] No, no! I'm joking! I'm totally joking! But they had no idea; they'd never heard of our show. No one had any marketing ideas, otherwise perhaps they would have. But I don't know if I would have been very keen on that since I was singing for the fun, and that's about it.

FAN: As always, it's a pleasure seeing you again. I wanted to ask you, I didn't think I had heard this question before, and because of my nerves, I forgot his last name, but Bill, from *The X-Files*, you said you were in his acting class . . .

LL: Oh, Bill Davis!

FAN: Yes, Davis. Thank you. And I was trying to find out how was it in his class?

LL: He's a marvellous teacher. My old drama teacher plays the Smoking Man in *X-Files*, and he's an awesome teacher. He taught me things that I use all the time. And I mark my script in the way that Bill taught me. I've picked up, like, two new things since . . . well, perhaps I picked up a lot, but the basis of how I approach a script is from Bill. He taught me such great things. Is anybody here an actor? Probably a really dumb question in L.A, isn't it?

AUDIENCE MEMBER: No, but I've met Bill! Very nice man!

LL: Oh you did? Wonderful man, and such a great teacher. I'm glad he got another chance to expand his career. I love seeing people get a second chance in life, like John Travolta, and a whole heap of people. And Dreyfuss and lots of people. It would be nice if that could happen to all of us, unless of course there's no *need* for a second chance! *[Laughter.]*

FAN: Lucy, I wanted to ask you, with what little free time I have, I tape the *Xena* show and I watch it, and I watch *Hercules*. And I wanted to ask you, what do you watch with what little free time you have?

LL: What I watch is the news, and CNN, and the Discovery Channel. I know that sounds awfully PC, but I don't have any need for any more fantasy in my life, ya know? *[Laughter.]*

FAN: You're living one!

LL: I'm living one! And I realized . . . there was a psychiatrist. My friend asked a psychiatrist, "Who would you rather treat: rich people or poor people?" and he said, "Rich people." And he said, "Why?" And he said, "Because only rich people know that money, or the lack of it, is not the root of their problems." And I realize that because I have all of this, I know that for sure, that all of this hubbub is not the meaning of life.

FAN: Money means nothing.

LL: Oh money's useful stuff! Don't get me wrong! *[Laughter and applause.]*

FAN: Money means nothing because it can't buy you anything else.

LL: That's right, but it can keep you comfortable, and can get your kids education.

FAN: You can't buy love, and you can't buy anything that really means anything.

LL: It really can't. You can buy a yes-man, if you want that sort of thing.

FAN: My name is Chris. I am from the Phoenix Xenites, and hello from all of us.

LL: Hello Phoenix Xenites!

FAN: There's about five or six of us here, and I just wanted to ask you, how hard is it, or how difficult is it for you to portray Meg, Diana, Leah, and Xena?

LL: *[She hunches over and laughs like Meg.]* Meg is so like me in my working days. Kinda true. Sad but true. It's not, it's such a pleasure to get, to break up, and we've got another one coming up, but it won't be on the air for quite some time, I guess. I love to do those, because it refreshes me, and I love to see Xena and Gabrielle pitted against some hag . . . some character, and I especially love that I'm playing the hag, because I am so good at it! Yeah! Yep

yep yep. You know a whole lot more about me this year, don't you?

FAN: What was your first television job?

LL: My first television job. Oooh! I did this really bad cheesy commercial for travel, and I wore this bathing suit, and I am not a bathing suit girl! Yeah I did this embarrassing sort of video commercial, made a videotape, but they seemed to like me and I got another one after that. Anyway, my first real acting job was in *Funny Business*, in a skit show. That was great fun. Comedy was my first real acting job.

FAN: What kind of plans do you have for your wedding? Is it going to be a big one, small one?

LL: I'm wondering what you expect me to say?

FAN: You know, do you have like a big party planned?

LL: You know, the truth is, yes we do because we don't ever plan on doing this again. And we want to really celebrate this day, we are two of the happiest people in the world, and we want to share that with our family and friends.

FAN: What are the colors going to be for your wedding? *[Laughter.]*

LL: I won't even tell my mother-in-law who'll be there! She keeps asking what I'm going to wear and I was going, "I don't know, Pat. I don't want to think about it. I'm busy doing Christmas decorations or something." And she said, "Because, I'm going to wear teal." "Yeah, wear teal, Pat. That's real cool idea." And then I hear later of course she's coming (she thinks it's a real Hollywood wedding), and she's wearing sequins! Like really big teal sequins! Imagine what those look like! *[someone asks what color 'teal' is.]* What color is teal? Light blue. Ducky blue. Yeah, wear teal. Yeah that's perfect. Nah . . . she's really neat, but we did have to dissuade her from the teal sequins.

FAN: Since I don't think that there's really anyone in the world they could have gotten to play you, I mean Xena,

CATHERINE M. WILSON

Callisto, and Gabrielle, better than they did, so I was wondering, are you a firm believer in determinism and fate?

LL: I believe in the ability to spot opportunity.

FAN: I mean, with dealing with all the pressure that goes into the acting repertoire.

LL: Oh no. I do believe it's all written. Too many accidents.

FAN: Too many happy coincidences.

LL: Too many happy coincidences, especially in my case, ya know? If Rob hadn't walked across a parking lot and into somebody who'd just come back from New Zealand filming a commercial, it would never have gone there. *Hercules* would never have gone there and so I'm afraid I can't say it's one way or the other.

YOUNG FAN: My name is Anthony, and I was wondering, how do you talk without doing your accent?

LL: Because when a camera rolls, it just seem so natural to me. I have a lot of difficulty, believe it or not, acting with the way I talk normally. Perhaps it's too personal, but I'm not often called upon to use a New Zealand accent anyway. I don't know how that happens! You just practise, it all takes a little bit of practice. Because to say the letter "R" in an American accent is very difficult to us, so just practice, you can do anything! Just stick at things, that's all.

FAN: My question was, off-camera, is there a friendship between you and Hudson?

LL: Yes! I have. I mean, we don't ring each other every day, but I have a deep love for Hudson and affection that isn't displayed by the amount of time we spend together. But I'm very fond of her. And she's a marvelous talent, and she's a wonderful ingredient to the show.

FAN: I'm kind of nervous. Mainly I wanted to tell you that I love the show. It's something that the intelligent person can watch. Also, I wanted to ask you, you don't have to do it if you don't want to, but could you do my favorite line, which is, "You don't want to make me mad now, do you?"

LL: The Lucy way, or the Xena way?

FAN: The Lucy . . . uh . . . the Xena way.

LL: *[In Xena's deep, whispery voice.]* "You don't want to make me mad now, do you?" *[Applause.]* Meg would do it like *[in Meg's voice]* "You don't wanna make me mad now, do ya?" Man, I've said that too, like outside the door of *Grease!*, I used that line. Twice, I think.

FAN *[dressed as Salmoneus]*: G'day! First off, I wanna tell you, my daughter's got to be, I don't care what anybody

AMY PUTNAM

says, your biggest fan. Three walls in her bedroom are dedicated to you and we have to bow and genuflect every time we walk by her room. *[Lucy laughs.]* My question is this, it's as much a comment as it is a question. In the show, and some writers are over there, right? I know that you must and I hope you continue to keep the children in mind. There are a lot of adult references and jokes in the series, I'm sure you know what I'm talking about, and you gracefully keep them obscure, and we as parents appreciate that. And please continue to keep them obscure, and you know what I'm talking about.

LL: I do know what you are talking about, but I've got another comment on that. You have to screen this show, because . . . [Applause.]

FAN: I can't screen *Xena*, she's going to watch it, believe me, she's gonna watch it.

LL: It's not so much the innuendo or anything that you're referring to, but there's are some very adult themes coming up. I mean, you've seen it in "Gabrielle's Hope." Some children are frightened by that kind of content, and you know, I would urge parents to be very careful of their children and the influence.

FAN: Thank you very much.

LL: Thank you. And yes I will. I will think about you.

YOUNG FAN: Do you have anything in common with Xena?

LL: Do I have anything going with Xena?

YOUNG FAN: No! Do you have anything in *common* with Xena?

LL: Oh in common! Quite a lot actually [Laughs.] I can't do flips! In fact, I did a forward roll the other day, and everyone was just laughing! It was to start going into a stunt, and they were rating me a three. A three for me, but . . . . Otherwise, a lot of Xena, when actors often think that to play a character, you have to be somebody completely other than yourself, you have to go read books up on subjects and become something different and I don't believe that's true. The whole idea is to experience yourself, the whole spectrum of yourself. The one thing that you can be, you need to keep that and just say, "This is who I will be, in this situation." And just be yourself in an extraordinary situation. So, yes Xena is . . . well, not all the flips and all that stuff, but Xena is possibly who I would be if I lived in that kind of world. I would at least be that tough. At least, I think. *[Laughs.]* I'd have trouble being as nice as Xena if I lived in that world, I think.

ANOTHER YOUNG FAN: Lucy, I made you a card.

LL: Thank you! They'll give it to me later.

YOUNG FAN: Has anyone been hurt when they're filming?

LL: Yes. A stunt woman got . . . had to have a bit of plastic surgery on her nose the other day when *somebody* hit her with a staff, and it wasn't me. Somebody bad! *[Laughter.]* No names. And otherwise, it's just me really that gets hurt, and stuntmen. I have to admit, you know, I'll . . . kick somebody in the head. Very seldom done. *[Laughter.]* Not very often. It doesn't often happen that we have accidents.

YOUNG FAN: If you can change anything on the show, what would it be?

LL: Xena could wear like a lycra, a long lycra dress. I wouldn't change a thing! What would you change? Do you want to change something? You tell me. I'll make it happen. *[Laughter.]* Hair color? Sidekick?

AUDIENCE: No!!

LL: *[laughing]* She's not going anywhere. Don't get rezzed! I'd be lost without Reneé.

FAN: I can't imagine having a mother like you, I was wondering how your daughter Daisy deals with this?

LL: Oh she doesn't! This is not part of our day-to-day life. She's not very thrilled about sharing her mummy all the time, but she tolerates it now, and she understands it. She's not threatened by it.

YOUNG FAN: What do you do in your spare time? If you have any.

LL: I do conventions . . . *[Laughter.]* No, we go fishing a bit. We go fishing. Every weekend, I have Spice Girls conventions out of my house! I have kids, loads of girls at my house every weekend.

FAN: I'd like to know that, if you and Reneé have any kind of relationship outside the show?

LL: Great, great friends. She's certainly my best friend on the set. But usually like on weekends, I'm doing Spice Girls conventions, and Reneé is moving into a new house.

AUDIENCE MEMBER: When's her wedding? *[Laughter.]*

LL: I don't know. But, yes she's one of my best friends. You can't help it, you know, you spend three years working with somebody that closely together, and we rely on one another. We keep one another on the straight and narrow, keeping a good attitude about . . . whatever.

FAN: If you could take up any hobby, what hobby would you take up?

LL: Hobby? I'd really like to be able to rollerblade. I used to go around like Hollywood *[holds her arms out and pretends she can hardly keep her balance]*, and skate and think "please don't let anybody recognize me, please!" I'm such a bad skater! But, I would sure like to be able to do that, 'cause those people have the best legs, don't they? That would be my hobby of choice.

FAN: It's a pleasure to meet you. Could you do the Xena yell?

LL: ALALALALALA SHEEEEYA!

FAN: Ares was telling us about his work-out regimen earlier, I was just wondering what yours consisted of?

LL: I taught Kev all he knows in the work-out department. Do you know I walk, I hike a bit, hand weights, a little bit of weights. That's about it. That's about it! If I go on holiday, and I'll be walking . . . like at Christmas time, I just let myself go to hell. I just eat ice-cream every day. Do nothing . . . maybe go fishing for a few minutes. And sleep the whole time! And I'll go in to buy . . . into the groceries . . . and there's this woman, and she works in a wine shop.

She's got dark hair and blue eyes, and she's cut beyond belief! She's some kind of a body-builder. And Rob's sister asked me, "How do you feel when you go?" because people look at me, and I'm kind of pudgy and white. You know when I come back to work I have to be on the wagon again, and get sort of back in shape, but at Christmas I'm really not in shape. I just think, "You poor woman! You do all that work and you're *not* famous?" *[Laughter.]* Yeah . . . you don't have to be a great martial artist or you don't have to be a muscle man to kind of look like one. I guess. Maybe you do, whatever. I just act.

FAN: I saw "Warrior . . . Priestess . . . Tramp" last night and I loved it, and I was just wondering, where did you get the inspiration for the mannerisms, and the way the characters talk?

LL: Well . . . ya know, Leah was kind of a cheap shot on my part, I have to admit, you know, the wheeled-out speech impediment. *[Laughs.]* Because we get the script the day after I've just come in, we get the script a couple of days before we go to shoot it or that's when I read it. I don't have a lot of time to develop a character and it develops over the course of the first two days. Which means I can always tell what we filmed first by how well-developed the character is in her scene. And . . . some things like Meg . . . Meg goes back to high school. I did Meggy-type things in Biology. Marist Sisters College in Bio. Just . . . I don't know. I'm always looking for new characters, better things pop up.

YOUNG FAN: What was your favorite episode on *Xena?*

LL: Oh . . . There's a lot of them now. Usually I like . . . the hardest ones are usually the best. And though they give me, though they are very difficult to shoot they're physically uncomfortable. You're always cold, you're always wet, you're always something. They are always the most rewarding as well. And I like the pure comedy ones, cause

. . . I don't know, I love playing Meg, and I love to be stretched as an actress.

FAN: I don't tell this to many people, but you are drop dead gorgeous! *[Loud applause and clapping.]*

LL: She's lying! She didn't drop dead! *[Laughter.]* This is a Hudson pose *[Stands seductively.]* Well thank you very much.

FAN: I have a question. I heard or read somewhere that Daisy was in an episode?

LL: Not really. She was an extra on a *Hercules* cross-over episode, because I suppose she had a day off from school, and she went to work with me. But she has no desire to act at this stage, and that's just fine with me. She likes to be an extra. She likes to hang out and Kevin's awfully nice to her, and to all the kids on set, considering they're always badgering him! And, um, he's really good with kids.

FAN: What or who inspired you to become an actor?

LL: We were doing a parable. A parable of The Prodigal Son at school when I was ten, and I thought for the first time, "Wow I really like this. I like doing this in front of people." It wasn't as scary as I thought. I just always wanted to do it.

YOUNG FAN: I just wanted to ask, what was the most fun show you ever did?

LL: The most what?

YOUNG FAN: The most fun.

LL: Well it would be . . . the most fun ones are always the ones where I play dual characters. And it just depends on who the director is, how much fun that was. Because some people really set you free. Directors have more or less to bring to you. Some are very strong in cinematography, some are very strong in acting. Everybody's strong in something, but some are particularly fun. Those ones are all great. I think "Warrior . . . Priestess . . . Tramp." Yeah. Josh Becker directed that.

YOUNG FAN: My name is Jackie. I just wanted to ask . . . why did you want to become Xena?

LL: I couldn't turn her down! [Laughs.] Because all actors want to work all the time. Because it was a great role in a wonderful company. Because at the time, I was just a young actor in New Zealand, and the company, Pacific Renaissance, had a very good reputation for paying people on time to provide a very good atmosphere for people to work in, and that continues. So I couldn't have turned it down. It would have broken my heart. Imagine!

YOUNG FAN: What was your favorite, when you were doing the animated, what was it like watching yourself, and what was it like hearing yourself when you were in the animated?

LL: Oh yeah that's a very strange feeling! I'm quite accustomed to seeing Xena in live-action, but to see a cartoon talking like you, and she's got some chin, hasn't she? I loved it. I love all that merchandise stuff. It's a big old thrill . . . who would have ever thought . . . Where's my PEZ dispenser? [Laughter.] Never happened, did it? Who ever thought they'd be on a cup, or a T-shirt, and . . . it's cool. It's very good. Thank you for asking, hon.

FAN: I wanted to know what your reaction was at you getting all the publicity after your first show on *Hercules*?

LL: Um . . . Well, I didn't know anything about it. Did I? [Someone shouts out an answer for her.] Yeah, somebody knows! I know it was a good episode, so it got attention, but of course you're pleased!

FAN: Oh, yeah! That's me and my friend's favorite show, *Xena*.

LL: Aw, thank you.

FAN: I'm just wondering, who is the favorite around the *Xena* set?

LL: The favorite what?

FAN: The favorite person.

LL: Um . . .

AUDIENCE MEMBER: Argo!

LL: You know, to be fair to all the other people, and Reneé would agree with me, and Ted and Hudson, everybody would agree, that there is no one person who's a favorite. Everybody's really loved on the set. There's a lot of people that you don't even see and they are working their backsides off, setting up dollies, and holding booms to catch the sound and every person is valuable.

FAN: I loved the "Warrior . . . Priestess . . . Tramp" last night, and I think Rob mentioned that there might be a poet in your next character add-on?

LL: [to the audience] What poet would that be, girls?

ALL: Sappho!

LL: [playing dumb] Who? You're right! . . . there is a poet.

FAN: There is? Can you enlighten us a little bit?

LL: Well, I don't know. All I know is that it's coming up. I haven't read the script or anything. But it'll be a fun episode. The man in the Salmoneus costume? [The man who had asked about keeping the show safe for kids.] We'll be thinking about you, we'll try to make those jokes obscure, but there's gonna be a lot of them! [Applause.]

FAN: Wow! This is about as big as an ego boost as anybody can get!

LL: It's pretty nice.

FAN: What I'm wondering is, if you could go back in time to when you were a small child, what would be one thing you would tell yourself to maybe make your life a little easier?

LL: I wish I could tell myself that what other people think doesn't matter. But, nobody told me that. That's probably it. Yeah, pure and simple.

FAN: It doesn't matter.

LL: Well, it does matter, but if you believe what you are doing is right, go for it. Go hard.

YOUNG FAN: Off camera, who is the funniest person you work with?

LL: Oh! Ted. Ted Raimi. There was someone else the other day. Who else is really funny?

AUDIENCE MEMBER: Bruce!

LL: Oh, Bruce. *[Laughs.]* Bruce is just a crazy man. *[Long pause.]* Let me think about that! Michael Hurst is a very funny person too. Didn't you think Reneé was funny in, oh, no, no, no, I was watching another . . . well, anyway, Reneé is really funny. *[She was probably going to mention ROC in "The Quill Is Mightier," then caught herself when she remembered it hadn't aired yet.]* She's just a great comic actress. But I don't think anybody much beats Ted off-screen.

YOUNG FAN: Hi, I'm Vanessa, and I just wanted to know what your favorite sport was, and what's your favorite team in that sport?

LL: Red Wings, hockey. I don't know I never really had a favorite sport because I was never any good at it. I really stunk at sports. I've gotten much better, though! Apart from the frisbee catch, I can truly catch things. Quite fluid now.

FAN: I was able to come last year, and I told you that I would one day I'll have a daughter, and that I would have her watch the show. I was wondering, do you let your daughter watch the show, and at those Spice Girl conventions, do they understand the difference between Lucy and Xena?

LL: Oh they know! They know! She doesn't even . . . unless like Ted's in it, she doesn't wanna watch the show! That's about the size of it. She doesn't watch it much unless it's . . . Ted, kinda likes Meg. No . . . Mum's not much of a draw card I'm afraid. *[Laughs.]* She just drives the car and buys the tickets.

FAN: I wanted to ask you, what is your favorite sci-fi movie, and why?

LL: Oh I saw this great movie the other day, *The Prophecy*! Has anyone seen *The Prophecy*? Whoa! What a scary movie! Kind of R-16, just because of the script. Another one? I like *Predator*. I saw the *Aliens* again the other day.

AUDIENCE MEMBER: *Blade Runner*!

LL: You know, I'm sorry I just didn't catch on to *Blade Runner [talks in a quiet baby voice]* "Do you know anyone who talks like this?" The show kind of . . . I just didn't get it. I didn't understand it at all. It didn't move me, is what it was.

FAN: G'day Lucy. My question is, about your fall, do you have any residual pain from it?

LL: No, I don't. Thank you very much.

FAN: I unfortunately also had an injury similar to yours, and I was wondering if you used any alternative or non-western medicine in your healing process?

LL: We have a lot of homeopathy in New Zealand, *[muffled]* vitamins, and really good attitude, I think.

FAN: Yeah, that helps. I'm still recovering, it's going to take several more years, unfortunately. Reneé signed my pelvis, so . . .

LL: Those are *not* child-bearing hips!

FAN: These are not, no not wide enough. So security's saying absolutely not. No good luck signing.

LL: No, I'm sorry, we . . .

FAN: That's okay! It's cool. It never hurts to ask. Take the risk.

LL: That's right . . . if you don't ask, you don't get.

FAN: I was wondering, outside of *Xena*, do you have any other projects? Movies?

LL: Aw, shall I tell you a secret?

ALL: Yeah!

LL: It's not a good secret, it's a real bummer. I had a great offer recently to work with a really terrific director and his children, who love the show, and that fell through for one reason or another. So, the heartache of being an actor doesn't stop. It just doesn't stop. You just gotta pick yourself up and start all over again, I realize it's just gonna happen my whole life. What a lot of actresses do, when they are 40, 45, you run your own production companies, because nobody is looking out for you. But . . . I'm happy. I'm here. I'm healthy.

YOUNG FAN: Since you had so many boyfriends, or whatever, on the show . . .

LL: Pardon? Oh, on the show. Huh.

FAN: Are you ever going to have one that's . . .

LL: Oh, I don't know. That's out of my hands.

FAN: I heard that you are going to have one that you fall in love with in a future episode.

LL: Oh the "King Con." No. It's another wash.

FAN: So they're just gonna leave?

LL: No, they die or something. We can't have a man hanging around! That's not our show! *[Applause and cheering.]* The vehemence of your response is a little shocking! Yeah, um, sorry I really don't know what's coming up. It's all in very broad terms. Let's have five more questions, and then off.

FAN: How is it working with Kevin Smith?

LL: Lovely. He's great.

FAN: I just wanted to tell you that you're a great actress, and I look forward to watching your show every week.

LL: Thank you. And I've got to tell you, Kevin's got more talent in his little finger than just about anyone I could name. He's a great guy, and a family man and we're very fond of him. *[Applause.]*

FAN: To answer your question from earlier, yes I am from L.A., and yes I do have acting [experience], and I'm working on it. I have a question. Who do you like?

LL: Well, I've often said it, but . . . Susan Sarandon, Helen Mirren, John Cusack, who's the tall guy in Spike Lee's new film? John Turturro, wonderful director, amazing actor. I like a lot of actresses.

FAN: Do you have any advice, because obviously you're the one to ask?

AMY PUTNAM

LL: Well, um . . . the truth of it is that it's 5% talent, 15% skill, and 80% hanging in there, it's just sticking it out.

FAN: And looks. It's true, unfortunately.

LL: Depends what medium you want to work in. But, you know when you go into an audition, or a job interview, you . . . the first thing they ask you, they go "so tell us about yourself." And you go, "Uhhhh . . ." What do you do, you go in there and you say "Hi" what's your name?

FAN: Samantha.

LL: Samantha who?

FAN: Hale.

LL: Hale? "Hi, I'm Samantha Hale, and lately I've been doing da-da da-da da-da." Something that is true, something genuine, that excites you. You don't have to go "Oh, I haven't done very much work before." You say, "I'm a new face." You should promote the most positive, but the most genuine spin on things. Don't apologize for anything, and people will just dig your energy.

FAN: You know, I come from a long line of actors, so I . . .

LL: Oh, bummer!

FAN: Bummer? No, *good* actors!

LL: Yeah, like in my case, I didn't have anybody else's reputation to live down. Good luck, sweetie! It's tough, but it's good fun.

FAN: If Xena were to switch bodies with another character on the show, who would you really like to play?

LL: I would play Reneé's character! The things I would do! *[Laughs.]* But I'll tell you what, because you guys are gonna tell me, "Don't you pick on Reneé!" Reneé is *so* tough, she gives me such trouble! Everything is like . . . everything I ever exposed. Because she came to us, and she was a nice girl from Texas . . . *[Laughter.]* Well, Reneé gives back ten-fold! Reneé gives it to you, don't be feeling sorry for Reneé. *[Laughter.]* She's wonderful! So everybody . . .

ALL: Aww . . .

LL [singing the Mickey Mouse Club closing song]: Now it's time to say goodbye to all my . . . You know, Reneé was a mousketeer once . . . [Laughter.] M . . . I . . . C — See ya real soon! — K . . . E . . . Y — Why? Because we like you [Audience is singing along now.] M . . . O . . . U . . . S . . . E. [Loud applause.] Thanks everybody!!

Lucy leaves to applause and the X:WP theme song.

RENEÉ

O'CONNOR

BIOGRAPHY

RENEÉ O'CONNOR

THE QUEST

Out in the East Texas town of lil' Katy, a blonde-haired, emerald-eyed bard was born on February 15, 1971. Her name was Reneé O'Connor, named after one of her mother's high-school chums. Although on *Xena: Warrior Princess* Reneé plays a character very different from Xena it is interesting to note how similar her background is to Lucy's. Her parents were Walter (a bank credit manager) and Sandra O'Connor. Sandra would eventually play the single most important role in her daughter's fame as Reneé got older.

In 1973, Walter and Sandra separated, and Reneé was raised by Sandra's second husband, Chuck Gibson, a businessman. Despite the divorce early in Reneé's life, she was a very happy child. Reneé vividly recalls the play fights she had with her older brother, Chris, where they would act out different action scenes: "[I]t's kind of funny, because sometimes when I'm playing the (show) with Lucy, it reminds me of when my brother and I were playing our simulated battles." Sound familiar?

Reneé actually started acting at an earlier age than Lucy. Sandra recalls her daughter's first acting experience at the tender age of eight. A travelling acting troupe called

Theatre on Wheels came through town and Reneé auditioned for and won the part of a caterpillar. Sandra went to the performance alone, naturally feeling nervous for her daughter. But her fears were quickly allayed when she saw

Reneé at the San Francisco convention, October 1997.
JOYCE BEZAZIAN

Reneé performing on the stage. As she later told Jacquie Propps, a writer for *Whoosh!*, "The moment I saw Reneé up there doing the best darn caterpillar in the world, I knew, 'OK, this is it! This is really what Reneé wants to do.' I mean, she even made her own costume, all by herself!" At eight years old, Reneé was already a girl of many skills!

Since she can remember, Reneé has always wanted to be an actress. She'd put on plays with her friends and entertain people, even when she was a little girl. Sandra fondly recalls, "I remember her borrowing my video camera to film scenes she created with her friends. She loved every aspect of theatre as well." Sandra immediately began to cultivate her daughter's interest, driving her to acting school, lessons, plays, and anywhere else she needed to go. She also enrolled her in dance classes, skating classes, and various sports. Whew!

At school, Reneé's exuberance and charm won her many friends. She was always a very popular girl, and she continued to entertain, but as she grew older her styles of acting became more mature. At the age of twelve, she enrolled in the Houston Alley Theater of Acting. For high school, she entered Taylor High School in Katy. However, she couldn't stay away from acting for long, and at sixteen she transferred to Houston's High School for Performing and Visual Arts. She would later modestly joke that at sixteen she was playing around in costumes, "but I started getting paid for it, thank goodness, at about eighteen or nineteen." Reneé doesn't talk about her high school years much, except to comment that she appreciates what she learned at the acting schools she attended. However, she did make the mistake of mentioning on a talk show that before acting she had a job dressing up like Porky Pig at a Six Flags amusement park. While the job probably didn't give her the acting practice she was looking for, it did give her an unmatchable opportunity to learn — the Porky dance. Perhaps this tidbit of information may be something she wishes she'd kept to herself, for whenever she makes a public appearance, fans mercilessly beg her to do the dance.

In late 1988, Reneé hooked up with a talent manager, Lee Peterson, who began getting her acting jobs. At the ripe old age of seventeen, after appearing in commercials for McDonald's and Exxon, she began filming "Teen Angel," a serial from the *Mickey Mouse Club* series. Reneé did such a good job in "Teen Angel" that she was asked to return for another episode, "Match Point." Filmed in Arizona, Reneé had to leave home (if not to go far) for her first job, and when she turned eighteen as filming was wrapping up, she decided that she liked her independence. In early 1989, she moved to Los Angeles.

Once there, and excited about her new life opening up, she was surprised at how similar it was to Houston. She kept to herself, taking jobs as a waitress and an aerobics instructor to pay the bills while she looked for acting work. She didn't have any friends who were actors because she wanted to focus on acting, not partying. "It's very easy to fall into that Hollywood club scene, and I didn't want to do that. I wanted to stay close to my roots."

Her methods worked. In 1990, she appeared in an episode of *Tales from the Crypt*, directed by the biggest star she had met until then — Arnold Schwarzenegger. Her role was small but Reneé remembers vividly how difficult it was learning her lines with Schwarzenegger: "I remember his thick accent and the line readings he would give me, and I would try not to mimic him as I said my lines." She also remembers what a talented director he was in his knowledge of the movement of the actors.

In 1991, Reneé's mother married Eddie Wilson, the owner of Threadgill's Restaurant in Austin, Texas. Her marriage with Chuck Gibson had ended in 1989 and when she met the lively and outgoing Eddie Wilson, she must have been swept off her feet. Eddie is as proud of Reneé as Sandra is (if that's possible) and the website for Thread-gill's features a picture of Reneé and a link to her *People* magazine interview. Reneé has only good things to say about Eddie: "I like him . . . I think he'll keep me around for a while." In the same year that Sandra and Eddie got married, Reneé earned a prominent role in the made-for-TV movie based on Danielle Steel's *Changes*. Reneé played Cheryl Ladd's daughter.

DREAMWORKER

By 1993, Reneé was being offered many roles, including the made-for-TV movies *Sworn for Vengeance* and *The Flood*, her role in the latter being the first that really got her noticed. She also played Julia Wilks in the TV movie *The Adventures of Huck Finn* and had a small but powerful role on an episode of NYPD *Blue* as the daughter in a family who had been killed while she was away at school. The look of shock and almost no emotion that is on her face during her brief time on screen shows how much Reneé had matured as an actress.

In 1994, Reneé got her big break, starring in the Sam Raimi/Robert Tapert production of *Hercules and the Lost Kingdom*, with Kevin Sorbo. Just as Lucy had been dis-covered by Raimi and Tapert when she appeared in one of the Hercules movies, so did Reneé. Reneé hadn't even planned on auditioning for the part and arrived at the last minute, having heard that an actress was needed in a show based on Greek mythology. It was O'Connor's contagious exuberance that won over the casting agents. "I remember standing up on a chair for the casting director and reciting lines with all the romantic energy that I could muster, and just enjoying myself completely." Sound like Gabrielle? Well, it should: the role of Deianeira is remarkably similar to that of Gabrielle. Deianeira is a slave girl who is about to be sacrificed to the fertility gods when Hercules saves her. Resisting with all her might, claiming that to die in order to save the crops is her destiny, she is soon won over by Hercules and becomes his sidekick, endlessly chattering away as he sets off to find the lost city of Troy. Reneé is very funny in this film, and she actually leaves a more memorable impression than Lucy did in *Hercules and the Amazon Women*, partly due to Deianeira being a more prominent role than Lysia.

On the set, Reneé was given an early chance to work with many of the people who would become her regular co-workers on *X:WP*: Eric Gruendemann, the producer; Kevin Sorbo, who would appear in crossover episodes with *X:WP*; Nathaniel Lees, who has appeared on *X:WP* as Manus and Nicklio; and Robert Trebor, who plays a slave in this movie, and would later star as Salmoneus in *H:TLJ* and *X:WP*. Trebor's character in this movie has a similar personality to Salmoneus's and there's a chance Salmoneus was based on the slave, given that the later role was written specifically for Trebor. Reneé would later say that the recurring cast members in various Raimi/Tapert projects is a result of Tapert's desire to get to know his actors personally and to cultivate their skills by casting them as various characters. An example is Bruce Campbell of *Evil Dead* fame appearing as Autolycus on *H:TLJ* and *X:WP*.

Reneé O'Connor was no different. Because of her comic rendering of Deianeira in *Hercules and the Lost Kingdom*, she was asked to play a role in the Raimi/Tapert direct-to-video movie, *Darkman II: The Return of Durant*. In it she plays a stripper — definitely an opportunity to expand her

Reneé attends a production of *Grease!*
during Lucy's Broadway run
JOEL JACKAL

acting skills! In one of the first articles written about her
in the *Toronto Star*, the writer said that Reneé had spent
five hours in the hairdresser's chair getting hair extensions
and braids: "O'Connor had to be tarted up, she was too
girl-next-door." It was precisely those "girl-next-door"
looks that would eventually land her the part of a lifetime.

Reneé parted ways with Raimi and Tapert momentarily
to appear in two more television movies: *Follow the River*,
where she played a woman who is captured by Shawnee
Indians, and *The Rockford Files*, starring as an arrogant
actress who hires Rockford as a bodyguard. This last appearance garnered one of Reneé's first glowing reviews in
a major newspaper, the *Washington Post*, which described

her as a sexier Melissa Gilbert and raved, "O'Connor is magnificently adorable as Laura Sue Dean, and she brings out a rueful warmth in Garner and in Rockford too." This comment summarizes Reneé's performance perfectly. As Laura Sue Dean, Reneé bears some resemblance to Gabrielle in her outgoing, chatty personality, but she somehow manages to be self-absorbed and lovable at the same time. In one scene she tells Rockford that her only friend in the world is her teddy bear, yet she states this as a simple fact, without trying to evoke sympathy. In this role Reneé was able to show off her comedic and dramatic talents that would be so important on *X:WP*. Finally, Reneé was getting a lot of attention.

Among her newest admirers were Raimi and Tapert, and within a year of doing the *Hercules* movie and *Darkman II*, she was being called back for another interview. This one called for a spirited, funny, and intelligent sidekick

WENDY SPARKS

named Gabrielle. The audition process was a long and
arduous one, and Reneé had to return several times as
the other women being considered for the role became
fewer and fewer. It was a difficult process, made easier by
the support she received from Raimi and Tapert. Reneé
remembers that "they were up front in saying, 'We are
looking at other people, so just hang in there.' It gave me
a sense of acceptance either way." She met Lucy at one
audition, and immediately felt drawn to her charisma and
sense of humor. Because the two actresses got along so
well, there was an immediate chemistry between them on
the set. Reneé's petite 5′4″ frame, standing beside Lucy's
height of 5′10″, made Gabrielle appear to be more of a
kid sister to Xena, which is how the pairing was perceived
at the outset of the show.

FOR HER THE
BELL TOLLS

As soon as Reneé was cast as Gabrielle, she seriously
immersed herself in the role. Up at 3:30 each morning,
jogging and lifting weights, she whipped her already fit
body into even better shape, believing that a girl who'd
been walking all over Greece should look the part. She
would also seriously study a script — which she still does
today — by reading it over three times, giving a final read
the night before filming a scene, just to make sure she is
"word perfect."

Reneé felt immediately comfortable with the character
because it was so well written, allowing Gabrielle to
mature in a believable way, as many reviewers have
observed, rather than changing overnight. Gabrielle
appealed to fans because of Reneé's comic skill and

Gabrielle's unwavering optimism in the face of everything negative that happens around her. In the first season, Reneé was very content with playing Gabrielle as the good character, because she liked the idea of Gabrielle being a role model for young women. In later seasons, Gabrielle would begin evolving into a far more complex character, but for now Reneé was happy just playing her as the good girl.

From the beginning Reneé wanted to be involved in every aspect of the show. "I wanted to fight, I wanted to get as involved in every part of the show *Xena* as I could which is very much like the character." Fans may remember the earliest episodes of *X:WP*, in which Gabrielle is constantly mugging into the camera and hamming it up. But Reneé admits that lately she's allowed the character to mellow, an indication that she has grown as an actress. In fact, at first many fans were annoyed with Gabrielle and wished the show could just be about Xena. It is thought that Ares' constant references to Gabrielle as "that annoying little blond" are poking fun at early reactions to her character. However, Reneé was soon able to win them over with Gabrielle's devotion to Xena and her kind, peace-loving ways.

Although Reneé enjoyed doing the fight scenes, she wasn't quite prepared for all the physical demands of the show. She still admits to getting nervous before a fight scene, but she loves the adrenaline rush she gets from them, "[e]specially being short and small you love the fact that you can be tough and staunch and men go flipping across the room, you know," she laughs. For the first few episodes, almost all of the stunt work was handled by stunt doubles. Now Reneé admits to being spoiled on the set, because often in a fight scene she hits the other stunt people by accident and never gets hit back. To help teach herself how to handle the stunts more adeptly, Reneé began taking up activities that demanded more physical aggressiveness, such as martial arts, boxing, and rock-climbing. She jokes that the first time she was hit by a sparring partner in the boxing ring she was completely taken aback: up until that point, she gave out punches, but never received them. Reneé does often have a lot of bruises, but she insists that not one of them is from *X:WP*.

Besides learning all the stunts, Reneé had to adjust to living in New Zealand. She was surprised how many luxuries she'd taken for granted in the United States that did not exist in New Zealand. She found compensation, however, in New Zealand's natural beauty. So much was different there, and she had to learn to adjust to Christmases on the beach, the family atmosphere everywhere she went, the "dry wit," and the language differences, which sometimes got her into trouble. "During a fight scene," she laughs, "I'll tell a stuntman playing a bad guy that I'm going to bonk him [a Kiwi-ism for having sex], and he'll turn white." Reneé considers herself a full-fledged Kiwi now, living in New Zealand year round and returning to the United States on her hiatus to see her family. Reneé admits that she feels homesick every once in a while and Sandra Wilson misses her daughter very much, although she does visit her occasionally in New Zealand. She is happy for Reneé, though, and is comfortable knowing that the cast and crew of the show are like a surrogate family for her.

It is to Sandra that Reneé owes much of the Gabrielle fanaticism. In January 1997, Sandra attended the first Xena convention in Burbank and set up a table devoted to her daughter. Up to that point she had been trying in vain to convince Reneé that she was as important to the fans as Lucy. Now she was determined to prove it. Armed with her charming smile and the details of how to join Reneé's fan club (run by Sandra, of course), Sandra drew in the fans and gave them a rare opportunity to meet the real-life family of "Gabrielle." Sandra took pictures of the fans who

Sandra Wilson, a.k.a. Momma ROC
CATHERINE M. WILSON

approached to tell her that Gabrielle was their favorite
character and later showed them to Reneé to prove how
popular she was. Sandra told everyone to write to Reneé
via the fan club e-mail and postal addresses, and to this day
Sandra reads the mail and passes it on to Reneé. Sandra
started a web site devoted to Reneé and her official fan
club, called ROCweb after the Internet term for Reneé,

ROC, and the fans began to gush on the mailing lists about how wonderful it was to have met Sandra, whom they lovingly dubbed Momma ROC. A mailing list entirely devoted to Reneé grew out of the Xenaverse mailing list and consisted of a group of creative people who would write fan fiction, poems, plays, and songs, all devoted to Reneé and Gabrielle. This mailing list set itself apart from other lists in that it was purely a creative forum in the spirit of Gabrielle's own storytelling. Soon two more lists appeared, and as a result Gabrielle has more mailing lists devoted to her than to any other character on the show, proving that Sandra was right all along.

Knowing that Sandra couldn't do all the promotion by herself, the fans on these mailing lists began banding together to try to promote Reneé wherever they could. When Xena and Hercules were featured on the American Literary Association's library READ posters, promoting reading for young people, the Gabrielle fans began a campaign to get her on the posters as well. After months of writing letters, they succeeded. They also got her a feature in *People Online*, and they constantly write letters to talk shows and entertainment magazines asking the producers/editors to consider Reneé for interviews. On the online polls where fans can vote for their favorite star, the best-looking star, etc., Reneé fans regularly vote and vote until she gets to the top, the result being that Reneé usually surpasses Lucy in these polls. As time goes on more and more people are recognizing the name Reneé O'Connor. These are the kind of fans — warm, creative, intelligent — that any star would be honored to have.

Despite all the new recognition, Reneé is still surprised at everything that has been happening. Even though Eddie Wilson puts Reneé's newspaper articles and fan mail into scrapbooks to show her, he says that "she's surprised that anybody turns out [to see her]." Reneé does admit to checking out the Internet to see the numerous websites devoted to her and her character. In an AOL chat, where she made a more direct foray into the world of the Internet, she said, "I think it is great that we can see the opinions of all the fans from around the world. We have a direct connection to you whether you realize it or not."

It is strange for Reneé to think of herself as anyone's idol, because she has been a fan of so many actresses herself. She has said she admires the work of Jessica Lange, Sally Field, and Holly Hunter, the latter being the star of her favorite movie, *The Piano*. In fact, one of the reasons Reneé was so excited to work with the cast and crew of *X:WP* is that many of them had also worked with Jane Campion on *The Piano*.

BEEN THERE, DONE THAT (FINALLY!)

The main reason that Reneé likes her character on the show is because Gabrielle and Xena are very close, and that sort of intimacy between two women is very rare on television. "In 'Callisto,' there was a scene with us sitting next to a campfire just talking. Seeing two strong women being close and intimate, as friends, is a nice change in television." What she hadn't anticipated was the fact that so many fans would spot lesbian innuendos in the behavior of Xena and Gabrielle. Once she did hear about the subtext issue, she thought it was interesting, and along with Lucy and the writers, decided to play along. "We accept it . . . as a subtext. I mean, there is a love between us, and as long as we play the innocence of that . . . people can believe whatever they want. We like to keep them guessing."

She acknowledges that the more overt intimacy between Gabrielle and Xena was in direct correlation to the amount of letters they received from lesbian viewers. Although occasionally Reneé flip-flops when discussing the subtext — saying how much fun it is one moment and then asserting she doesn't like being pigeonholed the next — for the most part Reneé and Lucy have fun with the lesbian aspects, playing it to the hilt in episodes like "A Day in the Life" and "The Quest." In fact, when she and Lucy heard about the Xena nights at the Meow Mix in New York City, they began joking that they would enter the lookalike contests to see if they'd win. In the end, Reneé and Lucy decided to keep the subtext alive in hints for fear of stereotyping the relationship of Gabrielle and Xena.

In October 1997, Reneé finally bit the bullet and appeared at her first Xena conventions in Valley Forge, Pennsylvania, and San Francisco, California. Although she was extremely nervous beforehand, the fans adored her and for weeks afterwards the mailing lists were buzzing with convention stories. For the online Gabrielle fans, finally getting a chance to meet their idol was a dream come true. After all, Lucy fans had been given the opportunity to see her at *Grease!* and at conventions, but this was the first public appearance for Reneé. To celebrate the event, the fans organized what they called "The First International GabGames," featuring such Olympian sports as the squid hurl and the BGSB race (BGSB is the Internet term for Gabrielle's top, the Bilious Green Sports Bra). Reneé thought that their enthusiasm was great, and the day before the convention she told an interviewer, "There's a group of people who love Gabrielle and they're having a picnic tomorrow and they're going to have a squid toss . . . and that's really funny because they took one aspect of the show that Gabrielle hates, you know, hates fish, hates to be on a boat, and embraced it and created this wonderful

Fans gather for The First International GabGames.
ROGER DUARTE

wacky world." The fans also planned to imitate the Gabby
dance of the Amazons. A highlight of the games was the
presence of Sandra, who could do the Gabby dance and
tossed her squid as well as the rest of them. It was a great
time for everyone, and fans were immediately begging for

Momma ROC doing the squid hurl
ROGER DUARTE

Reneé to make more public appearances where they could show their appreciation of her.

Working on *X:WP* has been a rewarding experience for Reneé. She has met many new people, become recognized all over the world for her extraordinary role, has developed ardent ROC fans everywhere, has moved to a completely different part of the world, and has a "Kiwi boyfriend." She and Lucy have become best friends, while Sandra Wilson couldn't be happier reading the loving mail that she passes onto her daughter. Gabrielle has also been turned into an animated cartoon (in the animated Hercules and Xena movie that was released earlier this year), and she was able to provide the voice for it.

Interviewers ask Reneé if she ever fears that she'll be typecast, but that is a problem that doesn't seem likely. In Gabrielle, Reneé is able to play comedy, tragedy, drama; to be involved in Greek mythology, Biblical stories, and actual history; to be feminine and yet strong; lesbian and straight. Other than Xena, there is perhaps no other character in television or movies who is as multi-faceted as Gabrielle. And Gabrielle just wouldn't have been Gabrielle without the talent and charm of Reneé O'Connor.

Reneé at the Valley Forge convention

CATHERINE M. WILSON

RENEÉ O'CONNOR AT THE VALLEY FORGE CONVENTION OCTOBER 5, 1997

On October 5, 1997, Reneé O'Connor appeared at her very first *Xena* convention. Fans had been anticipating her appearance for many months, for despite being able to see Lucy in *Grease!*, on television interviews, and at other *Xena* conventions, very few fans had ever met Reneé. The following is a transcript of Reneé's appearance at the convention.

Reneé comes out to the X:WP *theme song and loud cheering that lasts the entire song.*

ROC: *[Muffled]* . . . and here you are.

FAN: We love you!

ROC: He's my brother. *[Laughter.]* . . . So I've been told that all these people will ask all these questions, you know, "Oh it's so easy." Thanks so much for coming. Didn't Ted wear his pioneer hat? Didn't he? *[No.]* Oh. Yeah . . . up in Philadelphia, we were going on a history walking tour. We all wore our pioneer hats and we were all marching through, you know, battling on. *[Laughter.]* They said, "Are you from here?" "Oh, it shows through huh?" *[Laughter.]* Easy audience! So um, yeah, so here we are. *[Audience shouting.]* Yeah I know, Robert said, 'Oh yeah, she's the virgin con girl.'

AUDIENCE: We can't hear you!

ROC: Huh? You can't hear me. Ohhh. *[Speaks up in a deep voice.]* There you go. OK. Um, what do you wanna talk about? *[Yelling.]* What? Gabby rap. *[Cheers]* But you know I can't keep the beat, so you're gonna have to clap with me . . . *[Clapping.]* *[Note: The Gabby rap is something that Reneé talked about on Vibe. It was a song that she composed during the first season as a joke about what a rap song by Gabrielle would sound like.]*

There's a six-foot woman and her name is Xena.
You can bet you've never met anybody any meanah.
[Stops because she's laughing.]
She wears a lot of leather, armor made of brass.
If she . . .

OK, everyone close your ears if you're under 10.
If she flips in your direction you can bet she'll kick your ass. *[Cheers.]*
My best friend I call her, it's a gift I'll always know.
With her I learn to fight the baddies, hope that peace remains aglow.
Xena. *[Cheering.]*

You see, in Kiwi-land the warlords are called baddies. I've learned this, yeah, I've picked up everything. Presidents are called prezzies, mosquitos are mozzies. So everything's just shortened: 'Luce, grab the drinky so we can get out of herey.' You know.

FAN: Your first question for your first convention . . .

ROC: What's that?

FAN: I said it's your first question for your first convention. I was wondering, which show, director, or actor is your least favorite? *[Audience groans.]*

ROC: This is my opportunity to get back at everyone, isn't it? Irritating blonde jokes, yeah. Uh, least favorite. I'd have to say that Gabrielle still has a problem with Callisto. Yeah, that will be forever in her life. You know one husband down . . . you can't take forgiveness on that one. But she's a nice woman . . . I'm sure you've met Hudson. *[Cheers. Note: Hudson had just left the stage.]*

FAN: These next people are wondering if you can speak French.

ROC: Do I speak French?

FAN: *Bonjour* Gabrielle, we come from Belgium.

ROC: Fantastic!

FAN: *On vient de Belgique pour vous voir, et uh . . .*

ROC: What? *[she looks sceptical]*

FAN: *Nous vous aimons beaucoup parce que . . .*

ROC: A lot. That's a lot.

[Bunch of people yell "We love you a lot."]

ROC: We love you a lot. OK.

FAN: *Parce que vous êtes jolie, marrante, et que vous êtes bien avec Xena.*

ROC: He loves Xena? He loves Xena. He's Belgian.

TRANSLATOR: Alright. He said that they are from Belgium, and that you are a wonderful character and that you are amazing and they think you're the best. *[Note: The translation is actually closer to, "We came from Belgium to see you and we love you very much because you are pretty, funny, and you are great with Xena."]*

ROC: Thank you very much.

FAN: *J'aime bien que je me comprend la passion ambigue entre l'amour et l'amitie, j'adore ça. Je voulais vous* [muffled] *. . . vont monter au cheval avec Xena, a serait à l'écran. J'aime toujours tous les deux.*

TRANSLATOR: OK, she too loves your character and thinks you're amazing and that the relation between Xena and Reneé, I mean Gabrielle, is amazing. Oh, and she wants you to ride the horse. *[Note: Translation closer to: "I enjoy the ambiguous passion that is somewhere between love and friendship, I love that. I would like to see you riding the horse with Xena, to see that on the screen. I'll always like the two of you."]*

ROC: Well, yeah, I like to walk. You know what, the horse wranglers, they have this conspiracy going on here. They were trying to find a shaggy miniature pony for me for a while. So that was my only option for a horse. I said oh, yeah, well I really like to walk. So yeah.

AUDIENCE: What about Tobias?

ROC: Tobias! *[Laughs.]* He was um, actually he embarrassed me quite a few times because I have a problem sometimes hitting my mark. They put a mark on the floor, and you know, we're supposed to hit it and talk and do other things at the same time. So I'm always a couple inches forward, to the side, I bop around and they're used to me now, but Tobias hit the mark perfectly *[laughter]* each time while turning a corner. So I thought, you know, I have a lot to learn, so. Thank you though . . . *[Next fan steps up.]* Hi. That's not Lucy is it? *[The woman resembles Lucy. Laughter.]*

FAN WITH HER SON: Hi Reneé. *[She introduces her little boy who is holding flowers.]*

ROC: Hey there!

FAN: He e-mails you every week, and every week your mom is so wonderful, she e-mails him back. He wanted to present these to you but they said we can't.

ROC: Thank you very, very much.

FAN: He gathered them himself. He looked all over Pennsylvania to find these flowers for you.

AUDIENCE: Aww!

ROC: Ah, come on up! *[Cheers. Reneé takes the flowers and hugs him.]*

ROC: No one, no one in New Zealand is ever going to believe this. *[Laughter.]*

Reneé receives flowers from a young fan.

CATHERINE M. WILSON

FAN: Hi, I was just wondering when we are going to see Gabrielle's spin-off TV show? *[Laughter.]*

ROC: I think it has to be a talk show, funny enough. *[Laughter.]* I have to think about this. How about Gabrielle talks and Sophocles comes on, you know, Salmoneus, some of those people. But it'll have to be like, you know, thirty years from now when I can't move anymore, I can't fight. Something to look forward to, right? Yeah, how's that?

FAN: Hi, Gabrielle, it's nice to be able to speak to you in person . . . I would like to ask you, would you ever seriously consider, having seen one side of the camera, would you consider directing?

ROC: Um, I would love to direct, um, not exactly a *Xena* because I watch *Xena* directors and it just takes so much work because it's an hour show, and we do a lot of stunt work, so we have two crews going at the same time. So I think I should come up with more experience before I try a *Xena*. But I would love to do, um, low-budget films, dialogue-type films, one day, I know I won't be acting forever so I might as well, you know, try something new, one day.

FAN: Would you pose for a picture? [Audience groans and yells "No!"]

ROC: Oh, they're gonna throw me outta here . . . sorry. [Note: The audience wasn't being rude here: in the autograph lines at conventions, you can take your picture with the actors, so when people ask to take their pictures with someone on the stage, they are wasting the already limited time that person has up there.]

FAN: How ya doing, Reneé? I'm a vendor here. First I'd like to thank you and the other cast members for making this possible. I wanted to give this staff to you, I was hoping maybe you could use it in one of your shows.

ROC: Um —

FAN: I know sometimes they're props and sometimes . . .

ROC: Yeah, you know it's funny, usually they're funny about it because it has to be part of the period. It looks like a magician —

FAN: No, it's actually solid wood.

ROC: Hey, you never know.

FAN: Maybe you could twirl it for us.

ROC: Sure. [Cheering.] First ten rows, I am sorry for anything that happens. [Laughter.] I've been known to lose stuff.

AUDIENCE: Put the mike down!

ROC: Oh, put the mike down. [She twirls the staff for a bit.]

FAN: Hi, do you have any comments or suggestions that you could give to somebody who is interested in having a career in acting?

ROC: I think, um, I was very fortunate because I started off in Houston and there's a small acting community there and I started working after going to a performance high school. I was about . . . seventeen? So I would start in the area where you live, maybe go to a university, try a lot of student films if you want to go into film and television, do a lot of plays.

FAN: Yeah, I've been in some plays.

ROC: Oh really, that's fantastic. Do you live here in Pennsylvania?

FAN: Yeah, I live in Pennsylvania.

ROC: Yeah, I would try and stay here as long as you can, and get experience, a lot of people go to L.A. or New York and they find there are so many actors it's hard to get work. So um, yeah, try to find the best experience, best classes, and always try to keep learning.

FAN: Hi Reneé.

ROC: Hello.

FAN: What's your favorite meal at Threadgill's?

ROC: *[Heavy Southern accent.]* What's mah fav'rite meal at Threadgill's? Um. *[Someone yells.]* What? What was that? Eggplant? No, no, well that's pretty good actually. It's um, it's good in a chicken-fried casserole. I love chicken fried steak, all of the greasy wonderful things: gravy and mashed potatoes and peas. After you have all that you have to go to bed, though. Actually they used to have fried green pickles *[audiences moans]*. It was great. Now hang on, hang on . . . they have that flavor of the dill pickle and then you take um, red sauce that you dip it in, it's good . . . *[Audience member says something.]* Nutbread, nutbread. *[Laughter.]* I swear, I get all these weird eating scenes, you know, there's one coming up that um, Gabrielle eats, I shouldn't tell you this, Gabrielle eats chicken livers and cherries and cheese sauce and all this stuff all at one time, oh it was just . . . Everyone kept saying, "OK now, take twenty, Reneé. We have more for you," you know. It was fun.

FAN: Hi Reneé. I just wanted to let you know I gave you and your mom a sweatshirt; I gave it to your mom and on the front it says Philadelphia. My question is, when you had to eat the squid, when you were chewing on the squid —

ROC: Yeah, oh yeah.

FAN: What was it, actually?

ROC: It's funny because we call it squid right, but it is actually octopus. I know you all know that. And, um, it was a marinated octopus, so — [audience moans] Yeah, real good, too. I finally just gave in to it and thought, "OK, how can I eat this? I might as well try to gross out every person on the deck," and I did too. I just kept eating it and eating it.

FAN: They weren't the only ones grossed out. [Laughter.]

ROC: Thank you.

FAN: Hi, I heard about your rock climbing and I was wondering if you do any of it in New Zealand?

ROC: Actually I do. My mom, funny enough, is going with me to the south island of New Zealand, we're going to go to a place called the Marlborough Track. I heard it's supposed to be one of the most beautiful places in the world, so, um, it's not so much of a rock climb, or mountain hike as we did before, but it will take about six days. There's supposed to be a lot of waterfalls . . . so I'm looking forward to that. Thank you . . . um, I was trying to think . . . how am I doing up here, OK?

AUDIENCE: Yeah!

FAN: Hi Reneé, I think your work is wonderful on the show. I'd like to know, what is your favorite aspect of the Gabrielle character, and do you have a least favorite aspect?

ROC: I love to torture Ted. Yeah, he's great, 'cause he just kinda goes, "Now could you just try it a little bit softer when you're biting on my ear, you know." Literally after I was, you know . . . finally I had to bite him so many times that three days later he had this black and blue swollen ear drum, and he stayed way away from me, but um —

TED [From backstage]: Yeah, sure I did. [Cheers. Ted comes on stage] Sure, now that's the version that Reneé enjoys telling. Let's tell it how it really was, shall we?

ROC: What are you doing?

TED: I'm here, Reneé.

ROC: Yes, Ted.

TED: To set the record straight. About many bruises I have had *[muffled]* . . . *[Audience moans.]* Now I'll have you know. Do you remember that scene in "Callisto"?

ROC: I remember.

TED: Do you know what Reneé told me? I've done this a million times. *[Laughter.]* Won't hurt a bit.

ROC: It's a soft stick.

TED: It was a soft stick, you're right, it was a soft stick, I admit it. But then . . . *[Someone yells out to get a microphone.]* I will. Where? Here? *[Reneé and Ted get the microphone and both trip on it.]*

ROC: The two clowns on the show.

TED: Yahoo. *[Cheering.]* Do you remember in "Callisto" when I got my brains beat out by her?! We all remember that. *[Audience cheers.]* That's when I fell on my nose. It hurt, it hurt a lot! Ah, OK, that's all. I just wanted to set the record straight.

ROC: Do you know what Ted does to me every time that, um *[laughs]* —

TED: Yes Reneé? Go on, come on.

ROC: We're, ah, sometimes when we're not working, that sounds funny, but I mean there might be a couple hours when we're waiting around so we'll go back to the trailer and Ted will pop out of his door and say, "So Rachel, how are the kids this evening? Can I borrow some sugar?"

TED: That's right we do the, ah, so-called Kiwis love to see us do our Bob and Jane Johnson imitation, you know. I say, "So, how's that pot-roast? Did Bill make the team?"

ROC: "Yeah, he'll be coming over with young Fred and Wilma."

TED: *[Laughing.]* "Sure! He just made top of his class."

ROC: "I heard that, and so did little Sonya."

Reneé and Ted Raimi duke it out on stage.
CATHY HOFFMAN

TED: "Ah, she's a knuckle-head, the little cutie."

ROC: "Yeah, but we love her anyways."

TED: "We do."

ROC: Anyway, so that's how we amuse ourselves there.

TED: Yeah. *[Cheering.]* All right, I just thought I'd come in and, you know, rain on her parade as much as possible. No, actually, it's not like that at all, we're very close. In fact, her fists connect *this close* to my face. *[Laughter.]* That's all, just wanted to set the record straight. Bye, all. *[Leaves.]*

ROC: He's crazy. Yeah. Funny.

FAN: Do you have any personal feelings for Ted?

ROC: *[Laughter.]* Ted, are you still here? Just kidding. Um, no, I mean yeah, you know, he's Ted, um — *[Laughter. Ted just came out on the stage, hiding. Reneé spots him.]* He's the most amazing man. If you ever see him in his suit — *[Laughter. Ted shows off his suit. Someone cat-whistles.]* No, no. I don't think he can hear anymore after that . . . No, Ted and I are very good friends, very good friends. Thank you. What's with the cameras? *[Laughing.]*

FAN: I think your work is great. Are you inspired by any actor or actress?

ROC: I um, I love a lot of different people, but I must admit, I love strong women, funny enough, you know. I love Jessica Lange, I love . . . Holly Hunter's one of my favorites, she's amazing. Um, Lucy, she's a comedian, I guess you all know that. Especially for those who've seen *Grease! [Cheers.]* There's a whole other side of her that you just rarely see. *[Audience member asks if she's seen it.]* Not yet. I'm going this week, hopefully.

FAN: I just wanted to say that I love you and I think you're great. I was wondering if Gabrielle had any love interests coming up?

ROC: He'll probably die! No, no. No love interests that I know of, but we've only recorded partway into it, so that might change.

FAN: Hi, Reneé *[laughs nervously]*, I just wanted to ask you, I'm also an actress, I just wanted to say that I know what it's like growing up; there was always a role that I've always wanted to play, stage, screen, whatever, there was always this one role and I was like, "It's mine!" What is that like for you?

ROC: I would love to be in a musical, and dance in the background or the chorus —

FAN: I've felt like that!

ROC: Yeah, I mean it's not, I would just love to be a dancer. That would really make it for me. I mean I love what I am doing now, but I mean, that would probably be something.

FAN: I will see you on Tuesday, my radio station's going to be doing an interview with you.

ROC: OK, that's right.

AUDIENCE: What station?

ROC: What radio station?

FAN: It's a kid's radio station, it's a network across the country . . . it's called Oz World Radio.

ROC: Oz World Radio.

FAN: Oz . . .

ROC: Do you have, um, is it syndicated?

FAN: Actually it's a network, it's a full network. We've got an affiliate . . . Wednesday morning it will air 8:40 Eastern, around 8:40 Eastern. Check ROC Web. All the affiliates are listed.

ROC: Check the ROC Web. *[Laughs.]*

FAN: Definitely check the ROC Web, for more than that. But, uh, the New York affiliate is 1660 AM.

YOUNG FAN: Hello Reneé, my name is Michelle. I just wanted to know why you think *Xena* has become such a hit?

ROC: I remember — Rob Tapert, you know, our executive producer? Yeah, yeah, okay. He, um, he, one of our first days he came and took me to lunch and gave me the speech. "So you know, there's never been a woman warrior, or a woman hero since Wonder Woman" so *[muffled]*. But it still came as a surprise, and now I think it's made quite a difference in people's lives.

FAN: I just wanted to let you know I love your character . . . I love the way she moves . . . I love the way . . . *[Audience is giggling and whistling.]*

ROC: I've never been complimented like that!

FAN: . . . and I've got some roses for you, twelve of them. I think your character's really hot. *[Cheering and whooping.]*

ROC: I never considered Gabrielle hot. Thank you, thank you, I guess. Thank you.

FAN: Hi . . . you guys must have such a good time on the set, can you tell us anything?

ROC: Um, it's funny because a couple of months before Lucy went off to do *Grease!* she was singing all the show tune songs. Lucy would just sing away, and I can't sing very well so I just kept humming in the background. She's just, that's her, I mean, even before she got on the show [*Grease!*] she's always . . . she jumps around a lot. I think I'm kind of more quiet. So I think our characters are kind of more opposites as we are on screen, she's so stoic and she's wacky off-screen, but I'm quirkier on-screen, but, um, I don't know, just different. On the set, you know we, um, we work and have a good time.

FAN: It must be great fun.

ROC: What's that? Oh, yeah.

FAN: Hi, um, could you tell us if Gabrielle will ever have a relationship with Iolaus?

ROC: Iolaus? I don't think so, I think he's more of a confidant. I think he's told to be a mate towards Gabrielle. Yeah, I don't think so. But uh, we started that in the beginning, which you know, but it just didn't quite work out as a romantic relationship, it's more of a friendship. I think that everybody liked Hercules and Xena's relationship.

FAN: Hi, Reneé.

ROC: Hello.

FAN: What places would you recommend if someone were to take a remote trip to New Zealand? I'm taking a trip to New Zealand.

ROC: I would, um, I would definitely go to South Island. Take a car, drive, take the ferry . . . there's a place, a glacier called . . . thank you — the Fox Glacier and the Franz-Joseph Glacier. You just drive across, there are hardly any people on the road, but careful, you'll become very lazy, and all of a sudden a truck will pull out in front of you!

It's just beautiful, there are very few people there — it's gorgeous. We used to have this place where we'd do extreme sports. I tried this one called sledging, it was very — you take a boogie board. Have you done this before? Nah? Anyway, you go down a river and it's like surfing or something, so you're travelling instead of on a raft on this wonderful body board. It's just the most amazing experience because you're actually part of the water and it's frightening, but not dangerous. It's quite fun, you might want to try that.

FAN: What American slangs have gotten you in trouble in New Zealand?

ROC: Ah yeah. Um, well, the bonk one, yeah. I still say it, I never learn. But it's, um, you get in the middle of a fight and you're going bam, bam, bam, bonk, bam, bam! And the guys just *[opens her eyes wide]* . . . they think it means something sexual. *[Laughs.]* So I get in trouble with that. What else, what else, what else. Actually I'm getting in more trouble here in America right now because I'm bringing all these Kiwi terms with me so I say, "Can I please have a white coffee? What? What? You know, white — coffee with milk? Thank you." And um, I say "I do heaps of work," you know, just little things like that. Oh *[laughs]* another one. In New Zealand they call their boyfriend their partners, and here "partners" mean something else. So I could say yeah, my partner and I came around, and um, you know, you say that in a hotel and stuff and people just don't understand what gender that is. So that's another one that gets me in a lot of trouble. *[Lots of cheering.]*

FAN: *[Muffled.]*

ROC: That's great. It's funny, because a lot of things that you start to enjoy about the show the rest of the country is now coming up on, so we heard a lot about the friendship by reading the Internet, just different things, and the rest of the fans and writers start appreciating it.

FAN: Speaking of appreciating it, do you go onto the Internet?

ROC: I do, I usually go in on Saturdays because usually Friday afternoons and Friday evenings it's just packed and you can't get in. So I go in and check out some book sites. Sure, sure. Thanks for tuning into the show. I wish you well. *[Applause.]*

YOUNG FAN: Where did you learn to twirl your stick?

ROC: Well, in one of the first episodes Gabrielle needs to learn how to fight, and I was learning with her. So, literally I was hitting myself. Um, believe me I was not a pro at all. But I just started doing a couple movements, then they started repeating some of the things over and over again, and now I love it. I love having to turn and things. So you just take, you take a stick, maybe your mom's broom or something — *[laughter]* and, um —

TED *[yelling from backstage]*: You bash the first person you can find with it! *[Reneé starts laughing.]*

FAN: Out of all the episodes, "A Day in the Life" is one of my favorites, I just really enjoyed it. *[Cheering and applause.]* In the scene with the eels and the fish were flying, what exactly did they use? Were they alive?

ROC *[sighing]*: Oh, no, no, no. They were dead fish. *[Audience groans.]* Even better, yeah. Live eels, mind you, so. First of all the live eels came. Lucy was hilarious trying to pick them up out of the water. A lot of that was Lucy not being able to hold them, and they used it for the show which is quite funny because those were her natural expressions because she couldn't hold the eels. So this lake, after we work, I think it has like ten or fifteen eels that live in there, and just recently Michael Hurst was working — he's directing a TV movie over there — and they were talking about placing actors in the lake and that there was a concern about eels. And I heard some people say, "No, no, there are no eels in that lake," and I thought, "Sure

JOAN STANCO

there are! We put them there!" They're definitely there. But anyway, there were live eels and dead fish. It was funny because Michael Hurst was directing that episode and he ended up using the first take where they're throwing fish — dead fish — at me. But for some reason he kept doing it over and over again. *[Laughter.]* Why? Eight takes later I had scales in my hair and my eyes, it was great, yeah, yeah. Everyone was staying clear away from me as I walked back to go home, you know.

FAN: Welcome back to America.

ROC: Thank you.

FAN: I just wanted to let you know that you and Xena have saved me tons of money in therapy. *[Laughter.]*

ROC: *[laughing]* Me, too.

FAN: I have four brothers and I'm the only girl. My question is: Is Michael Hurst a good kisser? *[Oohs.]*

ROC: Uh, yeah, oh yeah. No, Mike? It's kind of hard for me to say, you know, because these are like, like my little brothers, you know, it's kinda . . . it's funny because I was thinking about it, okay, I've kissed Michael, I've kissed Ted — *[laughter because the audience is thinking about Lucy.]*

ROC: I um, well, I, I didn't, well, Lucy ah — *[Cheering.]* We didn't really — I'm probably gonna get killed for this — but um, well, sorta, but um, but not really, but um, see what happened is . . . *[laughter.]* I was crying . . . so I had all the tears and stuff around me, and Lucy did not want to get close to me, I can't imagine why. So there's her, and then Kevin Sorbo's the only one I haven't kissed. Funny that.

AUDIENCE MEMBER: What did Lucy kiss like?

ROC: I'll never tell. *[Screaming and cheering.]*

FAN: Outside of your family and friends, what do you miss most about the United States, and what do you miss most about New Zealand now?

ROC: Usually when I'm in New Zealand, especially for a long period of time, I miss my friends. More so than the cities or the states, so I could just come back here and hang out with them. So this trip back, that was amazing, so finally since two-and-a-half years ago I've been able to do that. And in New Zealand, right now I miss the crew, being here, I miss Lucy, I miss being able to be back in my comfort zone, you know.

FAN: I saw you on *Vibe*, I was just wondering if you planned on doing any more television while you're here.

ROC: I'm doing Regis & Kathy Lee tomorrow morning. *[Cheering.]* I'm going there and that's it, that's it for me.

FAN: Can I just come up there and get a picture of you?

AUDIENCE: NO!!!

ROC: Survey says —

AUDIENCE: NO!

ROC: I'm sorry, oh man!

FAN: At the Los Angeles convention I asked Lucy if she had any plans for singing and she said no, then bam! she gets a Broadway hit. So, I am going to ask you the same question . . . are you going to follow in everyone's footsteps?

ROC: If I can help it, no. *[Laughter.]* No, I don't think so, I don't think so. Then again, you never really know what's going to happen in Xenaland, so. We could all be singing, who knows? *[Note: Hinting at "The Bitter Suite"?]*

FAN: How about that "Deep in the Heart of Texas"? That could actually —

ROC: What? "Deep in the Heart of Texas"? *[Note: The fan could be referring to a clip on the blooper tape where Lucy and Reneé are in their bacchae teeth for "Girls Just Wanna Have Fun" and they're singing "Deep in the Heart of Texas" for the camera.]*

FAN: That could actually work like "Deep in the Heart of Amphipolis" or something like that. Just change the words a little.

ROC: Change the words? "Deep in the Heart of Kiwi"?

FAN: Amphipolis — for the show.

ROC: Amphipolis. I do talk better than I sing, but who knows, maybe there will be a Gabby song, I don't know. Thank you, you never know.

FAN: Hi, Reneé. I am lucky enough to see your show four times a weekend.

ROC: Lucky? *[Laughter.]*

FAN: One thing I really want to know is, how much of Reneé is in Gabrielle?

ROC: It's funny, when we first started, you know, back at the first season, she was different, and I actually used — a lot of, you know, my mom *[cheering]* . . . but I actually took a lot from my mom and put it in Gabrielle. There's this

little, my mom does this dance and I made it the Gabrielle
dance in one of Amazon episodes in the very beginning.
[Cheering.] And my mom's funny, she's just, she's fun. And
Gabrielle, just the little things, my mom knows. One day
she'll call and say "Reneé." "So did you notice, did it look
familiar?" and she said "Oh yeah." So that was a little
different. And then Gabrielle became more relaxed, more
sure of herself, um, and um —

FAN: Is that Reneé?

ROC: Well, um, I think. More comfortable, older I guess.
Gabrielle became a little bit older and I felt more comfortable playing her. Especially "A Day in the Life," that's
one of my favorite ones, because it's the first time that I
really let myself come out more in Gabrielle and really
worked off Lucy. It was great. That's how Gabrielle started
to grow up a bit more. Now it's very comfortable, she's
very similar. Um, coming up, there's some things coming
up that um, it's, uh, the first time that I've actually found
it very challenging to play Gabrielle because I didn't agree
with a lot of her choices, so that'll be interesting. But I
know that, you know, Gabrielle's human, we're all human.

FAN: Thank you, I am looking forward to more seasons.

ROC: Thank you.

FAN: Thank you for coming.

ROC: Sure.

AUDIENCE: Porky Pig Dance!! *[Cheering.]*

ROC: The Porky Pig dance! *[Cheering.]* Well, it's funny
how these things come out — What's that?

YOUNG AUDIENCE MEMBER: Xena rap!

ROC: Oh, we did Xena rap didn't we?

AUDIENCE: Yeah!

ROC: If I have to do the Porky Pig dance I think everyone
should have to do the Porky Pig dance. *[Laughter.]* Oh, you
know, it's so easy. Let me show you. OK, everyone stand
up, come on. *[Everyone stands.]* Now let's get your legs

moving. You kind of skip. Come on everyone, come on guys. Yeah. If you did it you're a good sport. That's it, that's the Porky Pig dance. *[Everyone sits.]* On the *Vibe* show they asked me what my worst experience was, and, um, I think it was the Porky Pig thing. I had this ceramic head and my first time out it broke. So the head started spinning and all these kids were just horrified. It was terrible.

EMCEE: There's a phone call for you.

ROC: Really?

EMCEE: Yeah, there's a phone call for you. Let me see if we can work it so we can all hear the phone call. *[Cheering.]*

ROC: Who is it?

EMCEE: Let's find out.

CALLER *[voice that sounds like Mel Pappas]*: Hello? Hello? *[Cheering.]*

ROC: Hello?

CALLER: Reneé?

ROC: Yeah?

CALLER *[obviously Lucy]*: ALALALALALALALALALALALA!! *[Screaming/cheering/laughter.]* Hey Ren, how ya doin'?

ROC: Oh, all right!

LUCY: Good, I'm missing you, when are you coming?

ROC *[laughing]*: Can you hear everybody?

LUCY: Yeah, could you all pipe down? I'm trying to have a conversation with my friend!

ROC: Oh, she's a star.

LUCY *[in Gloria Swanson voice]*: Don't you know who I am?!

ROC: I do!

LUCY: Hey Ren, how ya doin'?

ROC: I'm good, I'm good.

LUCY: You having a good time?

ROC: Yeah, yeah.

LUCY: Cool! *[Laughter.]* When do I get to see you?

ROC: I'm coming, I'm coming soon, Luce, very soon.

LUCY: When? Tuesday?

ROC: Yeah, thanks Lucy, Tuesday. *[Cheering.]* You're gonna have a full house. *[Laughter.]* How's it going?

LUCY *[laughing]*: Well, they'll be coming to see you as well, so, I can't wait till you get here. It's going great, um —

ROC: Two more weeks.

LUCY: Yeah, I only got two more weeks, um, so it's the big countdown. And um, I don't think I'll be making it my job because I just, I realize more and more since I've been outside, here, how much I love our show —

ROC: Yeah, I know, actually.

LUCY: And I keep warning everybody that we've got a very challenging episode for the two friends coming up, and I think it's going to challenge our audience a lot.

ROC: Yeah, I think so.

LUCY: With the friendship under a lot of strain. But you guys aren't allowed to hate either one of us 'cause the script, the writers made us do it. *[Laughter/cheering.]* In the China episode —

ROC: *[Laughs.]*

LUCY: I don't want you hating anybody.

ROC: She's worried about me. She thinks you'll all give me a very hard time. *[Audience yells, 'No!']*

LUCY: Is everybody having a great time there?

ROC: We miss you though, you should be here.

LUCY: I know —

ROC: Aren't you supposed to be on stage?

LUCY: I have two shows today —

ROC: Two shows.

LUCY: — so it wasn't possible. But I'm doing great and I'm loving New York, and, um —

ROC: Well, I'm going to come see you so, hopefully —

LUCY: OK.

ROC: Yeah.

LUCY: OK.

ROC: Everybody says hello, and we're having a great time here. It is fun, it is fun.

LUCY: It is? It isn't too often that you get the opportunity to . . .

ROC: What's that?

LUCY: Don't get many opportunities to be at a convention for a show that you're working on —

ROC: That's true.

LUCY: — and meet everybody. Reneé and I really appreciate the whole phenomenon. [Cheering.] OK, Reneé, well I'm gonna look forward to you getting here —

ROC: Me too.

LUCY: OK. And Teddie's got some information for ya.

ROC: Where is that man?

LUCY: Hiding probably. [Ted peeks his head through the curtain.]

TED: I've got some very special information for ya, which I cannot reveal at this moment.

LUCY: Put the neck pinch on him, Ren.

ROC: What?

LUCY: Do that little, uh, that little neck thing I showed ya.

ROC: OK. [Reneé puts the neck pinch on Ted. Cheering.]

LUCY: Just a little tid-bit. [Note: Could it have been the announcement of her engagement?] Anyway, goodbye everybody.

AUDIENCE: Goodbye!!

LUCY: See you in New York.

ROC: Bye Luce, thanks for —

LUCY: Is Ted coming as well?

ROC: Sorry?

LUCY: Is Ted coming as well?

ROC: No, Ted's not coming. He says hello and he wishes you well, and —

LUCY: Gravy!

ROC: What? Gravy?

LUCY: OK, all right, well it will be great to have you come here anyway.

TED: Bye Lucy, it's Ted, bye.

LUCY: Bye Teddie! Bye, everybody.

ROC: Bye Lucy! *[Cheering and people doing the Xena yell.]* It's great. Fun, yeah.

FAN: Hey Reneé! I'd like to know, you seem like a jeans and T-shirt kind of gal. Do you like all this publicity that you're getting? And do you do your own housework?

ROC: Housework? Yeah, you know, somebody has to. Yeah. I love to be casual. This is fun, it's something completely different, it's nice to interact more one-on-one because sometimes with, um, some journalists, you know most of them watch the show or have heard of the show, but it's still growing, and they don't know all the details of different episodes and they're not likely to spot as much as you guys. So that's what's fun about this, it's always fun to do the on-line chats, because, you know, if it's a specific question, it's easier to answer.

FAN: Is it scary for you?

ROC: Yes. Yeah, I was really nervous coming up here. But its been, you know, uh — no it's fine, ya'll are great, but different.

FAN: On the interview with *Vibe* you said that you were allergic to the medication for climbing sickness. Did any of that prepare you for sea-sickness?

ROC: Wait, did the — ?

FAN: Did the climate prepare you for the episode "Lost Mariner"?

ROC: Where I was sick? Um, well it was altitude sickness. No, that was really weird, no, no. You know, it's funny because I love boats, it's really strange, so um, you know, you have to kinda psyche yourself out into thinking this is the worst situation ever . . . but that was no problem at all. It was very . . . I love boats. And altitude sickness, I was very lucky that I didn't suffer from that at all.

FAN: Thank you.

ROC: Yeah, sure. It's funny because we met a bunch of people from around the world that were climbing Mt. Kilimanjaro with us, and there were these guys that were taking the altitude sickness pills, and they were from — The Netherlands? So anyway, they, they were great, hilarious, they were walking up and these guys had their fingers in the air while they were walking up this mountain so you could always spot where we were going to be in two hours because we were much slower but it was hilarious because your fingers tingle, and what they give you, they cause vivid dreams. So every night these guys sat by my mother, and it would plummet my health because we couldn't eat and we had these symptoms, and one of the symptoms is you can lose your appetite, so they would just sit next to us and just, you know, eat all her food, and then we'd hear about these wild dreams they were having. [Audience snickers.] You guys! [Laughs.]

FAN: You know when they call you an irritating blonde?

ROC: Oh yeah.

FAN: I don't get it, you're a redhead.

ROC: So what am I?

AUDIENCE: Redhead!

ROC: Yeah, uh . . . I think, um, you know . . .

AUDIENCE MEMBER: Gorgeous!! [Laughter.]

ROC: I guess a bit of both.

FAN: [Asks ROC if Gabrielle would strike out on her own.]

ROC: I don't think so. I don't think so, I think Gabrielle will always be the friend of Xena, and that's her place in the world. [Applause.]

FAN: [Muffled.]

ROC: She's very honest . . . she seems quite staunch and

quite hard on the show sometimes, but she's actually very affected by people.

YOUNG FAN: Hi, Gabrielle.

ROC: *[giggling]* Hello.

YOUNG FAN: I'm the youngest member of your fan club. *[Crowd cooing about how cute she is.]*

ROC: Thank you, thank *you*. What's your name?

YOUNG FAN: Katie.

ROC: Kaylee.

YOUNG FAN: Katie! *[Laughter.]*

ROC: Katie!!

YOUNG FAN: Hi, I was wondering what Gabrielle's favorite food was?

JOAN STANCO

ROC: I have to say she had a great time with nutbread. *[Laughter.]* Apples, apples are easy, easy to eat. *[Someone yells.]* Cherries. *[Laughter.]* Yeah . . . um, it's funny, um, I'll tell you a secret, those actually aren't cherries. It's funny because they take grapes and take stems and pop them into the grapes and we eat them. It's very bizarre but that way there's no seeds.

YOUNG FAN: I'm your biggest fan.

ROC: Woo hoo! Yeah. Thank you.

ANOTHER YOUNG FAN: I wanted to know if you were scared when you first tried it? *[Audience whistles and cheers.]*

ROC: Wait, I don't get it, was I scared the first time I tried . . .?

AUDIENCE: The show!

ROC: The first time on the show! It's funny because I was the only American there, so I tried to go and do my job the best I could do.

At this point Reneé's time was up, and she left accompanied by a roomful of wild cheers. Afterwards she proceeded to sign autographs for everyone who wanted one. People came to this convention expecting a lot from Reneé, and I have a feeling that no one went away disappointed. She exuded a charm that is very rare in show business, and she definitely succeeded in winning the crowds over at her very first convention.

THE GREASE! CHRONICLES

by Bonnie Fitzpatrick
a.k.a. Dragon Lady

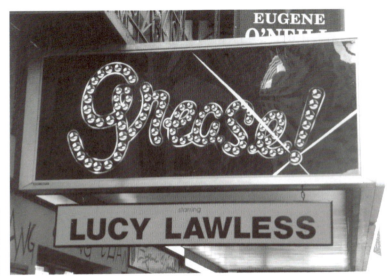

AMY PUTNAM

PART ONE: THE SHOW

I originally didn't intend to see *Grease!* sixteen times. When
I heard Lucy was coming to Broadway I bought four tickets
(opening night, closing night, and two weekends in between). Then I heard that Actor's Equity was questioning
Lucy's star status and she might not be able to do the play.
After that was settled, I read that some theatre type said
that none of Lucy's shows had sold out, thereby questioning Lucy's drawing power. To me it sounded like the theatre

snobs were looking down their noses at the TV star and that made me mad. I decided to support Lucy by doing what I could to increase her box office; so I bought some more tickets. During the course of her run someone (a non-Xenite) asked if I was getting sick of seeing the same play so many times. One of the nice things about the theatre is that no two performances are exactly alike. Sometimes the actors are on, sometimes they aren't. The actors flub lines. Props don't work. The response of the audience impacts what happens on stage. (In fact, outside the stage door Lucy said she and the rest of the cast noticed the mood of the audience and remarked on it to each other. "Whoa, what's going on here?" were her words.)

Lucy played Betty Rizzo, leader of the Pink Ladies and Kenickie's girlfriend (he of the Burger Shop Boys). Although she's secondary, I think she's the most interesting character. For most of the play she's very tough. She picks on Patty Simcox (head cheerleader, who's too dense to pick up on the comments being thrown her way). She also torments Eugene (nerdy, four-eyed geek). Rizzo is also very independent. At one point Kenickie tries to make her jealous by taking another date to the prom, but Rizzo turns the tables on him by going to the dance with Zuko. Towards the end of the play, however, Rizzo has a pivotal scene with Sandy during which we see Rizzo's emotional depth. Rizzo thinks she's pregnant and her friends (the rest of the Pink Ladies and the Burger Shop Boys) try to offer support. Although she's obviously scared and very much wants their help she tells them to "flake off and get the hell out of here." Which they do. Sandy is the last to leave, and as she's doing so she wishes Rizzo good luck which sparks a confrontation. The songs "There Are Worse Things I Could Do" (sung by Rizzo) and the reprise of "Look At Me, I'm Sandra Dee" (sung by Sandy) were the highlights of the show. The two characters bond by daring to show each other that they aren't quite as tough as they seem and they care more than they've been letting on. In Rizzo's case it also seems like she's settling on Kenickie because she's not going to waste her time waiting by the phone for Mr. Right to call. At the end of the play, all the couples end up together (Rizzo finds out she isn't pregnant and she reconciles with Kenickie) and everyone sings the *Grease!* finale.

As Rizzo, Lucy had three solos ("Greased Lightning" reprise, "Look At Me, I'm Sandra Dee," and "There Are Worse Things I Could Do") and sang as part of the group in seven other numbers. (*Grease!* trivia: Lucy had five costumes and seven changes. Her costumes were: black-and-white dress, black stretch pants with a black-and-white striped blouse, black negligee, black jeans, black leather bra with black leather vest, and a black velvet prom dress.)

It was great seeing Lucy perform on stage, stretching beyond Xena and singing. If you ever needed proof that Lucy is more than Xena, this was it. In an *Entertainment Tonight* interview, done when it was announced she would be doing the play, Lucy indicated she was afraid. In another interview she said she lives in fear. She shouldn't. From what I saw (and I was looking) I think Lucy has the talent to pull off any role she wants. There were Saturday nights when I went home after the theatre, watched *Xena* and thought that, aside from a certain physical resemblance, if I didn't know better there was no way this could be the same person I just saw in New York. In this play Lucy was surrounded by actors who had been doing this for a long time (some of whom originated their roles) and she more than held her own. Lucy has stage presence and brought real depth to the role of Rizzo. Specifically, for me, Lucy's performance/run could be broken down into three phases:

I. The beginning. Lucy was obviously nervous at first (in fact her hands were shaking during her opening night performance). Based on what I saw later, I would characterize her first couple of performances as workmanlike. There were shows when she was "on" from the instant the curtain went up. There were other times when Lucy seemed to be walking through the first part of the play. But regardless of how the rest of the show was going, when it came to the scene in the rec room (when Rizzo and Sandy confront each other) Lucy was always firing on all cylinders. I don't know if that was because this scene revealed the emotional depth of her character, giving Lucy more material to work with, or maybe, because the difficult choreography was over, Lucy could concentrate on her acting. Whatever the case, you could tell by the expression on her face as the curtain was going up on the scene that there were going to be fireworks. And this scene (especially the song "There Are Worse Things") always got to me and my heart went out to the character every time. You would think after seeing it several times I would become used to it. Nope, never happened. That was how good Lucy was. She got me every time. I was also impressed at how well Lucy was handling distractions. For example, despite flash-bulbs going off in her face, and someone wolf-whistling during her big song, Lucy maintained her concentration and her performance never wavered. During the course of Lucy's run the play underwent some fine tuning. For example, at the beginning of the play the characters come forward and introduce themselves. Lucy was in the middle, but the ovation for her character was so loud and lingering that the introductions of the rest of the cast were drowned out. By the third show they moved Lucy to the end, making hers the last character introduced. After each performance Lucy made essentially the same curtain speech. She indicated she was enjoying her stay in New

Grease! billboard in Times Square

AMY PUTNAM

York and appreciated the support of her fellow cast members. She also sometimes added that there were probably some people in the audience who didn't understand what all the fuss was about. At the show I took my parents to (my dad loves *Xena*, thinking it very funny) she included those remarks.

As soon as she said it someone in the back yelled, "We love you, Xena." We were in the front row and Lucy looked at my father and said, "That's who I am." My father hit his head in mock recognition and said, "Oh, *that's* who you are," and Lucy laughed.

II. The middle. The second phase started approximately two weeks into the run. It began when Lucy started smoking during the bathroom scene (prior to that her cigarette remained unlit). By this time Lucy was relaxed and appeared to be having fun. She wasn't walking through performances anymore. On the other hand, she wasn't letter perfect anymore either. She flubbed lines now and then. She started adding flourishes to her songs. She was obviously more comfortable with the dance numbers. She and her fellow Pink Ladies (especially Marissa Jaret Winokur, who played Jan) seemed to really hit it off. When the spotlight/action wasn't centered on them, they were talking and seemed to be having a great time. At the beginning of the play (when the characters were at lunch) Rizzo, Jan, and Marty developed a ritual where they would each put a hand on one of the bowls on Jan's very full lunch tray, and close their eyes for several seconds (wishing for a good performance?). The audience always reacted (loudly) to the Xena yell in the second act prom scene. While the audience was reacting, Lucy started making faces. This always elicited another (loud) audience response. One night Lucy started laughing while making the faces and had to put her head down for a while before she was able to collect herself. The audience was loving every moment of it. During another performance after a fight with Sandy, during which she almost lost an earring, Lucy looked like

Curtain call, 18 September 1997

AMY PUTNAM

she wanted to laugh, but she didn't. One night Lucy slipped coming down the stairs. The audience held its collective breath. During her curtain speech that evening Lucy said "Break a leg. Break a pelvis. Anything to entertain you." At the end of several shows Lucy received flowers. One night someone wasn't satisfied with the usual method of delivery (handing them to her), opting instead to throw them at Lucy. They hit her in the arm and she reacted in pure Rizzo fashion. Whenever someone did give her flowers Lucy always made it a point to make eye contact and say thank you.

III.   Homestretch. The last couple of weeks. Fun and games were over. There were no more flubbed lines. No more laughing. It still looked like she was having fun, but she was all business now. Her songs and dance numbers were completely fleshed out. At the end of the first act instead of twirling the hula hoop, Lucy started jumping through it as if it were a jump rope (and she made it look easy). I guess variety kept things as interesting as possible. Lucy started saying "quarter" more like a New Yorker. (Prior to that her pronunciation always belied her origins. It sounded like she was saying "qwata.") Her last couple of performances had a "no holds barred, go for broke" feel to them. She was getting down to the wire and she wasn't holding anything back. During her big scene with Sandy, for example, her eyes would well with tears. During her last shows the tears flowed. Her last show was very emotional, especially her song "There Are Worse Things." Marissa (Jan) was watching Lucy's big scene from the wings and during the song their eyes locked for several seconds. Lucy was crying. (So were several members of the audience.) "There Are Worse Things" and the reprise of "Look At Me" blend into each other and, prior to the last couple of shows, the audience always held their applause

Curtain call, 13 October 1997
AMY PUTNAM

until both actresses were done and were heading up the stairs ending the scene. During her last performances the audience started applauding after Lucy's portion. At first this drowned out Sandy's part. By the last show Sandy (and the orchestra) paused during that applause and waited until it died down to continue.

The rest of the cast were really good. Several of the actors had great voices (Melissa Dye, who played Sandy for example). The rest of the cast standouts (in my opinion) were Kevin Anthony, in a show-stopping portrayal of Teen Angel (for those who saw the show, he was the first of three Teen Angels), and Christopher Youngsman, who played the klutzy nerd Eugene to perfection.

Of all the performances I was lucky enough to see, Lucy's opening night was my favorite. During her run, while the audience was filled with her fans, there was an air of anticipation and expectation on opening night that wasn't duplicated in any other performance.

Because of the depth and emotional impact, I will miss Lucy singing "There Are Worse Things" the most. The cost of the tickets was worth it for the opportunity to see her perform that scene and sing that song. In several interviews, Lucy mentioned that doing this show was therapy for her to help her get over her fear of singing. Well, I for one would welcome it if Lucy extended that therapy into an album.

PART TWO: BY THE STAGE DOOR

On the nights I wasn't going to see *Grease!* with anyone I knew, I enjoyed striking up casual conversations with the people sitting around me. I also enjoyed watching the people standing outside the stage door. Through this I was able to gain a real appreciation for the incredible diversity of the *Xena* fan base; if ever there was a physical manifestation of the *Xena* demographics, this audience/crowd was it. Whether in the theatre or by the stage door, this was a mixed group. There were men and women in their twenties dressed in leather standing next to Long Island matrons. Professional men and women next to teenagers. Kids all over the place. I remember seeing a woman who looked to be about 60 hanging on the lamp post, camera in hand, waiting for Lucy. Standing not far from her was a mother holding her four-year-old who was asking, "Mommy, where's Xena?"

I was surprised at how many non-Internetees made up the audience (actually they seemed to make up most of the audience). They invariably referred to Lucy as Xena. They were usually accompanied by family members who were indulging them by coming to see the play. I was usually asked how tall Lucy is, where did I get my chakram necklace, and about the official *Xena* fan club. I loved seeing their reaction to the Xena yell during the prom scene in the second act. During one performance a child kept saying

Lucy at the stage door with her fans.
AMY PUTNAM

to her mother, "It's Xena." At another show one child was very restless until Lucy came on stage. Then she was riveted. After the NYC convention, during which Lucy asked the men in the audience why they watched the show, I decided to take a very unofficial poll. The men I spoke to were divided into two groups. One group watched the show because their daughters did. One gentleman in from Utah on a business trip explained he had extended his trip just to see Lucy in *Grease!* He said that every weekend his daughters had "*Xena* time" during which all activity in the house would stop while the entire family watched the show. He said his daughters had Xena everything. He hoped to get Lucy's autograph as a present. (He succeeded and was left with the tough decision of deciding in which daughters' room to hang his prize.) The other men I spoke to thought the show was very funny and think Lucy is beautiful (although they usually only admitted the latter upon the urging of their wives). There was a noticeable difference between weekday and weekend audiences. The weekday audiences always seemed more relaxed and responsive. The weekenders were more reserved. For some reason Tuesday night crowds were the best.

Meanwhile the crowd was gathering outside the stage door. At the beginning of her run, there were usually only a few people waiting for Lucy to arrive at the theatre. Even if she was running late Lucy always signed as many autographs as possible and seemed to take the time to talk to kids. (Although, in her haste to get to as many people as possible Lucy was scrawling her initials instead of signing her complete name.) The crowd after the show was something to behold. They started gathering before the play started and by intermission the barricade leading from the stage door to Lucy's car was completely occupied. Before the show ended, the crowd would be two to three deep around the barricade. They would be joined by the people leaving the theatre after the performance. Very often the crowd spilled into the street and blocked traffic. I remember buses stopping across the street so the people inside

AMY PUTNAM

AMY PUTNAM

could get a look at Lucy. The waiting crowd started out very calm. Then as time passed the tension would mount; Lucy mania was taking hold. The play usually ended at 10:40 and, unless she had visitors, Lucy would take just long enough to change her clothes before leaving the theatre. As she walked out the crowd would erupt. Suddenly everyone was screaming (usually "Xena") and people were jostling each other trying to get an autograph or a picture. I'm surprised Lucy could see given all the flashbulbs going off in her eyes. Almost every night several people would do a Xena yell, trying to get Lucy to do one. In the beginning she frequently obliged. People asked questions and Lucy took the time to answer while signing as many autographs as possible. She seemed very relaxed and friendly. She worked both sides of the barricade and over the roof of her car trying to get to everyone. She would sometimes recognize the face of someone she had previously given an autograph to and not sign anything for them, opting instead to sign something for an unfamiliar face. Sometimes she signed for as long as 15 minutes before

she said good-bye, disappeared into her car and was driven
off. After Lucy left, the snippets of conversation I over-
heard always centered on how nice it was of her to take
the time to sign all those autographs. Some of the people
lucky enough to get autographs would literally bounce
their way back to groups of waiting friends or family, their
hands shaking. One girl even kissed the theatre walls after
Lucy left. It was amazing to see how incredibly important
making that momentary connection to Lucy was to everyone. There were downsides, though. For example, one guy
nearly knocked people over trying to get autographs, and
after Lucy left he tried to sell them for $15 each.

Sometimes Lucy would leap out of the stage door and
do high kicks. The crowd loved it. And she didn't always
arrive in her car. Sometimes she would walk up the street,
pass among us and be in front of the stage door talking to
her security guard before being recognized.

About half way though her run I wondered if the novelty
of the stage door routine was wearing thin. There were
times she wasn't feeling well, or didn't appear to be in the
best of moods, but she was always gracious to the waiting
fans. (There were only a handful of nights when she went
out another door bypassing the waiting crowd. That only
happened when she had to be somewhere.) I wondered if
she felt like she was facing a gauntlet.

As her run progressed the crowds by the stage door
increased. People brought folding chairs to sit on while
they waited for Lucy. Then, with about a week and a half
to go, it seemed to dawn on people that she was really
leaving. This was their last chance to see her. A kind of panic
set in. Her last few shows were standing room only. There
seemed to be a perpetual throng of people by the stage
door. The security people had to barricade both sides of
Lucy's car (I heard someone tried to climb in the window
at her). The crowd extended half way down the front of

the theatre. I have never, ever seen crowds as large as these. Security was tightened. Extra police were brought in. We hardly saw Lucy at the end. She would go into the theatre early and only sign about ten autographs after the show before being whisked away. What an experience (for Lucy and us)!

PART THREE: FUN AND GAMES

While Lucy was in *Grease!* New York City felt like the center of the Xenaverse. It feels like we've been through a seven-week long XenaFest. This had all the elements of a good Fest:

1. Hanging out with/meeting other Xenites. Every weekend there were groups of Xenites hitting town. People were coming in from all over: New Zealand, The Netherlands, various points in Canada, and all over the United States. I wish I could list everyone's name, but it would be impossible. There were several pre-show dinners which included between 20 to 40 Xenites. I had met a lot of the visitors before (at Fests for example) and it was great seeing them again. I also got to meet people I had only "talked" to on the 'net. It's always great to put a face with the handle and have a face-to-face conversation with someone. Because people made this their vacation they were here for extended periods of times. Between the show, Xenite social activities, and conventions, I think I was home one night during these seven weeks and that was the only night I managed to get more than four hours sleep. We became well known at several places in New York. For example, when I would show up at what became our usual restaurant to make dinner reservations, the hostess and manager were greeting me by name even before I had a chance to say anything. Our last night there (just before

Lucy's last performance) we endeared ourselves to the other restaurant patrons and the management by entertaining them with our practice renditions of "I'm An Old Cowhand" which we were going to serenade Lucy with. (We thought it would be a perfect tribute, to show Lucy our appreciation, to serenade her with the song that got her in *Grease!* And how often on Broadway does the audience sing to the actors?) Luckily the atmosphere at the restaurant was such that it went over fine and the other people thought it was very funny. Hey, this *is* New York!

2. *Xena* episode viewing. This was done at the several special *Xena* nights held at Meow Mix in honor of the visiting Xenites. Because the *Xena* nights have become so well known, MM became one of the most often Xenite-visited NYC sites.

3. *Xena* panel discussions. Usually held while hanging out at the barricade by the stage door waiting for Lucy. To ensure we had prime spots some of us would gather sometimes four or five hours before the show ended and Lucy came out. (Sanity was not a prerequisite for joining these little discussion groups. Actually, come to think of it, it was frowned upon.) The discussions were free-wheeling and all-encompassing. Topics included the direction of the third season. Howard Stern bashing was a favorite. Photos were often exchanged at these gatherings.

4. Guest appearances by members of Xenastaff. Steven Sears made it to a MM *Xena* night and graciously signed posters, etc. Several weeks later Robert Field hit town. He caught the play and also came to MM. Both gentlemen were very nice, leading me to the conclusion that niceness runs rampant among Xenastaff. Rob Tapert was at several Saturday shows and was at the last four of Lucy's peformances. He was also very nice and very accessible. (Side note: I can't help but wonder if we'll see any

Lucy and Reneé at Grease!
BONNIE FITZPATRICK

of Lucy's fellow *Grease!* cast mates in some future Renaissance production. Rob seemed to really enjoy the show. Unlike others in the audience, he wasn't only watching Lucy. He seemed to really enjoy the character of Eugene.) Bottom line is everyone in this group were really nice people and I throughly enjoyed talking with them.

At several points during these seven weeks it was remarked that this was a magical time. What are the odds that Lucy is ever going to do another Broadway show? We are never going to have this kind of exposure to her again. And what are the odds that such a group as we will ever again come together? For that reason I gladly sacrificed sleep and abandoned the rest of my personal life. Would I do it again? Without a doubt or hesitation. Boy, I had fun. Who would have thought seven weeks could pass so quickly and in such a blur? I loved meeting everyone I did and truly hope our paths cross again.

XENITES JUST WANNA HAVE FUN: FAN CLUBS, MAILING LISTS, AND OTHER FAN-BASED ORGANIZATIONS

In this section you'll hear from fan-club presidents, organizers of XenaFests, administrators of web sites and mailing lists, and the head of the Sword and Staff foundation, an organization that collects charitable donations from fans and donates them to various charities in the name of stars from *X:WP*. Perhaps by listening to these fans tell their stories, you'll find out how to start a *Xena* organization of your own!

Venator, Administrator of the Chakram Mailing List (and revered inventor of the term "Xenite")

Back in mid-December of 1995, the very first Xena mailing list started. I had helped the list moderator, Arbiter, in running the list once, so when he no longer had time to run the list in May of 1996, I picked up the ball and ran with it, using his same list guidelines and naming the list "Chakram." When the first incarnation of the list ended, it had about 250 members on it. As of December 1997, we had nearly 1,500 members from close to 30 countries on the list. Thankfully, the list has remained unchanged in terms of the guidelines over the years. The only two things that had to actually be added were points stressing that we *are* a subtext and Joxer-friendly list . . . in other words, the two subjects that cause the most controversy are welcomed.

Unlike the other mailing lists, Chakram must have someone (myself) constantly monitoring it. People send posts to me, I make sure they are in accordance with the list guidelines, and then I send them out to the entire list. This assures everyone that the quality level of the posts will be high, and the quantity of posts low. Originally, I would spend all day long with an eye on my mailbox, but I've been able to wean myself down to between 5 and 8 hours a day, all free of charge to list members.

Why do I do it? Simple . . . it provides a great service to the fans of the show because it's the only list like it out there. "The first, and still the best," as they say. I've even received a few compliments from various members of Xenastaff about the quality of the list, so I know that I must be doing something right.

Mary Draganis, Administrator of Web Sites and the GabChat Mailing List

I started GabChat around August 1997 and there were a handful of subscribers. There are now over 100 members and it's growing every day. Creating and maintaining a mailing list is quite a challenge: there's always something going wrong, either with the server being down or people wanting to unsubscribe or subscribe.

The web site went up December 15, 1996. It took me initially four or five hours to create the site, which at the time consisted of the main page and about six sections. Since then, of course, it's grown. The fan fiction section has had the most growth in the first year. The site is by invitation only, which means I don't accept submissions and I usually invite the author to join what I call The Bard's Corner. If I know the author's prior work, I'll jump in and ask them, and coding the additions to the fan fiction takes an hour or two depending on how many pieces I get. Montages, which are clusters of photos from each episode, take a lot of time. They usually require about two hours each depending on how involved the episode was. And of course there is the GabChat mailing list which takes time in unsubscribing, chasing up error messages and basically being there and reading the messages. It's a good list and everyone is very nice.

I've had over 85,000 hits to my site in the last year, which started off very slowly but has grown. What makes it stand out? Firstly I aim it at Australian Xena fans — without, of course, excluding other fans — and I have the montages, which are a unique aspect of the Xenaverse. I wanted something different when I first created the page and montages were it. I also endeavour to update the site nearly every day so people will want to come back. Recently I've added a bulletin-board style of chat system and a postcard center which has been a big hit with those who return to my site. If you're going to create a web site, you would want people to return to it and you must make it accessible to everyone, even to those who don't have the latest browser with all the wizzbang applets on them. Make it visually a nice place to come to. I guess the number-one rule I have is that I create the page the way I want to see a page done. If I go to a site and it's geared towards Australian members, I would like to see some Australian content. And mine has just that.

Kym Masera Taborn, Administrator of *Whoosh!*, the online journal of the I.A.X.S.

I released the first Xena Media Review (XMR) 03/29/96. XMR is a world press review of Xena media citations with commentary and anything else I could think of to put into it. I was releasing it weekly at first. In May 1996, in an editorial in XMR, I announced that it would be cool to have an organization with a journal devoted to fan *non*-fiction. By the end of the month we had started taking members in the International Association of Xena Studies, and had set up a web site (Tricia Heintz was the IAXS webmaster). The requirement of membership was to have access to an e-mail address and to submit an article to the journal at least once a year. There are even members of the production staff and actors on *X:WP* who are members of IAXS. By September 1996 we released our first *Whoosh!* at the *Whoosh!* web site (Betsy Book is the *Whoosh!* webmaster). We currently get around 60,000 monthly visitors which works out to over 1.5 million hits, averaging 2,000 a day. Anyone who wants to write an article is welcome to. We have never refused an article unless it did not fit into the guidelines, although we do not take fiction or poetry.

When we first introduced *Whoosh!* (**http://whoosh.org**), we were lucky in that *Web Magazine* had done a review on the IAXS site in their premiere issue (10/96). That meant we always had a healthy amount of visitors. When we first set up we were getting over a hundred a day. After the first Burbank Convention (01/97), we were averaging over 400 per day. Our highest visitor count for one day was Thursday October 23, 1997. We had 4,070 visitors.

Having so many visitors to the site means we spend a lot of time keeping it up. I used to spend more time on it, but now that *Whoosh!* has a staff of about 30 people, I spend about 10 hours per week specifically on *Whoosh!* projects. We have groups working on the Xena FAQ, the episode guide, a gossip area ("News Gossip Rumors"), the convention reports ("On the Road"), and preparing the journal articles for publication. We are also always developing new areas of interest for the staff and fans. And of course we have about 10–15 articles per monthly issue. So, each month about 45–50 people are involved in making sure the issue gets out.

Sword and Staff is an organization of *Xena: Warrior Princess* fans dedicated to making a difference in the lives of the people in their own communities. In just six months, through charity auctions, raffles, fundraising drives, and volunteerism, *Xena* fans have benefited the greater good by contributing over $25,000 (and uncounted hours) to organizations providing aid to those less fortunate than ourselves. Born shortly after the New York City XenaFest in March 1997, the Sword and Staff originally defined its mission as one of tracking the donations made by fans in the name of the show and its stars. Since then, Sword and Staff has since expanded its mission to include organizing fundraising drives and supporting and participating in charity events organized by fans and fest committees.

Sword and Staff has reached out around the world in an effort to have all segments of *Xena* fandom represented. As a result, members of Sword and Staff currently hail from the United States, Canada, Great Britain, New Zealand, and the Netherlands. By forming alliances with XenaFest committees, fan clubs, and individual fans, Sword and Staff has drawn on the strengths of the incredible group of caring and giving individuals who inhabit the Xenaverse, and the result is an enormous amount of good being done in the name of show, its stars, and its fans.

Sword and Staff has 'adopted' The Elizabeth Glaser Pediatric AIDS Foundation and will continue to contribute to that organization in the name of *Xena* fans.

For additional information about Sword and Staff, see our web site located at:

http:// xena.simplenet.com/swordstaff.html

Or write to Sword and Staff at the address below. You can also send your questions or comments via e-mail to Debbie Cassetta at **cassetta@ix.netcom.com**. Anyone wishing to join with the members of Sword and Staff in making a donation to the Pediatric AIDS Foundation can do so by sending a check or money order made payable directly to the Pediatric AIDS Foundation to:

Sword and Staff
P.O. Box 224
Floral Park, NY
11002-0224

Julie Ruffell, Co-Organizer of the Pacific Northwest XenaFests

A XenaFest is a gathering of Xenites organized by Xenites. It is *not* a convention (we pray for the stars, but it just doesn't happen). Basically, it's a way for Xenites to meet others in the area, make new friends, and have a good time.

How did I become one of the organizers? I had just joined *Whoosh!*, and in the message I received it said that members had a say in conventions. I thought that maybe this would mean I could voice my desire (along with the desire of many others) to have a Convention in the Pacific Northwest (preferably in Vancouver or Seattle).

I was then told of the XenaFests. I contacted the woman organizing the New York Fest at the time, and she told me about the plans for the Pacific Northwest XenaFest and gave me Rita's e-mail. I contacted our Amazon Queen that night, and soon received a call. I had been invited to the first meeting. That Saturday, I gathered with the others at a restaurant and met the other organizers: Donna, Stephanie, Rita, and Ann (Fern also helped with the Fest, but was not at this meeting). Things took off from there and we got started.

The First Pacific Northwest XenaFest was held on March 29th (Lucy Lawless's birthday), 1997 in Vancouver. We plan to have one every year. Fests range in organizing time, but the longer we have, the more time we have to plan and contact Xenites.

We contact fans through the Internet, but are searching for ways to reach those who are not online. Putting a Fest together takes a lot of work, but those who join the committee work really hard to make Fests a blast! Every Fest has different events, however most will have a viewing of episodes, games, trivia, and no matter where you go, you'll meet new, exciting Xenites!

Now that we've done one Fest, we are trying to raise money for those in need. For more information, you can visit *Whoosh!* and read, "The First Pacific Northwest XenaFest: A Committee Members Experience," in issue nine.

Also, anyone with e-mail access can e-mail Xena Torres/ Julie Ruffell at: **norman_ruffell@bc.sympatico.ca**. And for those without access, can send a SASE to Rita Ma at:

5200 Clifton Road
Richmond, B.C.
Canada
V7C 3B9

If you are interested in arranging a Fest in your area, I would recommend talking to Xenites nearby and finding out how many would attend. XenaFests aren't cheap, and you have to watch that budget. Make sure people will come before putting down money for a hotel room. Contact people any way you can, whether online, through newspapers, or if you have a TV station that runs adds for events happening in the area, drop them a line. After that, find yourself a committee, because a Fest is *not* a one-person job (believe me!). Find people to help manage money, find the location right for you, create events, and so on. I would also not recommend trying to arrange an auction or any fund-raiser that would dig into your pockets for your first Fest. It's a noble idea, but find your footing before you set your foot down. Do it once and understand where the money will need to go, and how everything flows. The less you put on yourself the first time, the less stress you'll incur while organizing it. Creating a XenaFest is no easy matter. If there is already someone in your area that handles Fests, try contacting them instead of trying to run your own. They'll have the experience, and you'll have the new ideas. I wish you all the best of luck!

Deb "Neuf the Goof" Neufell,
President of the Lucy Lawless Fan Club

I started The Lucy Lawless Fan Club in August of 1997 after realizing that Lucy didn't have a fan club, as her official club closed after a few months of operation. It didn't seem fair that other stars of the show had fan clubs but Lucy didn't. So I decided to change that!

Since we're not official and don't have Lucy's input into the club, we work extremely hard to keep the club interesting and fun for all of our members. I'm involved in the majority of the fan club development. Some of my tasks are: writing articles for the newsletter, designing the layout for the news-

CATHERINE M. WILSON

letter, getting the newsletters copied, creating the membership certificates, ordering the photos, putting the membership kits and newsletters together and shipping them out, maintaining our web sites, handling e-mail from our members and potential members, managing club funds, and creating our club logo.

My vice president, Sue Steinike, also writes articles for the newsletter and edits the newsletter. Together we discuss the content of the newsletter and our ideas about what little goodies to give to our members.

Our membership fee is $15.00 for U.S. residents, and $20.00 (in U.S. funds) for non-U.S. residents. To join send your name, address, e-mail address (if you have one), and appropriate membership dues to:

> The Lucy Lawless Fan Club
> 65 Edwin Road
> Waltham, MA 02154

Also, let us know what name you'd like on your membership certificate (some people like their nicknames or screen names on there). We are open to Internet and non-Internet fans. Please make your check or money order out to The Lucy Lawless Fan Club.

Since we are not an official club we do not have contact with Lucy. Lucy's fan mail should be sent to:

> Creation Entertainment
> 664–A W. Broadway
> Glendale, CA 91204

You can access our web site at:

http://members.tripod. com/~LLFC/index.html or
http://members.aol.com/LLFanClub/LucyClub.html

Our e-mail address is **LLFanClub@aol.com**. The Lucy Lawless Fan Club is a member of The National Association of Fan Clubs.

ROCweb: Reneé O'Connor's
Official Fan Club

The fan club is run wholly by Sandra Wilson, Reneé's mother. She opened a P.O. Box for Reneé's fan mail in Austin in August 1996. After attending the Burbank convention in January 1997, Sandra more or less promoted the fan club as officially launched, and handed out some really nice flyers about how to join, etc. The fans really appreciated getting to meet Sandra. Her being there as an ambassador of sorts for ROC was well received. Shortly thereafter, Sandra endorsed starting a webpage for Reneé which was created on behalf of the fan club for the sole purpose of disseminating information about ROC and the fan club via the Internet.

Sandra has received (and continues to receive), *many* generous offers for help with the fan club. All have been sincere and much appreciated by Sandra. She has one or two helpers in Austin — where the fan club is headquartered. ROCweb — which is comprised of a couple of folks — handles the webpage and e-mail.

Reneé's webpage (a.k.a. ROCweb) was first launched in about mid-February 1997, just after ROC's birthday, and it's

Sandra Wilson and Reneé O'Connor

WENDY SPARKS

updated periodically. Sandra and her Austin helpers handle the snail mail and are responsible for keeping the fan club database current. As for the time involved, Sandra handles all the fan club packages, autographed photos, special requests, and a lot of other business on Reneé's behalf. Time spent by ROCweb (the webmaster) is only a couple hours a week as long as there are not any web site updates to be done. ROCmailer (e-mail responsibilities) takes about an hour or so a day.

The other form of fan club communication is obviously the newsletter, which is intended to be quarterly; however with personal time constraints on both ROC and Sandra, sometimes it gets out when it gets done. The newsletter is a collective effort by several people involved with the fan club.

The exact number of fans in the ROC fan club is not quite nailed down. As Momma ROC has somebody helping her handle the huge volume of mail in Austin now, she's not sure what the total current number is. We do know the fan club had passed the 2,000 mark *before* the conventions this past October. So the membership estimate is probably somewhere between 2,000–2,800 at this date.

Reneé's participation in her fan club consists of an interview periodically for the newsletter and when time allows, a message for the webpage. ROC personally autographs all the photos that go to the new members.

Reneé also checks her webpage periodically to make sure the info is accurate and not too crazy. Direct fan club contact with Reneé is typically done through Sandra, who talks to ROC at least once a week. They do not however always talk business (i.e. the fan club) when they talk since Reneé gets so much of *Xena* during her work week.

Anyone interested in joining the fan club should do so via regular mail, as we do not process memberships via e-mail. Send a letter with all the pertinent info and a check or money order to:

ROC Fan Club
P.O. Box 180435
Austin, TX 78718-0435

The cost is $10/yr for U.S. citizens and $12/yr (in U.S. funds) for the international fans. There may be a small price increase in the works for next year, but so far nothing definite to report on.

For this you will receive:

- Membership Certificate
- Membership Card (wallet size)
- Autographed photo of Reneé
- Copy of the first fan club newsletter (4/97)

During the year you will receive copies of the Un-Quarterly fan club newsletter and any special announcements that the fan club sends out. It should be noted that the standard turnaround time for the fan club packages is at least eight weeks due to the delay in sending mail to and from New Zealand.

Anyone wishing to visit the Official ROC web page should surf on over to:

http://rampages.onramp.net/~Rocweb/

This is a new URL, we just recently moved the site, and up-dated the information and photos on it. E-mail to Sandra, ROC, or ROCweb can be sent to either **Rocmailer@aol.com** or **Rocweb@aol.com** (although this latter e-mail address should be used for communication about the webpage. Fan mail and other fan club inquiries should refer to the ROCmailer e-mail).

Jan Holbrook, President, BC CENTRAL, The Official International Bruce Campbell Fan Club

I already knew Bruce, having met him in 1994, before BC CENTRAL was officially sanctioned in September 1996. I knew that Bruce was a terrific person and very easy to talk to, and knowing that his popularity was growing and he didn't have a fan club, a few of us decided it was high time he did. I contacted

Lucy and Kevin Sorbo

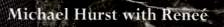
Michael Hurst with Reneé

Hudson Leick

Kevin Sorbo and Lucy

him about the club in August, outlining everything that we
planned to do with the club, and he was receptive to the idea.

At the time of this writing, the club has 400 members and
people can join by sending a SASE for info to:

BC CENTRAL
8205 Santa Monica Blvd., #1–287
Los Angeles, CA 90046

Or they can go to the fan club page on The Official Bruce
Campbell Web site at:

http://www.bruce-campbell.com

When you join the club you receive a membership card,
membership certificate and photo both personally signed
by Bruce; Bruce's biography and filmography and the official

Bruce Campbell
CATHERINE M. WILSON

newsletter, *Stay Tuned . . .* , which will now be coming out quarterly. I do have a fan club staff, but I handle all of the memberships and mail and mailing out of membership kits and newsletters. Club members are encouraged to send in articles for the newsletter.

In addition to handling Bruce's fan club, which is a voluntary effort, I also actually work for Bruce. I maintain his web site and set up some of his personal appearances. I also handle his fan mail and autograph requests. The "autograph requests" is a feature that is on the web page at: **http://www.bruce-campbell.com/e-mail.html**. If anyone would like an autograph, they should send their full name and mailing address to: **bcautographs@bruce-campbell.com**. Bruce loves to interact with his fans, so if they would like to write to Bruce they may do so at: **bcquestions@bruce-campbell.com.**

For those not online, they may write to Bruce at:

Bruce Campbell
14431 Ventura Blvd. #120
Sherman Oaks, CA 91423

Our web site, which started out as a small fan-club page, has become a huge web domain with the club having its own section on the site. The web site is more like an on-going newsletter for those fans with Internet access. They can go there to find out "everything they have ever wanted to know about Bruce" including all of his upcoming projects.

The web site has a separate staff from the fan club and Bruce and I work together to get the info onto the site in a timely manner. Though Bruce has a very busy schedule, he always finds time to give me any info I need for the newsletter including writing a message to the fans and answering questions.

I also do all of Bruce's online publicity and when fans join the club, I request that they also give me their e-mail address. I send out periodic e-mail memos about upcoming TV shows and convention appearances and any other thing that is apt to come up quickly. If those not online would like those same memos sent to them, then they should send in SASES often.

Fan clubs are a lot of work, but they are definitely fun!

Danielle Cormack

CATHERINE M. WILSON

Bret Rudnick, President of the Danielle Cormack Official Fan Club

The story of the origin of the Official Danielle Cormack Fan Club is one of high drama, pathos, subtle comedy, and a ton of subtext.

No, not really. It was a complete and total accident.

I work for *Whoosh!*, an online webzine that is the journal for the International Association of Xena Studies. Although my contribution to *Whoosh!* started as a graphics editor, I sort of fell into a niche of doing interviews. Kym Taborn, publisher of the magazine (and, for a change, *my* prime assistant in the fan club) one day mused out loud if we could ever do any interviews with cast or crew for the webzine. We were thinking "Third Spearholder From The Left" kinds of interviews to start with. I volunteered for that, and it turned out to be a very successful venture.

One of my interviews was with Danielle Cormack. For me, this was a very important interview, because I quite like Danielle Cormack's work and I think she is an underrated actress, certainly Stateside. In the course of the interview, we chatted about how very popular her character Ephiny was, not only in the USA but wherever *Xena* was shown in the world. She laughed and found that very hard to believe since, as she put it, she is cut off from the rest of the world living in New Zealand and *Xena* was shown at a very "unsociable" time in her own country and few people there knew she was on it. She has quite a lot of notoriety in New Zealand for other things she has done (not the least of which is winning the 1997 New Zealand Film and Television Award for Best Film Actress for her work in *Topless Women Talk About Their Lives*). I volunteered to put together a fan club for her and she quite happily agreed. Her agency had gotten a few inquiries from fans Stateside, and a fan club would help to be a central organising point for fan mail, etc. So the Official Danielle Cormack Fan Club was born in August of 1997. We have a homepage at:

http://members.aol.com/dancorfans

And people can write to us at:

> The Official Danielle Cormack Fan Club
> 297 Boston Post Road, Suite 141
> Wayland, MA 01778

I've spoken with her agent on a number of occasions and we have a very good working relationship. He and his office have been very helpful to us in getting started. They didn't even have any pictures of Danielle that a fan club could use, since no one had ever asked before! We continue to communicate regularly; a couple of times a month I will send a bundle of new memberships down and Danielle will personally autograph each one, then I'll get the bundle back and redistribute. Fan mail is handled the same way — I'll collect a batch and mail it to Danielle and she'll respond when she can. It's a gentleman's agreement right now; we are the official fan club unless or until Danielle doesn't want us to be. Some fan clubs have had to sign agreements and work out legal arrangements, but we're not in that ballpark by any means. We're just a small group of people who like to help out.

Right now, the fan club is fairly small, so it's been very easy to work with. But I expect we will grow quickly and very soon — Danielle appeared at her very first convention in Burbank in January of 1998 (she was going to attend a convention in Washington, DC last year but had to cancel because of a work conflict). Fortunately, I have Kym Taborn to help me, and now Stacey Robillard as well. None of us has ever run a fan club before, so we're learning as we go. I couldn't ask for better help, though.

At the moment our primary work is the collection and redistribution of autographed pictures and fan mail. We're also getting a newsletter off the ground, and we keep people up to date on Danielle's latest work, awards, and appearances primarily via the homepage.

Danielle is very appreciative of the club, and as we continue to gear up we are seeking more of her participation. She does write in her spare time, and we want to share that talent of hers with her fans. She's a delightful person, a lot of fun, completely unpretentious, and just a genuinely nice and talented person. From what I've been able to piece together, native New Zealanders tend to be low-key in their fandom and appreciation of same. They don't quite know what to think of some of the . . . more enthusiastic . . . fans up here.

Laura Morris, President of the Official Robert Trebor Fan Club, "Palindrome Pals"

Palindrome Pals, The Official Robert Trebor Fan Club, started a year ago. In addition to working with the fan club, I am a convention organizer. In December of 1996, Bob was one of our media guests at Stellar Occasion 3 in Dallas, Texas. As Executive Assistant, one of my pre-convention jobs is to make

Robert Trebor

JOAN STANCO

sure that any of the guests' needs are taken care of. I spoke to
Bob numerous times over the telephone prior to the show.
Upon arrival in Dallas, I served as his guest liaison, making
sure that everything was taken care of for his visit. At the
conclusion of the convention, Bob asked me if I had ever had
any experience in running a fan club. I have been in one kind
of science fiction fandom or another since the early days of
Star Trek, so I told him yes, I do have experience. He asked if
I would be interested in running his club, and so Palindrome
Pals was born.

Since Bob approached me about the club, and since it is his
club, rather than that of a character from the show, sanctioning
was easy. Universal has known almost since the beginning that
we exist. At the present time, our club has 75 members. We
have been steadily growing this year. To become a member, one
needs only to send some basic information about themselves

to the fan club address with payment of $14.41 (U.S. funds) for dues. Our club address is:

> Palindrome Pals
> The Official Robert Trebor Fan Club
> 3352 Broadway Blvd #538
> Garland, TX 75043

Our membership packet includes:

- Membership certificate
- Welcome letter
- Bob's Biography and filmography
- Laminated membership card
- Autographed photo
- Quarterly newsletter

Right now, I have three other "officers." One handles newsletter publication, one handles the web site, and one deals with some of the publicity duties of the club. Since Renaissance also sends Bob's fan mail to me, that tends to keep me rather busy. I send all letters and any thing else he may receive to him. Speaking of which, if you are interested in receiving an autographed photo, please include a SASE in the package, or you may not receive one. Bob is *very* active in the club. From the beginning, he has been involved in everything, from having a say in the color of paper for the membership cards to supplying the newsletter with a column for each issue.

Debbie K. Mills, Liaison for the Official Hudson Leick Fan Club

Hudson Leick and I first met at a sci-fi/fantasy convention held in Fairfield, California in early May of 1997. At that time, I was in the process of putting together the first Hudson Leick newsletter for the unofficial Hudson Leick fan club and Reginald Mathusz's Hudson Leick Resource Page web site (the very *first* Hudson Leick/Callisto web site to go up on the Internet, in November of 1996). At my initial meeting

Hudson Leick

CATHERINE M. WILSON

with Hudson, I found her to be extremely intelligent, warm, friendly, witty, charming, and totally unpretentious. At all of Hudson's convention appearances everyone leaves feeling fantastic, and this convention was no exception. Seeing Hudson in person is an experience that no one will soon forget. Her sheer energy, enthusiasm, and exuberance for life are refreshing and infectious. And her mere presence "lights up" the entire room. Hudson patiently answered every question asked, signed every autograph, and posed for numerous pictures with everyone, myself included.

I then found out that Hudson would be coming to another convention in my area (Sacramento, California) within a month of the Fairfield convention and I interviewed her there. During my interview with Hudson, I found her to be very honest, thoughtful, and candid, to my sometimes personal and probing questions. As was the case in Fairfield, Hudson was very gracious and generous, both with her time and herself. I had by then completed the first issue of the Hudson Leick news-letter, which I presented to her at the end of our interview. Shortly after that interview with Hudson, Eric Christman, the fan club liaison at the time, had to resign from his fan club obligations and asked if I would be willing to take over his responsibilities as unofficial fan club liaison. I agreed, and Hudson's agent, and Hudson, were notified of the change.

Within a few weeks of my taking over as unofficial fan club liaison (mid-July 1997), Hudson called and expressed an interest in the fan club. During our conversation I asked Hudson if she was interested in making her unofficial fan club an official fan club. Hudson accepted my proposal, and a verbal agreement between us was made at that time, with the written agreement following soon after.

The Hudson Leick Official Fan Club (HLOFC) now has about 650 members. Anyone can join the HLOFC by logging on to the Internet and going to the Hudson Leick Official Fan Club site:

http://www.hudsonleickfan.com

and then clicking on the "Fan Club" button. Or send e-mail to: **HLOFC@hudsonleickfan.com**. There is no fee to join the Hudson Leick Official Fan Club and no yearly dues. The Hudson Leick Official Fan Club Web Site (HLOFCWS) is run by Wes Reiser, Bret Dedmore, and an entire HLOFCWS Maintenance Team that all do a fantastic job of running and maintaining an accurate and up-to-date Official Fan Club Web Site.

Once you are a member of the Hudson Leick Official Fan Club you will be notified of all the latest "Hudson News" and fan club information via e-mail. Hudson shares current information with her fans through the HLOFC and takes a very active interest in the fan club and its members, so everyone receives a lot of input from her, as well.

Since the Hudson Leick Official Fan Club is still so new, HLOFC membership packages are still in the process of being put together. The exact content and price of these packages will not be known until they are completed, but they will definitely include an exclusive, autographed, 8x10 color photo of Hudson, her biography, filmography, official fan club membership certificate, and a membership card and/or membership button.

Currently, the only way to join the Hudson Leick Official Fan Club is on the Internet. But you may send mail to Hudson, or inquiries about the Hudson Leick Official Fan Club, to:

Hudson Leick Official Fan Club
P.O. Box 775
Fair Oaks, CA 95628

Lana Andrews, President of the Ted Raimi International Fan Club

The Ted Raimi International Fan Club (TRIFC) formed in the spring of 1996, and we established our anniversary date as being June. Four members of the *SeaQuest* mailing list came together (*SeaQuest* being the television show that Ted starred in before *X:WP*) and then I was invited along and became the last of what has come to be called "the founding five." We started out to be just an Internet-based club but quickly grew into a full-fledged organization. The international part of our group stems from the eight countries in which we have members. Right now our club is relatively new so it doesn't "do" much. We do meet each other at conventions and make a habit of going to dinner after the cons so we can get to know one another, and we have a snail mail club, e-mail list, newsletter, and various other things. We also run a web page with a gossip page for members to share updates. Ted does his best to stay in contact with me when he's got the time because he's terribly busy. He seems to be very happy with TRIFC and has asked us to be his "official" club, a process we are still working on. To join send a check or money order for U.S. dollars made payable to Lana Andrews to:

Ted Raimi International Fan Club
c/o Lana Andrews
555 Surby Ave
Battle Creek, MI 49015

Cost is $4 for U.S., $6 for Canada & Mexico, and $8 for rest of the world until June 1998. Included in this is a quarterly newsletter and a membership card. The membership package may change for the next year which starts in June 1998 for everyone. For more information visit our web site at:

http://www.stgenesis.org/~inga/TedRaimi

Please be sure to type it in exactly as seen here: the address is case-sensitive.

Once you become a member you will receive a quarterly newsletter and a membership card. We started out small so we could see what all we could accomplish. At this time, there are some discussions with Ted and other officers about changing the package for next year, so this may result in changes in the dues. At this point we are still quite small but growing steadily.

Ted Raimi

JOAN STANCO

We also have a large Internet following as the most current information can be found on our web site and with the gossip page and e-mail list, the updates are usually done almost constantly.

I obviously don't run the entire club by myself: I am helped by vice-president A.J. Adair and secretary Christina Scurti. Others who help out are Sherry Loeffler, who is the editor-in-chief of the TRIFC *Tribune*, Melissa Cavanaugh, the convention table consultant, Jeane Noriega, the club designer, and Michelle Vincenti and Valerie Perez, who maintain the list. Ted helps out, too, by sending updates about one to two times per month about his professional activities. He is very happy with TRIFC and is working to make it his official club. He has also discussed some other possibilities for the future.

Beth Gern, President of the
Kevin Smith Official Fan Club

When I first conceived of starting a fan club for Kevin Smith, I didn't anticipate how long it would take to get it off the ground. After a couple of false starts, I finally wrote to some-one whom I met through the Internet who works on the set and knows Kevin personally. The false starts began around December of 1996, but I didn't get to start the fan club officially until April 1997.

I had been in contact with Kevin and his manager down in New Zealand for a couple of months but they weren't comfortable agreeing to the fan club until they had actually met with me face to face. Kevin was in the L.A. area last spring with his manager on business, and one of the things they wanted to do was have a meeting with me! So I drove up to Hollywood (I'm in the San Diego area) with a friend. I was incredibly nervous and was hoping I would make a good impression. My friend and I got to the restaurant before Kevin and his manager did, so we were sitting there at a table waiting and looking at every approaching passerby. Finally, I saw him come around the corner; my heart jumped into my throat! The first few moments were a little awkward, I think for all of us, but soon we were chatting away like old friends. I wanted to be able to talk to Kevin on a human level, not just as a star-struck fan. I wanted to find out who he is as a person, and find some common ground. Over Italian food, we talked about all kinds of things: our kids, his work and his family, funny things, life in general, what I wanted to do with the fan club, and more. I had a wonderful time and I think they did too. Initially they had said that they only had about an hour, but I think they stayed close to 2 hours. He and his manager are both incredibly warm, down-to-earth and charming people! I asked Kevin and his manager to sign a simple agreement that they approved of the fan club and that I had their cooperation, and the fan club was born!

Of course, I don't do everything alone. My friend Sue Ball is the editor for the newsletter, and I have another friend named Danielle Walther who contributes a lot by way of articles and other assorted tasks. We have a girl named Tamara Brayton who coordinates the tables at conventions and made the banner and pictures for our fan club table. Another girl named Katie Buller helped out initially by making up the bio. I keep track of the memberships, mail, web page, and information gathering; and various other tasks. And we love to get contributions for the newsletter from fan club members. I probably spend 10–15 hours a week at it.

Kevin helps out, too. He calls me about once a month or so just to touch base and let me know what he's up to. He is really good about cooperating and contributing. I fax him frequently to ask questions, and he also writes a column for each newsletter and answers a long list of questions directly from fan club members.

Right now the fan club has about 125 members, but we get more every week. People can join by sending an SASE to the fan club for info at:

Kevin Smith Official Fan Club
9880 Magnolia Ave., #126
Santee, CA 92071

Kevin Smith

CATHERINE M. WILSON

or by following the instructions on the fan club web site, which is:

http://www.inetworld.net/zepgirl2/fanclb.htm

When you join the club you will receive a quarterly newsletter, Kevin's bio, an FAQ about Kevin, filmography, membership card, and an autographed photo. We have contests in the newsletter, such as one where you could win a phone call from Kevin, and we had a fan club members' group photo taken with Kevin at the Warriorcon convention in Washington, D.C. Being in this fan club is a lot of fun, and you really get the feeling that you're up close and personal with the actors, something that's rare in a lot of others.

INTERNET
SOURCES

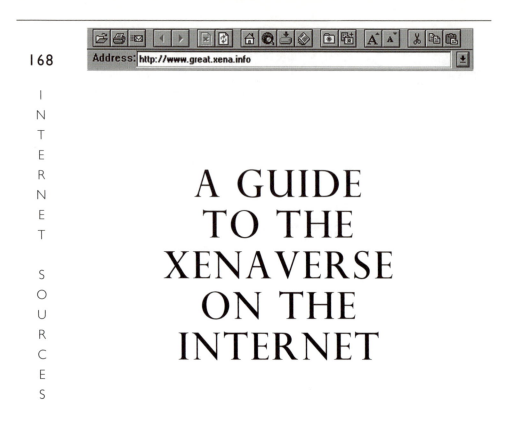

Address: http://www.great.xena.info

A GUIDE TO THE XENAVERSE ON THE INTERNET

Web sites

The Internet fandom that surrounds *X:WP* is vast and contains some of the most creative work devoted to a show and characters that you'll ever see. There are new *X:WP* web sites popping up every day, so this listing is by no means exhaustive, but contains the essential web sites that are overflowing with information, as well as a few quirky web sites that stray from the norm.

Whoosh!
http://thirdstory.com/whoosh/
Whoosh! is the online journal of the International Association of Xena Studies, the closest *X:WP* has come to academia so far. "Whoosh" is the sound Xena's head makes when it turns, the sound of her sword, the sound

of her chakram . . . well, you get the idea. There is an issue of *Whoosh!* each month (back issues are available) that include articles, interviews, essays, reviews, and analyses of *X:WP*. The site also includes an episode guide, list of air dates, a *X:WP* FAQ (Frequently Asked Questions), a rumour mill, and more. This site is a monumental achievement in the vast Xenaverse.

Tom's Xena Page
http://www.xenafan.com/
Considered by many to be the *X:WP* page, Tom's Xena Page has it all — FAQ, sounds (hundreds of them), thousands of images from the show, a collection of fan fiction, the Poteidaia Post Office (a great place to send *X:WP* electronic postcards to friends), an art gallery of fan artwork, videos of *Xena* bloopers, and much, much more! This site also boasts the weekly "Battle On!" comic strip by Jeanette Atwood.

Xena: Warrior Princess: A FAQ for Subtext Fans and the Loyal Opposition
http://members.aol.com/daxwtesq/faq/faq.htm
For anyone who is still hazy on what the subtext issue might entail, this site answers all your questions about

I
N
T
E
R
N
E
T

S
O
U
R
C
E
S

the lesbian innuendo in *X:WP*, including what it is, which episodes have the most, what LL and ROC think about it, why it's so popular, etc. It also keeps track of magazine articles where a cast or crew member may have mentioned the subtext.

Texas Xena Mafia presents The Bubba's Guide to *X:WP*
http://rampages.onramp.net/~ccgddos/txm/
This site is definitely one of the strangest sites you'll find in your travels through the online Xenaverse, but it contains my favourite webpage. "Bubba's Episode Guide" is the single most hilarious episode guide you'll ever read, with the explanations written in a "Bubba Elucidation." Only certain episodes are available, but your sides will be splitting when you read, for instance, the guide to "Don't 'Member Nuthin', " where they review "Remember Nothing," from Season Two: "It commences with our gals Xena 'n' Gabrilla goin' tuh this Temple of the Fates. I reckon thass prolly like th' temple my momma goes to, the Faith in Our Lord Jesus Temple in Waco, Texas." This is the most cleverly written *Xena* material I've seen yet.

Logomancy: XENA fandom
http://plaza.interport.net/logomanc/XENA/
This is one of the *Xena* mega-sites that takes a more serious look at the show. With links to sites about Greek myths and Ancient cultures, you can learn more about the issues and history behind the episodes. This site also features the fantastic credits guide menu, which is the only complete listing of those impossible-to-read credits (and without which the episode guide in this book would be much smaller), puzzles, an online bookstore, an entire calendar to print out, images, interviews and a message board where you can leave notes for other Xenites. Logomancy is an essential *Xena* site. Don't miss it.

Xena: Warrior Princess Information Page
http://xenite.simplenet.com/index.html
An absolutely extraordinary page devoted to the show
and dedicated to Australian Xenites who have the mis-
fortune of being slightly behind North Americans in the
episodes. This site includes transcripts of articles and
newspapers, fan artwork, upcoming appearances of LL
and ROC, and the best selection of fan fiction on the
Internet. It also features site administrator Mary Draganis's
famous episode montages, where she puts various images
together from particular episodes, to make a dazzling
picture. Highly recommended.

Coffee Tawk
http://pc-rschnepp.pepperdine.edu/rizzo.htm
Rita Schnepp is one of the most hilarious and clever
Xenites on the web. This site is based on the *Saturday
Night Live* skit with Mike Myers, where he plays the
Jewish lady with the impeccable New Yowk accent,
Linda Richman. This site features "interviews" with Lucy,
Reneé, and many others, where Linda gangs up with
other guests and drives the interviewee insane. Schnepp
is also the creator of the Encyclopedia Xenaica, a brilliant glossary of Xenite terms, taken from interviews, the
episodes, and the mailing lists. The E.X. can be accessed
from this site.

The ROCzone!
http://www.impulz.net/~ragnarok/roc.htm
This site was the original ROC web site and contains all
sorts of quirky information about "the goddess," as they
call her, including her actual résumé before she starred
in *X:WP*, her horoscope, poetry and songs dedicated to
her, print articles, and much more. If you're a diehard
Gabrielle fan, check this one out!

Rate-A-Xena
**http://arcane.eng.ohio-state.edu/bgaynor/
xenarate.htm**
Finally, a place that allows you to rate *Xena* episodes
from best to worst! This great site allows you to rate
episodes from 1 ("I'd rather be watching flies molt") to
10 ("I laughed, I cried, it was better than *Cats!*"). You can
also rate your favorite characters, and after you vote
you can check out the totals to see how others have
voted. Great fun!

http://www.xenite.org/xenaonln.htm
In my opinion, the #1 *Xena* page on the web. This page
has absolutely every link you could possibly think of to
guide you to articles, photos, Lucy sites, ROC sites, sites
devoted to secondary characters, fan clubs, mailing lists,
FAQ's, usenets, merchandise, interviews, and more. This
site is a truly astounding accomplishment and an absolute must-bookmark for new fans, and fans who think
they've seen it all.

Xena Media Review
http://www.xenafan.com/xmr
If it's *Xena* in the media that you're after, forget all those
other listings of articles: nothing is as comprehensive as
the XMR, which has been around since March 29, 1996.
In what must be a gargantuan ongoing task, Kym Taborn
(who is also the editor-in-chief of *Whoosh!*) and her team
of helpers compile articles, interviews, television appearances, and any mention of the show and its crew into
this concise and informative listing, which includes anno-
tations and complete transcripts of the articles. The

XMR is the perfect tool for armchair researchers, and is one of the many Xenite achievements that proves *X:WP* fandom is unique.

Gabbygab and Mariner's Look at *Xena: Warrior Princess*
http://gab.simplenet.com/xena/
This site has it all — photos, episode guides, articles, movies, fan fiction ... what sets this site apart from the rest (other than its constant evolution) is the look of it. The banners for each section are stunning, and every page is decorated with pictures and wallpaper. This site is a lot of fun — and boasts plenty of awards to prove it!

A Day in the Life . . . (of a *Xena* Addict)
http://xena.simplenet.com
This site provides links to all those sites that offer quirky downloads from an onscreen Lucy Lawless calculator to a funny little online *Xena* game. This site is worth checking out just for Lucy singing "I'm An Old Cowhand" on *Rosie O'Donnell*, which begins playing when you enter the *Grease!* page (it takes a while to download the first time, but on return visits it automatically comes on). This site also features detailed links to other *Xena* web sites by character.

Chris Knery's *Xena: Warrior Princess* Web Page
http://knerys.simplenet.com/xena/start.html
The woman who runs this site is the image editor for various other *X:WP* sites, so you're in for a visual treat with this one! At Christmas she put little Santa hats on Xena and Gabrielle and had a picture of their stockings hanging up for Senticles. This site features the clever idea, "Find A Xenite," where you can click on a country and find other *Xena* fans in your area (and enter your own name). She includes animated pictures that she's created from screen captures, calendars you can print out that include images from the show, fan fiction based

Address: http://www.great.xena.info

on particular episodes, and the "Addiction Test," a group of 42 questions designed to reveal if you are a hardcore nutball. This site is updated regularly, so check it out often.

Clan MacGab
http://www.takaro.co.nz/macgab
This group of people comprise some of the most ingenious, creative, and eccentric *X:WP* fans around. Used in conjunction with the mailing list for the Clan MacGab, this site explains the rules of belonging to the list, the history, and the various positions certain members hold. But you don't have to be a MacGabber to enjoy this page. Read some ingenious filksongs (parodies of songs) like "Amphipolis Pie," "Don't Cry for Me, Mighty Xena," and "The Itty Bitty Bard from Potodeia [sic]." Look over the Gabberish Lexicon, with definitions of words such as "gabdoration," "gabvocate," and "bardiculate" (many of which are used in regular conversation on the mailing list). You'll spend hours looking at this site, and you just might want to subscribe to the mailing list and join in the fun!

The Xena Coalition Homepage
http://www.avalon.net/~bensor/intro.html
This is a wonderful site, however completely sacrilegious. Set up as a parody of the Christian Coalition, this site deifies Xena and the show, rewriting the opening of Genesis to retell how Rob Tapert created *X:WP* in seven days: "Then Rob said, "Let's make some dough"; and there was dough. And Rob saw that the dough was

good; and Rob separated the net from the gross." The holy trinity is made up of Xena, Gabrielle and Callisto, Gabrielle is prayed to as the Holy Virgin of Poteidaia (the wallpaper on this particular page is wonderful!), there is a hymnal of songs of devotion to the virgin and the goddess, a section that *insists* that Gabrielle and Xena are "straight as arrows," and many more. Especially brilliant is the Paradise Lost / Inferno section, where Marlowe, Dante, and Milton come together as never before. A must-see.

The History of Xena: Warrior Princess
http://www.xenite.org/xenahist.htm
Although we seem to learn about Xena's past life in bits and bites from various episodes, trying to keep the information straight can be more than a little confusing. Well, worry no longer. This site puts all the information together into a detailed biography of the warrior princess, starting with her humble beginnings in Amphipolis and moving through all the events of her life. Because of its detail, it doubles as an episode guide, albeit one that is focused largely on Xena. It also includes the genealogies for Xena's family, the Amazons, and Joxer. A huge and ongoing achievement.

The Xena + Hong Kong Connection
http://www.slip.net/~redbean/xena/xena_hk.html
This is an excellent site where you can see the direct connection between episodes of *Xena* and the Hong Kong movies that inspired them. Taking, for example, the gauntlet scene from the Brigitte Lin film, *The Bride with White Hair* and laying screen captures of it beside almost identical ones from "The Gauntlet," it's made clear that Tapert and Raimi have seen their share of Hong Kong flicks. Some amazing observations here.

Aida's *Xena: Warrior Princess* Page
**http://members.aol.com/xenagodesz/xena/
xena.htm**
Aida's site boasts some of the best *Xena* photos on the web, and is the recipient of numerous web site awards. The photos are split into galleries, including black-and-white photos, LL photos, ROC pics, Men of *X:WP* pics, and a page of *Grease!* photos. Also includes downloadable software, sounds, fan fiction, and links.

Mailing Lists

Mailing lists are a great way to converse with other *Xena* fans, talk about the show and the characters, find out about upcoming appearances and conventions, and make a ton of new friends. When you send out a message to the list, it goes to everyone subscribed on the list (which can sometimes be over 1000 people). To try to lower the volume of mail you receive, some lists offer a digest version, where someone compiles 30 or 40 messages into longer e-mails, so you receive one to five long messages a day, rather than 30-250 individual posts.

Chakram
This is a moderated mailing list, meaning the messages go to a moderator's mailbox and he sorts through them, only posting the ones that are relevant. Many people prefer chakram to other mailing lists because of the lower volume of mail, although some find it frustrating that their messages don't always get posted. To subscribe send a message to majordomo@frontiernet.net with subscribe chakram or subscribe chakram-digest in the body of the message.

Xenaverse

This list is the counterpart to Chakram, and is completely unmoderated so that every message is automatically posted to the list. An unmoderated list is an advantage because the subscriber knows that he/she isn't missing out on anything, but it's also a disadvantage, as many of the posts are completely off-topic or are "me, too" messages responding to a previous message. The digest version of Xenaverse is highly recommended. To sub-scribe send an e-mail to Majordomo@mlists.com with one of the following commands in the body of the message: subscribe xenaverse or subscribe xenaverse-digest.

Clan MacGab

This is a list for those who are completely devoted to ROC, Gabrielle, and the bard's peaceful ways. The list is intended for creative types and is a delightful playground where you can write poetry, plays, songs, and stories and be applauded for your efforts! The Clan MacGab has the feeling of a family, and all are welcome. Subscribing sometimes takes a while, but your patience will be worth it. Visiting the Clan MacGab web site (listed above) before posting is highly recommended. To subscribe send an e-mail to majordomo@po.databack.com and write subscribe macgab in the body of the message.

Herc/Xena

Although there seems to be more *Xena* discussion than *Hercules* on this list, this is a great forum for discussing both shows and talking about crossovers between the two. To subscribe send an e-mail to herc-xena-request@mythicalworlds.com with the following command in the body of the message: subscribe. For the digest version send the same message to herc-xena-digest-request@mythicalworlds.com

GabsClan

This list is similar to the Clan MacGab and seems to have a bit of news and a lot of fluff (fan fiction). The Clan MacGab grew out of this list, so there are similar ideologies behind the two, although where Clan MacGab splits subscribers up into guilds of creative writers, GabsClan has the option of joining regiments, where you bond together with other listmembers to write ongoing stories about your adventures. To subscribe send an e-mail to mlperkin@indiana.edu with subscribe gabsclan <your e-mail address> in the body of the message.

Gabchat

Where GabsClan and the Clan MacGab are devoted mostly to creative writing to express the "gabdoration" for ROC, Gabchat was set up by Mary Draganis to offer ROC fans a way of finding out about ROC in the news, on the web, and to tell fans of upcoming appearances. There is also plenty of discussion about the episodes themselves and Gabrielle's part in them. This is a great list as a complement to the fluff lists or just on its own. To subscribe send a message to majordomo@zip.com.au with subscribe gabchat in the body of the message.

TRIFC (Ted Raimi International Fan Club)

Devoted to all things Ted and Raimi. This is a fun list for Joxer lovers, and about once a month Ted writes a note to the list via the listowner and club president, Lana Andrews. A lot of fun. To subscribe, send a blank message to tedites-subscribe@stgenesis.org.

Down Under Xenites

The Down Under Xenites is the Australian section of the Xenaverse. Here Aussie Xenites can come together and discuss the show from their point of view, and it is the mailing list for members of The Xena Fan Club of

Australia. If you don't have online access, The Xena Fan Club of Australia is coming together with a quarterly newsletter. To subscribe to the mailing list send a message to majordomo@zip.com.au and in the body of the message type subscribe dux. There is also have a web site which is located at **http://xenite.simplenet.com/dux/index.html** where members are encouraged to send in their ideas and episode reviews.

Bruce Campbell Mailing List
A mailing list for Bruce Campbell fans, which enables you to discuss his work as Autolycus, and his numerous other roles in television and movies. To subscribe send an e-mail to brucecampbell-list-request@hypenet.com and write SUBSCRIBE in the body of the message.

Salmoneus List
This is a fairly quiet list, but when Robert Trebor appears in an episode of *H:TLJ* or *X:WP* the list lights up with fan commentary. Send a message to majordomo@precipice.v-site.net with the words subscribe sal in the body of the message. Leave the subject line blank.

Xena Scrolls
This is a list devoted to fan fiction based on both *H:TLJ* and *X:WP*. If you're interested in subscribing send a message to randor@cheerful.com to ask how long it would take.

Hudson Leick Mailing List
A heavy volume list that's devoted to Hudson Leick and her villainous little character, Callisto. Send a message to majordomo@hera.ecs.csus.edu with subscribe hudson-leick in the body of the message.

THE ENCYCLOPEDIA XENAICA

Reprinted with the permission of Rita Schnepp,
Administrator and Author of E.X.

ILLUSTRATIONS BY JEANETTE ATWOOD

chakram-cam (shah'-krum-kam') Am., N.Z. n. A bird's eye view of the chakram's path when a small camera is mounted behind it, allowing Xenites to follow its trajectory after Xena throws it. Ref. St. Louis Xenites, 2/96; *The David Letterman Show*.

flame (flame') Am. (flime') N.Z. n., v. Like Xena, this word "traverses the timelines" with its meaning. (1) One of Xena's many skills where she consumes a combustible liquid and skillfully blows it through a lit torch into the faces of her enemies. E.g. Xena

flames the harpies. Ref. "Mortal Beloved." Xena flames the renegade soldiers of Nemos. Ref. "Cradle of Hope." (2) An Internet term describing verbal abuse of or by Internet users. e.g. "Don't flame me for saying this, but don't you think Xena and Hercules should get married?" Ref. Netforum, 12/17/95, etc.

Hard-core Nutball

(hard'-kor nut'-bol) Am. (hed'-kaw nut'-bol) N.Z. n. Term coined by a New Zealand actress describing the early fans of Xena. E.g. ". . . hardcore nutballs who've been around since the dawn of time." Ref. Netforum, *Xena* Mailing Lists, March 31, 1996.

Momma ROC

(mam-uh rok') Am. (mum-r rok') N.Z. n. Real life ever luvin' mother of ROC (Reneé O'Connor), and the biggest ROC fan in the world. Founder and prez of the ROC fan club, frequently known to epitomize southern charm at its best. Ref., Momma ROC, submitted by Rowdy2, 8/9/97.

O.B.E.

(o-bee-ee) Am., N.Z. n. Acronym for "out-of-bodice experience." A paranormal phenomenon where individuals claim they can leave their bra, bustier, or T-shirt and travel through space using their astral body. It has attracted considerable interest among parapsychologists, costumers, and hockey fans.

Unlike an "out-of-body" experience where the 'OBEer' can see her own body from a vantage point somewhere above it, the "out-of-bodice" experience gives this vantage point to everyone *except* the 'OBEer' herself. "I didn't know about it till the next morning." Individuals who survive the out-of-bodice experience often report 'a cool breeze' blowing across their bare skin, 'nervous behavior' by people surrounding them and an exaggerated enthusiasm for "The Star Spangled Banner." An out-of-bodice experience is more likely to be had by uninhibited individuals who live life to its fullest and "go for it" (sans double-sticky tape). Ref., *The Tonight Show*, 8/18/97 and *Metro* Magazine, Auckland., 8/97.

Psycho Barbie

(sí'-kó bär'-bee) Am. (sí'-kó bäh'-bee) N.Z. See Callisto. Internet nickname for "Callisto." This Barbie says things like: "Here Comes Trouble!," ("A Necessary Evil"); "Why can't you just die like a good boy?," ("Surprise": *H:TLJ*); "Love is a trick that nature plays to get us to reproduce," ("The Return of Callisto"), "Now it's *my* turn to host the cook-out!," ("Maternal Instincts"). Ref., Shelley Sullivan; OMXena, The Netforum.

red shirt

(red'-shurt) Am. (rid'-shurt) N.Z. n. In the original *Star Trek* series, the unfamiliar, red-uniformed crew member who inevitably got killed on away missions. In the Xenaverse, one of Gabrielle's ill-fated lovers. Term used to describe Gabrielle's love interests, most of whom die shortly after falling in love with her. E.g. "Poor Gabrielle, I've had sex longer than she was married to Perdicus!" Ref. LisaJain, Xenaverse, 11/96; the 'Red Shirt' thread, Xenaverse, Oct.-Nov. 1996.

Rixxo

(rizz'-oh) Am., (reez'-oh) N.Z. n. The Lucy Lawless interpretation of *Grease!* character, Betty Rizzo, the tough-tawkin', gum-chewin', hand-jivin', heart-breakin', Kenickie-kissin', leather-wearin', post-Mycenaean bad girl. " 'Rizzo is a tough, hard woman with a heart', Ms. Lawless said, drawing the obvious parallel with Xena." Ref., *The New York Times*, August 31, 1997. Spelled "R-I-X-X-O" because of her singular, xen-esque battle cry which brought down the house on Lucy's opening night on Broadway, September 2, 1997. See also, battle cry. Ref., Margaret Fox.

ROC

(rok') Am., N.Z. n. Fan-generated acronym/nickname for Texas native, Reneé O'Connor. The shy but charming girl-next-door actress who plays Gabrielle, the stick-wielding bard on the television show, *Xena: Warrior Princess*. Not to be confused with RoC (acronym for Return of Callisto), ROC has single-handedly hoisted the term "sidekick" to an entirely new level of inspired, reverent endearment. Variable eye and hair color is common. See also, Abs of Steel, Momma ROC, and Austin. Ref., submitted by Rowdy2, 8/9/97.

sand spider

(sand' spi-dur) Am. (sand' spi-duh) N.Z. n. Giant, juicy arachnid skewered by Xena's dagger in "Girls Just Wanna Have Fun." American Xenites mimic the New Zealand pronunciation of "sand spiduh" because this is the way Xena says it. E.g. "... spiduh! ... *sand* spiduh!! ..." A corollary of the First Law of Thermodynamics, the "Linguistic Law of The Conservation of R's" states that r's are neither created nor destroyed. Thus, the extra 'r' in "Xener" (N.Z. pronunciation) is taken from words like "spidur" (Am. pronunciation) which then becomes "spiduh" (N.Z.). Ref. Xenaverse, 11/8/96, jspfadden, gthomas.

Seduction Rave

(sed-uk'-shun rave) Am. (sed-uk'-shun rive) N.Z., n. Provocative music, ancient Greek "rap," played at village festivals, ostensibly, to ward off bacchae. Ref. "Girls Just Wanna Have Fun."

stuntie

(stun'-tee) Am., N.Z. n. Kiwi name for stunt person. A stunt professional on the set of *Xena* or *Hercules*. The faces of some stunties have become quite familiar to Xenites. E.g., Sling-Blade Stuntie: the two-sword-twirling stuntie that Xena cuts down with her chakram in "The Debt I" was the same two-sword-twirling stuntie she reamed with a toy unicorn in "A Solstice Carol". See also, "Vicious Chic". Ref., Zobrion; Tigress; Dearcy, Anonymous.

Styrostone

Y'KNOW REN...
YOU'RE HEAVIER
THAN THIS ROCK!

OH HUSH
AND PLAY
THE SCENE!

(sti′-row-stone) Am., N.Z. n. The Xenite name for Styrofoam™. Light-weight, sponge-like substance used as stones, rocks, statues, boulders, pillars, banisters, parapets, walls, buildings, castles, cliffs, mountains, and "god-knows-what-else" on the *Xena* set. Styrostone has a way of jig-gling whenever a character makes contact with it. Ref., "Warrior . . . Princess": Xena bounces Philemon's head off the 'styrostone' palace pillar. Ref., "Warrior . . . Princess": Xena brushes against the 'styrostone' ram's head as she walks down the castle steps with Gabrielle. Ref, "Beware Greeks Bearing Gifts": Deophobus knocks Xena into a 'styrostone' wall during a sword fight. Ref., "The Black Wolf": Xena hurls a 'styrostone' boulder at Diomedes. Ref., "Giant Killer": Xena tosses a 'styrostone' wagon wheel at the Philistine army. Ref., Neuf The Goof. See also, Poly-Boxes.

The Look

(look′) Am. (luke′) N.Z. n. To regard with condescension, disbelief, confusion. Disapproving stare suffered by many Xenites when they reveal to non-Xenites that they love an "over-the-top, campy fantasy-fix" like *Xena: Warrior Prin-cess*. Ref., LDCorrea.

XCPR

Acronym for "Xena's Cardio-Pulmonary Resuscitation." A pre-Mycenaean first-aid technique invented by Xena. It saved Gabrielle's life in "Is There A Doctor In The House." Xena passed her XCPR knowledge on to Hippocrates. It later evolved into what is now known as CPR. It is a combination of rescue breathing (which provides oxygen to the victim's lungs) and chest compressions (which keeps the victim's heart circulating oxygenated blood). CPR, the modern-day version of XCPR, involves a cycle of two deep breaths and 15 chest compressions (after calling 911). Xena's original XCPR technique went as follows: (1) check consciousness of victim (shake and shout at Gabrielle) (2) open

air passages (3) press your lips to the victim's mouth and blow two strong breaths into the lungs (subtext notwithstanding) (4) apply one strong chest compression (a desperate, warrior-strength punch to Gabrielle's chest) (5) Kick Hippocrates' ass for wanting to give up (6) two more strong breaths into the lungs (7) six to seven warrior-strength chest compressions (8) repeat the cycle until the victim is revived (dialing IX-I-I is not an option). XCPR and CPR are best performed by those who have been trained in a (x)CPR course. Ref., *The American Red Cross First Aid and Safety Handbook*; The American Red Cross; Kathleen A. Handal, MD; "I.T.A.D"; Lpatti; JMcNickle, 10/16/97.

Xena Flu

(zee'-na floo') Am. (zee'-ner floo') N.Z. n. An acute illness which renders its victims too sick to attend work, school or other prior commitments, yet healthy enough to travel 3,000 miles by plane, six hours by car, and spend an entire day standing in the summertime heat. Though no scientific studies

have been conducted to prove this association, the Xena Flu appears to coincide with public appearances by Lucy Lawless. It spreads across the North American continent following the actress's itinerary. The Xena Flu struck Chicago Xenites during her "Planet Hollywood" appearance (8/14/96); New York Xenites during her *Rosie O'Donnell* appearance (8/16/96) and her opening night on Broadway (9/2/97); Southern California Xenites during her *Tonight Show* appearances (10/8/96, 10/30/96 & 8/18/97); and Orlando, Florida, Xenites during her "Universal Studios" appearance (7/10/97). The indications are as follows: highly contagious, marked by a sudden onset of forced coughing and drowsiness with a miraculous recovery within 12 hours after seeing Lucy on stage. There is no known immunity. See also, "Warrior Princess Haze." Ref., Lucia Correa, September 1996.

Xena Scrolls

(zee-'ne-skrols) Am. (zee'-ner-skrols) N.Z. n. Ancient manuscripts re-discovered in 1983 in a small village East of Macedonia. Possibly the oldest known papyrus writing, the Xena Scrolls tell the story of the legendary warrioress and her traveling companion. Xenites speculate they were written by Gabrielle. Ref. "The Xena Scrolls Website." In the words of Dr. Janice Covington, "The most important archaeological find of the century. Something that will revolutionize the way we

look at the ancient world. It has the power to turn myth into history and history into myth." (1940). Ref., "The Xena Scrolls." Note: although the final script describes the setting as "Macedonia: 1940," the opening title for the first showing of The Xena Scrolls reads "Macedonia: 1942." It is speculated that the post-production staff purposely changed the date from "1940" to "1942" just to see if Xenites were paying attention. The date was corrected back to "1940" in subsequent broadcasts. Ref., Anonymous.

Xena touch

(zee'-ne-tuch) Am. (zee'-ner-tuch) N.Z. n. One of Xena's most impressive skills. Adapted from ancient, oriental acupressure, Xena uses this skill as both a weapon and healing technique. She first learned it from M'Lila in "Destiny." When used in the extreme, she can kill a person instantly. Ref. "A Royal Couple Of Thieves," the finger fighting battle with Lord Sinteres. When used for humanitarian purposes, it allows her to relieve pain, even perform surgery without pain to the patient, Ref. "Is There a Doctor in the House?" She most commonly uses it as a neck pinch to "extract information from chaps by cutting off the flow of blood to their brains." Ref., *The David Letterman Show*, 4/9/96. See also, pinch interrogation.

Xenafest

(zee'-na-fest) Am. (zee'-ner-fist) N.Z. n. Large gathering of Xenites organized by the fans themselves. Xenafests usually include a group viewing of episodes of Xena or Xena-related interviews, swapping of xenabilia, and charity fund-raising. The first Xenafest was held on September 6, 1995, in a private home in St. Louis. Ref., Artemis.

xenaphobe

(zee´-na-fobe) Am. (zee´-ner-fobe) N.Z. n. A person unduly fearful or contemptuous of all things relating to Xena, often a dejected spouse in a 'mixed' Xenite/non-Xenite marriage. Ref., vschaefer, hhanneman.

xenatize

(zee´-na-ties) Am. (zee´-ner-ties) N.Z. v. To fill one's environment with xenabilia. To decorate the office, computer, car, home, clothing, body, etc., with anything 'Xena.' E.g. "I just xenatized my computer with Xena wallpaper, sounds, and icons." See also, xenabilia and xenastack.

XWS

Acronym for "Xena Withdrawal Syndrome." An addictive condition suffered by Xenites when they crave the next new episode of *Xena*. First identified on the Xena mailing list, January 6, 1996, by a sufferer named Gambit. Symptoms include bringing Xena into every conversation, acute restlessness, computer over-use, web-site building, extensive searches for dollies, and pre-occupation with Thracian music. Originally "Xena Weekday Withdrawal Syndrome," later modified to x.w.s. Ref. N.S.F. study submitted, 1/17/96, by Dr. Heparin, Seattle, WA.

YAXI

(yak´-see) Am. (yek´-see) N.Z. n. Acronym for "Yet Another Xena Inconsistency." Xenite term for both anachronisms and contradictions. E.g. Fork plants (GG), tomatoes, and steel swords in Ancient Greece; the missing chakram (COW), the CCDS (Centaur Caesarian Disappearing Scar, ITAD), the disappearing Amazon bird's head staff (H & H), the leaning tree, the curving knife (GJWHF), American accents, Kiwi

accents, Beverly Hills accents, British accents, Irish accents, Scottish accents, New York accents. Ref. Originated by C.J. Carter, The Netforum, 11/21/95; Geekgrrl, 9/97.

YIYIYIYIYI

In the early days of *Xena*, the Xenite's imitation of Xena's war cry. After two years of mystique, it was clarified by the 'Goddess of the Xenaverse', 9/29/97: "Really all they say, is 'ALALALALA', but very fast . . . a bastardization of an Arabic woman's cry . . . an all purpose ululation." This deafening sound is so intense, it often startles and frightens Xena's opponents (as well as talk show hosts). Xenites speculate that this ululation is Xena's instinctual attempt to evoke her dark side and change her fear into strength as she does battle. Lucy Lawless, *Live: Regis & Kathie Lee*, 9/29/97; The Xena Mailing Lists and Netforum, 1995–1997. See also, "battle cry."

This is a small sampling of the *Encyclopedia Xenaica*. Find the complete E.X. at

http://www.jps.net/mythology/xenaica/ex.html

INTO THE MIX: XENA NIGHTS, SUBTEXT, AND MISCONCEPTIONS

by Debbie Cassetta a.k.a Mistopholees

Perched on the periphery of what is known as "Alphabet City" in New York City's East Village, Meow Mix is the type of place one would expect to find in this tough inner-city neighborhood. It's small and dark. Its no-frills facade blends into the surrounding tenements and bodegas which stand as monuments to the nature and flavor of this section of the city. It's tough, it can be mean, and it is one of those sections of New York that many natives prefer to avoid. It is not an area that would normally draw large numbers of tourists. East side chic this isn't.

Once inside the bar, Meow Mix fairly reeks of alternative grunge. The room is dark and the lighting is practically non-existent. Dark curtains cover the windows blocking out the view of the busy street just outside. The bar stands before the back wall which is littered with assorted paraphernalia, including awards earned for various events held here, as well as items available for sale, like the trademark T-shirts with the

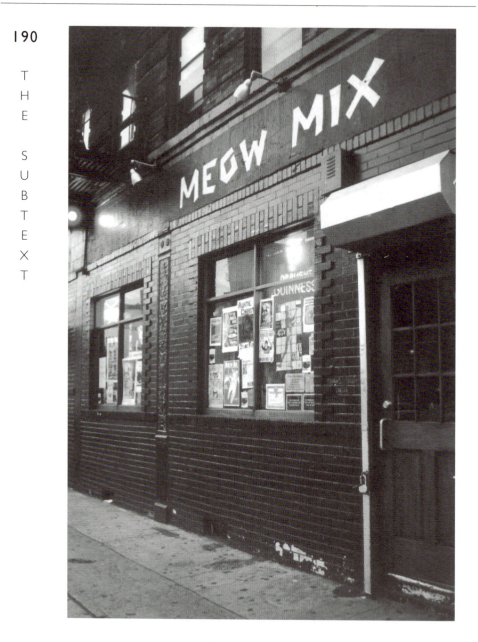

DEBBIE CASSETTA

words "Don't Fuck With The Ladies" emblazoned across the front. Off to the left is a stage which serves to showcase everything from alternative bands to poetry readings. This is a bare-bones bar with all the charm of a New York City subway station. So how is it that this no-frills, no-nonsense dyke bar has become the center of New York City's *Xena*-related activities? What is it about this place and the people who frequent it that has drawn national and international media attention to this otherwise unimpressive establishment, inviting the attention of the show's stars and its production staff? And why is it that on the second Tuesday of every month a rather unlikely group of people ranging in age from 21 to 71, many dressed in three-piece business suits and sporting leather briefcases, flocks to this bar to watch videos of a television show they can just as easily watch in the comfort of their homes?

To understand why *Xena* Night at Meow Mix is such a hit with New Yorkers, one must come to understand the two sometimes disparate aspects of the phenomenon that is *Xena: Warrior Princess*. The first is the show itself, which has struck a chord in the hearts of countless viewers the world over. Particularly popular among women, the show has been described most often as "empowering," encouraging women to strive to be all that they can be and not to allow limits to be placed on them by others. The two strong female lead characters making their way in the world have captured the hearts and imaginations of millions. But beyond that, the show has evolved into something else for many people who have been captivated by this action-packed fantasy that wreaks havoc on both history and myth. It has spawned what has come to be known as the Xenaverse, and it is this aspect of *Xena: Warrior Princess* that perhaps most defies explanation while exemplifying the very nature of the phenomenon.

Simply stated, the Xenaverse is the universe created around the show, one filled with people who have reached out across the world and forged relationships that they would otherwise never have had the opportunity to share. It is electric, it is compelling, and, if you ask fifty citizens of the Xenaverse what draws them to the show, you can expect no lack of variety in their responses. Other viewers will respond honestly that they don't have any idea why what makes this show so compelling for them. They only know that it is. And there is this sense of belonging to the larger Xenaverse and the camaraderie that the show affords its viewers that draw people to Meow Mix once a month to join a standing room only crowd in cheering on the show's heroes. This *Xena* night gathering offers fans the opportunity to enjoy what the show has to offer each of them, and allows them to share in the friendship and sense of belonging that is very much in evidence whenever *Xena* fans gather, and no more so than at this monthly gathering of friends.

New York City provides what can best be described as a view of the Xenaverse in microcosm. By virtue of it being the large population center that it is, the city has the advantage of being home to a rather large group of hardcore nutballs who love the show and enjoy sharing the experience with each other. They converge on Meow Mix to share their mutual obsession and as a result have bestowed on Meow Mix the rather dubious honor of being the focus for *Xena* fandom in New York.

The evolution of the relationship between Meow Mix and the fans of *Xena: Warrior Princess* has its roots in the mundane rather than the fantastic. The birth of Meow Mix's *Xena* Nights can be attributed to the notoriously miserable television reception which plagues many sections of the city. Such was the case for Andrea Kusten, an early fan of *Xena: Warrior Princess*. Andrea, known by the handle Big Mama Freak, was instantly drawn to *Xena* when it first aired. However, the reception in her apartment was horrible, and her then partner didn't particularly share Andrea's love of the show. Undaunted in her efforts to indulge herself, she began going to friends' homes and showing tapes of *Xena* to anyone who would watch. She soon realized that such group showings of *Xena* were an inordinate amount of fun and she approached her friend Brooke Webster, a part-owner of Meow Mix, with the idea of showing *Xena* at the bar on a slow night during the week so she could watch the show, and so could anyone else who might care to join her. They posted a notice of the event in *H/X for Her* Magazine, which describes itself as "the totally biased politically incorrect party paper for lesbians." On the second Tuesday of July in 1996, the first *Xena* night was held at Meow Mix. With only ten attendees, it was, to say the least, a rather inauspicious beginning. But it did draw some rather hardcore fans, and that first gathering provided the seed for what would grow to become one of the most talked-about and attended regularly-scheduled events in *Xena* fandom.

Among the attendees at that first *Xena* Night was "Montana," a library and archives student who had ventured over to Meow Mix from Brooklyn out of curiosity and because she too enjoyed watching the show. She met Andrea that first night, and after speaking for a while, the two collaborated on getting the episodes together (Montana had been taping all the shows and had clean, clear copies that could be shown). The two hit it off and began to work together on the preparation of the episodes to be shown each month.

The format of Meow Mix's *Xena* Night was set from the very beginning. Three *Xena* episodes would be shown (sans commercials) along with any television interviews that might be available. In addition, the evening would be topped off with a toy sword-fighting competition with *Xena* dolls, posters, or pictures being used as prizes. Eventually the festivities expanded to include an occasional look-alike contest, comic skits based on actual episodes — but with the twist of having *Xena* fantasy endings where the two main characters would invariably end up in each other's arms. *Xena* Nights at Meow Mix began to draw more attendees as the event was publicized, and particularly after the New York City newspaper, *The Village Voice*, published a couple of articles, one on the show itself, and another on the monthly Meow Mix event.

Andrea continued on as the hostess for the festivities through the rest of 1996 and was gratified with the increase in the size of the crowd with each successive *Xena* night. But sometimes life gets in the way of our ability to indulge our fantasies, and in January 1997 Andrea left New York City and moved to the West Coast. Not wanting the *Xena* Nights to end, Montana assumed the role of *Xena*-night hostess, but with one change. Shy about speaking in public, Montana did not want to face an audience every month so Lizerace, a New York City DJ and drag king, assumed the role of announcer, leaving Montana to concentrate on organizing the monthly event.

With the format set, the organizing committee began to meet once or twice a month to brainstorm and plan other events that they might introduce during *Xena* Nights. Marsha Weiler, a massage therapist from New Jersey and a member of the Meow Mix *Xena* Night Organizing Committee, explains that Montana decides on the episodes to be shown during each *Xena* Night, and she also edits interviews, bloopers, and other televised *Xena*-related events for viewing at the club. In addition, there are other items of interest which make it into the *Xena* Night line-up, such as fan-produced music videos, and Montana also attends to those. Marsha and Montana collaborate on the writing of the *Xena* fantasy-ending skits which are performed by people who come to the *Xena* Nights. It is truly a case of wandering bards strolling on stage and running with the material. It's intended to be fun, and simply put, it is. These skits are a howl and never fail to bring cheers and hoots from the audience. It is precisely this type of tongue-in-cheek production that makes Meow Mix *Xena* Nights so much fun for those who drop by. You never really know what will happen next.

By the second season, *Xena* began to emerge from the shadow of *Hercules: The Legendary Journeys*, finding its own audience and coming into its own. This process was hastened when actress Lucy Lawless was injured in a fall from a horse while filming a stunt for the *Tonight Show with Jay Leno*. The *Xena* star was seriously injured, having fractured her pelvis in four places. The accident sent *Xena* fandom into a tailspin. Concerned for Lucy's well-being and with the memory of Christopher Reeve's accident still rather fresh in people's minds, it appeared that whatever bonds *Xena* fans had been tentatively nurturing among themselves suddenly solidified and strengthened as they looked to each other for support, all the while hoping for a quick and complete recovery for Lucy.

To let her know that she was being thought of, fans sent all manner of gifts and get-well wishes to the hospital. The women at Meow Mix sent off one of their T-shirts with their best wishes for a speedy recovery. In mid-December, much to their delight and utter disbelief, Lucy called Meow Mix from Auckland, New Zealand to tell them she was wearing the T-shirt they sent her and she thanked them for it and for all their good wishes. The bar was closed at the time she called, but the answering

machine caught her entire message, much to the delight of the
Meow Mix staff, and anyone else who's heard it.

All the media attention that accident garnered propelled the
show (and Lucy Lawless) into the media spotlight. Nightly
reports on the actress's condition became the norm on the
television news magazines, and overnight what had been considered a campy little syndicated show with a cult following
was suddenly launched into the public eye to become a mainstream media phenomenon. What was especially worthy of
attention, at least to the national media, was that this show was
so popular among lesbians, an angle they could exploit in their
coverage of the show. And given that, they began to exhibit
interest in the little group of people watching the show down
in New York's East Village.

So who are these people who have captured the media's
attention, and have, for many, come to represent the typical
viewer of *X:WP*? The regular *Xena* Night crowd consists of
doctors, lawyers, professors, teachers, librarians, law enforce-
ment officers, nurses, investment bankers, public relations
professionals, social workers, and a myriad of other professional titles that looks more like a listing of a New York City
professional woman's organization than a bunch of obsessed
fans of a campy television show. There are also a large number
of students, some housewives, filmmakers, accountants, and so
on. So instead of finding a group of women who demonstrate
those expected negative stereotypes, they find a bunch of
relatively normal men and women, of various sexual orienta-
tions, who have gathered in the East Village to have a good time.
This is not some bunch of crazies who need to get a life. These
are people who have lives, who hold responsible positions in
the world, and who are delighted to have the opportunity to
spend some time away from the pressures of work and home,
to indulge themselves in an atmosphere that allows them to
enjoy each other and the show which draws them together.
Montana observes, "We behave just like everybody else and
they [the media] leave just a little bit . . . well, if not disappointed, they're saying they thought that at least it was going
to be weird. Or, 'Well, we can hype it up.' "

Xena night guests at Meow Mix watch "Orphan of War."

DEBBIE CASSETTA

Hype is not why New Yorkers flock to this club to watch *Xena*. There's something else happening, and that something else is the draw for this monthly gathering of fans. Whether it's your first time in the bar, or if you attend every month, it is the bond that quickly develops between and among people that keeps everyone coming back. Everyone shares a love of the show, but there's something else to be shared here as well. There's a feeling of community, of belonging. But that feeling was not something many of the women here felt before coming to *Xena* nights. They were reluctant to come down to this bar, many because they are straight and the very thought of going to a dyke bar was somewhat unimaginable. But most overcome any apprehension shortly after arriving for *Xena* Night.

Michele, a librarian and *Xena* Night regular, states frankly that her "first impression of Meow Mix was negative because of the way it looked. It was so small and dark . . . it just didn't strike me as someplace I would want to hang out. But that was before I met the people. They were warm and friendly and they made me feel fairly comfortable." Similarly, Marsha Weiler, a New Jersey resident, remembers her first trip to Meow Mix.

She laughs as she says that the idea of "going to New York City and going to a gay bar, which to me represented a possibly scary, heavy-duty lesbian/gay environment," was rather unnerving. But, she notes, "I ultimately found it harmless and wonderful. . . . It wasn't scary, and it was so much fun I knew I'd be coming back." Cathy, a computer programmer who lives in Brooklyn, had much the same experience and notes that she enjoys "the reaction of the people in the bar who are watching the show. It's the camaraderie." Marsha agrees. "My first evening there the women at the bar welcomed me with open arms and were friendly, outgoing, and warm." Bonnie Fitzpatrick, a member of the New York City XenaFest Committee, recalls what it was like going to Meow Mix for the first time. "I was uncomfortable at first because I wasn't sure how I would fit in. Now there are people there I know and like so I feel comfortable being there."

The club also attracts other segments within the New York City *Xena* community. For instance, the New York City XenaFest Committee stopped by after one of its early meetings, and a large part of that committee are now regulars at *Xena* Nights. Meow Mix serves as the meeting place for the many fans located in and around the city. In fact, Meow Mix has been unofficially adopted as the watering hole to be visited after other in-town events. For instance, the place was absolutely jumping during Lucy's *Grease!* run, regardless of whether or not it was a *Xena* night. With all the publicity and with the hope that Lucy might drop by, people began stopping in to have a drink or merely to say hello. On several nights following *Grease!* groups of *Xena* fans met at Meow Mix to spend the evening getting acquainted or to share a dance with other nutballs who happened to be in town. New York City hosted a *Xena* party for two months, and Meow Mix was a very popular part of that experience for many Xenites.

Why has Meow Mix gotten the type of attention it has? There are other clubs across the United States which host *Xena* nights. Some are straight clubs, others are gay establishments. But none has attracted the type of media attention that Meow Mix has. What is it about this particular club and this eclectic group of people that draws the media to it like moths to a flame? In part, the interest in Meow Mix can be attributed to the fact that Meow Mix hosted the first *Xena* night. And, of course, there is the notorious nature of Meow Mix, simply because it is what it is, a New York City dyke bar. As such, the bar carries with it all the stereotypical images of lesbians and the gay community, and provides the media with the type of sensational coverage they're sometimes looking for in their coverage of the lesbian community's relationship with *Xena: Warrior Princess*. In addition, much of the attention stems from the fact that *Xena* cast and production crew have spoken openly about the events at Meow Mix, and they have themselves stopped by the club to visit with fans and enjoy the party atmosphere that *Xena* Nights foster. Visits from the likes of Lucy Lawless, who in a NYC radio interview credited the crowd at Meow Mix with making the show hip; Steven Sears (Tyldus), supervising producer, who stopped by one night and spent several hours chatting with fans and signing autographs; and *Xena* editor Robert Field (Avicus) who spent an evening at Meow Mix sitting with the *Xena* Night regulars watching videos of the show, occasionally commenting on the editing process, the show's content, or the reactions from the people around him, have made this New York bar very visible to the Xenaverse. Visits such as these allow the fans to interact with Xenastaff and that accessibility of the cast and crew is a large part of what draws fans to the show and to *Xena* nights. Seemingly overnight, Meow Mix was transformed from an unknown alternative East Village bar into a tourist stop for every *Xena* fan passing through New York.

Lucy Lawless stopped by Meow Mix twice while she was in New York City during her run on Broadway as the tough-talking Betty Rizzo in *Grease!* To the dismay of *Xena* fans, neither visit coincided with a *Xena* night. The star's first visit was on August 19, 1997, her first day in New York. Unannounced, she arrived at the Meow Mix with a friend and a reporter from the *New York Post*. They ordered drinks and sat at the bar for a while before someone recognized Lucy and approached her. She spoke cordially with the people who were there and was described by those present as gracious and gorgeous. A week later, Lucy paid another visit to Meow Mix, this time with a *New York Times* reporter and a photographer. She spent about a half hour being interviewed up on the stage area for an article that appeared in the *Times*. After the interview she spoke briefly with the people at the bar and she was kind enough to autograph the *H/X for Her* Best Lounge Party Award that Meow Mix received for its *Xena* Night festivities, as well as two Meow Mix T-shirts, one of which has been awarded as first prize to the winner of a *Xena* Night sword fight.

Lucy appears to be at ease with the show's lesbian following, and her ready acceptance of the lesbian community has earned her the admiration and respect of that normally disenfranchised segment of the population. In an interview for *H/X for Her* Magazine Lucy described her experiences with the women at Meow Mix as incredible. But she does voice some level of discomfort with the way the media have focused on her and her relationship with the show's lesbian fans. Another reporter attempted an interview at Meow Mix, but Lucy stated in no uncertain terms that she was quite uncomfortable with the agenda the reporter appeared to be pushing. And she commented that she could not understand why so many people waste their energies trying to "out" her. Jill Falzoi expressed similar discomfort about the way some of the media people have addressed these issues when visiting Meow Mix and interviewing the regulars. Speaking about the television media, she noted that "they want the [*Xena* Night] participants to out Lucy Lawless or Reneé O'Connor, or they want to out the show as a lesbian show. They want simple answers as to why lesbians and feminists are attracted to the show." They seem unable to accept that there is no simple answer and as most participants in *Xena* nights will tell you, the reasons for their watching are many, and they differ from person to person.

So why do the subtext issue and the show's lesbian fans continue to fascinate the media? And why the continued attempts to out the show's stars? Perhaps, as *Xena* Night regular Susan Barnes notes, this is the backlash for Lucy's pro-lesbian, pro-gay attitude. In response to questions about the show's (and her own) lesbian following, Lucy delivers matter-of-fact responses and truly seems to have grown annoyed not only that this issue keeps arising, but that this is an issue at all for the media and some segments of the viewing public. Often when she has snapped rather short answers about being tired of this issue, the media has chosen to interpret these responses as her saying she's tired of the gay community raising these issues. But Lucy's statement at the *Hercules* and *Xena* Convention held in New York City on September 28, 1997, makes her feelings quite clear: she is tired of the gay bashing and wants to see it stop.

Like many of the *Xena* Night patrons, Lucy apparently has mixed feelings about the media attention that Meow Mix has received, and the way in which her visits to the club have been treated in the media. "If I go I want it to be because it's my own idea, out [of] goodwill and sense of fun and because I'm respectful of the women who run that place because I like those women. Not somebody else's little piece of manipulation because that means we're all being manipulated. And I think the women in the club are being used," she stated frankly in a *Lesbian News* interview. If the actress is angered by the attempts of the media to manipulate her and the Meow Mix crowd, the feelings are no less familiar to the group of people who have come under the media microscope at Meow Mix. They tolerate the media's depiction of them as representative of lesbians in general with a mixture of good nature and outright chagrin.

What does the media expect to find at Meow Mix, and how do the *Xena* Night regulars feel about the way they are being portrayed by the media? Those issues are among the topics of much discussion among *Xena* Night regulars who know that the media arrive with an agenda, one that usually involves exploiting the regulars by seeking to portray them as something less than normal, as people obsessed with the show and with Lucy Lawless herself. "We are being used, and we are very aware of that," says Montana, in a tone marked with resignation. "There are two reasons we agree to it. One, because we want to help Brooke, and if the place wasn't doing okay we wouldn't be able to have *Xena* Night. And second, a lot of the time . . . heck, all of the time the media has come here, they come expecting some kind of freaky, weird show with tons of people in costumes" and they arrive with preconceptions that include "all the stereotypes, negative stereotypes, about lesbians."

"From their questions they appear to have an agenda," says Jill Falzoi. "I think they expect outlaws, gender outlaws, perhaps. Or a bar full of people who don't have anything better to do than watch television. I think they're surprised that people here are actually articulate and can pick up on the subtleties of the show and articulate them better than the reporters themselves."

Falzoi's observations are echoed again and again by *Xena* Night regulars. "They're looking for off-the-wall people," comments Lauren Ecock. "Many of the people they interview are dressed in the extreme. They avoid the people dressed conservatively." What is also evident to Ecock is that "they're also looking for the 'lesbian angle.' What bugs me about this whole lesbian angle is that it assumes that two women can't be strong without being gay. That's a sad commentary on America."

Susan Barnes suggests that it is precisely because of Meow Mix's lesbian clientele that *Xena* Night and the people attending it are of interest to "the homophobic American press." She continues that Meow Mix "is a focus for the media because its reputation lends itself to the shaved and pierced crowd." An East Side dyke bar conjures up all manner of negative stereotypes, and thereby lends what Barnes refers to as a sleeze factor to this gathering of fans. "It provokes images of some kinky, weird sort of thing. So yes, they are disappointed to find normal people."

Whatever preconceived notions the media harbor when they walk through the door at Meow Mix seem to dissipate when they find a relatively normal-looking bunch of people. This reaction is not lost on the people at the bar. It is evident to the *Xena* Night regulars that many of the reporters and film crews are surprised at what they find at Meow Mix because it is not what they expect. "They don't expect normalcy," notes Falzoi. But if they're coming to find people attired in leather and battle armor and brandishing swords, they're definitely going to be disappointed. The range of fashion spans the gamut from business suits to jeans and T-shirts. More exotic dress is usually not seen unless it's part of a skit being performed or there is a costume contest being conducted. Nor are they likely to find in abundance the tattooed gender outlaws they often expect. "They're expecting freaks," states Tanya Dessereau. "Tattoos. Shaved heads. Obsessed maniacs. You know what I'm saying." Arlene Calandria agrees. "They have this stereotypical notion or idea that all these crazy lesbians get dressed up in costumes and go gaga over Lucy. They're just not. We just basically enjoy what she does and take Xena as a role model. As for Lucy as a person, well, we're just happy for what she's doing."

In one televised segment on Lucy's engagement to Robert Tapert, executive producer of *Xena: Warrior Princess*, the club and the *Xena* Night event were described in the clip as a predominantly lesbian bar where fans gather to hold a *Xena* Night and bask in the glow of the show's star, Lucy Lawless. It is just such types of statements that leave many of the people who attend these monthly gatherings cold. The nature of the questions asked in relation to this clip also caused much consternation among the fans. It was obvious to those interviewed that they were looking for negative reaction to Lucy's engagement. They were disappointed in that regard, given that the responses were wildly enthusiastic about her marriage. Yet the televised piece still suggested that it was the fascination for Lawless on the part of these women that drew them to the show and to *Xena* Night at Meow Mix. The portrayal of them as a bunch of crazed fans lusting after Lucy Lawless ruffles a lot of feathers here because it again implies deviance and suggests that the draw isn't the show but instead is simply a sexual attraction directed at the stars. For most people who attend the *Xena* Night gatherings, that is not the case.

Reasons for women being drawn to this show vary significantly, but an almost universal response is that it is the nature of the relationship between Xena and Gabrielle that is so compelling. Pat, a *Xena* Night regular from the very beginning, notes that it is Xena's strength that draws her to the character and the show. That, and the strong emotionally binding relationship between the two main characters. Sharon, a social worker and another monthly attendee, likes the character's depth. "She's very complex. I really admire her strength, and I'm not just talking about physical strength. I'm talking about emotional and physical strengths. I think it's wonderful that she can go out there and make it in a man's world. I like that she faces her dark side as a challenge for her in every episode." Viewers find Xena's constant struggle with her dark side to be an attractive force in drawing them to the character. It often reflects the struggles they perceive in their own lives. Pat states with a quirky grin, "Quite frankly, the reason why I love Xena is that I wanted to be Xena. I want to be that strong woman who could just take care of business and not let her fears overwhelm her." To a large degree, Sharon sees this as a draw for most of the women she's come to know at Meow Mix. "We're all strong women with careers. We're all Warrior Princesses. We have had to fight that fight to get where we are at. I think that's a biggy: we all have that in common. I think we can sense that."

Pat adds, "It isn't about Lucy Lawless, it's about the character Xena. I've come to admire Lucy Lawless. I love her as Xena. But I really love the character Xena." This statement perhaps illustrates where the fans and the media part ways. There is very little confusion among these fans when it comes to differentiating Lucy Lawless, the actress, from Xena the character. The media too often assumes that the fans cannot make this distinction, or that for them the distinction is quite blurred. Perhaps more correctly, it is the media who are unable or unwilling to make that distinction, particularly given the amount of energy they expend in pursuit of this aspect of *Xena* fandom. For them, the lesbian element of *Xena* fandom and the stereotypical perception of what lesbians are makes good press.

The relationship of the fans to both Lawless and O'Connor is something the media seem unable to get their hands around. They are invariably surprised at the level of support the show's fans display for both actresses. They are amazed at how protective of the stars the fans are. And despite their best efforts, the media have been unable to get fans to voice any negative comments about either actress. One interviewer commented that she had never seen anything like it. There was no backlash whatsoever toward the stars, and that, she found, was very uncommon. They often can't understand that Lucy's sexual preferences are irrelevant to lesbian fans. She's straight, and that is her business. There are no hard feelings on the part of the gay community. Perhaps the media miss the irony in their assumptions. Lucy Lawless accepts the lesbian community for what it is and on their own terms. The lesbian community accepts her for what she is on her own terms. It is really that simple. And these fans appreciate Lawless and the level of support she has shown them, and you would be hard pressed to find any one of her fans uttering a negative word about her. The basis of the reaction of Lawless's fans is one of respect for the woman who has taken the time to give her fans far more than they ever expected she would. And as it is with the rest of the Xenaverse, Lucy's health, happiness, and well-being always take precedence over all else, including the show. While that may mark her success as an actress, it says far more for her success as a human being.

IS THERE AN ANSWER IN THE HOUSE? X:WP TRIVIA QUESTIONS

Compiled by Julie Ruffell, a.k.a Xena Torres

Test your *Xena* knowledge with these 100 questions, each worth one point. If you want to truly test yourself, don't look up anything!

RANK

100–95	Warrior Princess
94–80	Amazon Princess
79–60	Bard
59–40	Warrior wannabe
39–20	Warrior dud
19–0	Peasant

TRUE OR FALSE?

Answer each question with true or false, and correct the false statements.

1. *True or false?* The warlord Cortez attacked Xena's home.
2. *True or false?* The centaur that raised Solan is named Kaleipus.
3. *True or false?* Hudson Leick appeared in "The Greater Good."
4. *True or false?* Borias is the father of Solan.
5. *True or false?* Lao Ma taught Xena pressure points.
6. *True or false?* Gabrielle named her daughter after Xena.
7. *True or false?* Gabrielle married Perdicus, who had loved her since they were kids.
8. *True or false?* Meg calls Xena's chakram, "the round-killing-thing."
9. *True or false?* Meg's father died during childbirth.
10. *True or false?* Xena's first encounter with a flying monster was in "Mortal Beloved."
11. *True or false?* Gabrielle first rode Argo in "Chariots of War."
12. *True or false?* Gabrielle has a sister.
13. *True or false?* Phantes was a centaur.
14. *True or false?* Xena's descendant is Janice Covington.
15. *True or false?* Argo has been killed before.

THE CHARACTERS

How much do you REALLY know about your favorite Xena characters?

1. Xena is from what town?
2. The name of Joxer's twin brother.
3. Gabrielle is from what town?
4. Also known as "The King of Thieves."
5. Amazon Queen with a perm.
6. Joxer comes from a family of _____.
7. Who is Lila?
8. Which of Xena's brothers is dead?
9. Toris is Xena's _____ _____.
10. Xena's parents.
11. Gabrielle's husband.

12. Why did Draco give up being a warlord?
13. The salesman.
14. Xena is the _____, Diana is the _____, and Meg is the _____.
15. Centaur who fought Xena at Corinth.
16. Cupid is the son of which goddess?
17. The name of the baby centaur delivered by Xena.
18. Many believe this god is Xena's real father.
19. _____ the wonder horse.
20. Xena's slightly psychotic arch enemy.
21. Gabrielle's Amazon arch enemy.
22. Callisto is from what town?
23. "Callisto" featured the first appearance of this new warrior, who would reappear in later episodes.
24. This character must have been a fan of James Bond.
25. Cupid's trouble-making son.

EPISODE EVENTS

Every episode brings new adventures for Xena. Think back to the old ones and answer these.

1. In what episode did Ares make his first appearance?
2. Callisto first visited Hercules in what episode?
3. In what *Hercules* episode was Xena introduced?
4. In what episode did Xena debate changing her outfit?
5. Gabrielle's first costume change was in what episode?
6. Name the first episode where Gabrielle picked up a sword and made an attempt at Xena's yell.
7. In what *Xena* episode did we first see Xena in something other than her leather?
8. In what episode did we see a change in the style of Ares' beard?
9. In what episode did Xena fight her first monster?
10. Name the first episode in which Xena sang.
11. In what episode did Xena first get to face her dark side?
12. Name the three episodes that sent a baby down the stream.

13. In what episode did Xena sing her burial song twice?
14. Name the three episodes where Gabrielle hit Xena.
15. Name the episode where Gabrielle went crazy and the one where Xena did.
16. In what episode did we learn Argo's name?
17. What was the first line ever spoken by Xena?
18. In what episode did we first see Gabrielle kill?
19. Name the first episode where Gabrielle left Xena.
20. Xena gave Caesar a splinter in what episode?

LINES

Fill in the blanks to finish off these Xena quotes.

1. "I've just cut off the flow of _____ to your _____." (Multiple episodes)
2. "A ___ ___ ___ ___!" (Multiple episodes)
3. "Life is an _____ to be _____, and without _____, what's the point?" ("Dreamworker")
4. "Now I see why you _____ _____ _____." ("Hooves and Harlots")
5. "Son of a _____!" ("Been There, Done That")
6. "I'm sorry _____, but that hurt me more than it hurt you." ("A Comedy of Eros")
7. "You can't hide from me, _____! You can't hide from a _____!" ("A Necessary Evil")
8. "You don't want to _____ ____ _____, now do you?" ("Sins of the Past")
9. "You don't just _____ me and _____ _____." ("A Necessary Evil")
10. "We played _____ ____ _____, and she wasn't very good at it." ("A Necessary Evil")
11. "Gabrielle, you are a _____ ____ _____." ("A Solstice Carol")
12. "Please don't let that _____ that shines _____ of her face go _____. I couldn't stand the _____ that would follow." ("Return of Callisto")

13. "This _____ _____ you. I _____ you."
   ("Destiny")
14. "Didn't your _____ ever teach you it's rude to
   _____?" ("Altared States")
15. "This is _____! What did you expect, _____?"
   ("The Price")
16. "Yeah, he got _____ and fell off the _____."
   ("Warrior . . . Princess . . . Tramp")
17. "I could always stop _____ and wear _____
   _____ _____." ("A Day in the Life")
18. "Don't _____ me because I'm _____." ("Here
   She Comes . . . Miss Amphipolis")
19. "What do you _____? You don't _____ anything!" ("Is There a Doctor in the House?")
20. "_____. We've got to work on _____." ("The
   Deliverer")

THE PEOPLE AND PLACES
BEHIND XENA

You might know everything about the show *Xena*, but how much do you know about the stars, writers, directors, and locations?

1. What is the Xenite name for New Zealand?
2. Bruce Campbell had a small cameo in the Oscar-winning movie, *Fargo*. Who did he play?
3. When is Lucy Lawless's birthday?
4. When is Reneé O'Connor's birthday?
5. Who directed "A Day In The Life"?
6. Name the two geniuses who created Xena.
7. Lucy's first job with the *Hercules* crew was in what TV movie?
8. Reneé O'Connor also was in a *Hercules* movie. Which one?
9. Reneé O'Connor appeared in a Sam Raimi and Robert Tapert movie before she landed the role of Gabrielle. What was it?

10. What toon character did Reneé O'Connor bring to life at "Six Flags"?
11. What New Zealand comedy show was Lucy part of?
12. Name the movie with the strange fruit obsession in which Lucy appeared.
13. "A Day In The Life," "Warrior . . . Princess . . . Tramp," and "Ulysses" were written by _____.
14. "Girls Just Wanna Have Fun," "Return Of Callisto," and "Is There A Doctor In The House" were directed by _____.
15. Steven L. Sears' Internet name is _____.

SUBTEXT

We all know it's there, the subtext. See if you can answer these.

1. In what episode did Xena and Gabrielle share their first kiss?
2. In what episode did Xena and Gabrielle first skinny dip together?
3. Name the episode when Xena and Gabrielle shared their first bath.
4. What woman kept Xena hidden under water long enough to avoid being seen, by putting her own head under water to give Xena air, allowing Xena to hide longer?
5. In "King of Assassins," what famous woman of history seemed to make a pass at Xena?

XENA: WARRIOR PRINCESS EPISODE GUIDES

"You can make 'em laugh, you can make 'em cry, but don't bore 'em."
— Robert Tapert, Creator and Executive Producer

What is it that makes *Xena: Warrior Princess* such a popular show? Simply put, there is nothing else like it. The friendship between Xena and Gabrielle is unique to television, and the fact that they are two strong women has become secondary to their relationship. During the first season, the writers are careful to make the development of both women believable and gradual. The emphasis is on Gabrielle's growing sense of independence and how she learns to fight for herself. We don't see her pick up a staff and become adept at using it overnight, but instead we watch a progression that is slow, yet determined. As the season progresses, so too does her maturity and her sense of herself in the world. Xena, on the other hand, is engaged in a constant struggle with her dark side, which makes her more appealing than the usual good guy/bad guy stereotypes. As she struggles to suppress her desire to kill, she becomes more trusting of people and allows Gabrielle to be an important part of her life. Although she lapses back to her previous warrior ways in "Ties That Bind," by "Is There a Doctor in the House?" she realizes just how important Gabrielle is to her, and that episode establishes the relationship between the two women as the focal point of the second season.

The overarching storyline of the second season was interrupted by Lucy's accident, and writers were forced to rethink the general direction of the show. The new focus is on the emotions of the characters, and because Lucy was unable to move about comfortably, it offers an opportunity to take the focus off of the action plots. Joxer becomes more of a central character, Callisto stays around to haunt Xena and remind her of her past, and Gabrielle becomes such a skilled fighter that there is no need to further explore that aspect of her character. We are given more insight into Xena's past and a glimpse of Xena and Gabrielle's day-to-day life, and as the two women become very comfortable with one another and start noticing little things that bother them about each other, the stage is set for the third season.

Season Three contains the most difficult episodes ever on X:WP. The rift saga overshadows everything else on the show, splitting up the pro-Gabrielle and pro-Xena fans everywhere. The focus now is on the strains in the relationship, and the episodes are far more complex, with deep storylines that require extra thought. Where the first season shows the two women growing together and the second season sets them up as two women against the world, the third season pits them against one another, and Ares becomes a main character. The third season, in other words, is dominated by war. However, the clever writing on this show prevails, and the rift saga is concluded satisfactorily, leaving Xena and Gabrielle's relationship stronger than ever. The writing, acting, directing, and music are all combined throughout each episode to make *Xena: Warrior Princess* the freshest, most original, and campiest show on television, and considering how much the actors themselves have matured, there's seems to be no end to the fun in sight.

This episode guide will provide you with background information to the myths underlying each episode. You'll learn about Greek mythology, Judeo-Christian stories, and the actual historical context in which certain episodes are placed. They do not include comprehensive plot summaries because a summary of the plot of an episode could never replace watching the episode itself, so this guide is meant to complement your viewing of the show. Any opinions and interpretations of the show are mine only, and feel free to disagree with them at any point. That said, there are some spoilers ahead as well, so if you don't want to know anything about the episodes you haven't seen, you probably don't want to venture any further. At the end of the episodes I have included various little points of interest. The TIME section in no way implies that the show follows a logical timeline, but instead is a fun way to see all the eras and discrepancies that appear on the show. To create a timeline would be pointless. GABRIELLE'S FIGHTING SKILLS are tracked during the first season, where her development as a fighter is a focal point of the show, but they are mentioned occasionally in later episodes. YAXI stands for "Yet Another Xena Inconsistency," where something happens that is in direct conflict with events from another episode. The NITPICK section includes those little things that still bothered me after watching an episode, but most of them are meant in fun, and the same goes for the OOPS section, which points out any bloopers I may have noticed. The INTERESTING FACT includes knowledge outside of the show about the actors or certain circumstances, and the DISCLAIMER section, of course, lists those humorous disclaimers that appear at the end of every episode. I enjoyed writing this section, and I hope you enjoy reading it.

Battle on Xena!

THE HERCULES:
THE LEGENDARY JOURNEYS
XENA TRILOGY

109 The Warrior Princess

ORIGINAL AIR DATE: March 13, 1995
WRITTEN BY: John Schulian
DIRECTED BY: Bruce Seth Green
GUEST CAST: Kevin Sorbo as Hercules
Michael Hurst as Iolaus
Lucy Lawless as Xena
Elizabeth Hawthorne as Alceme

Hercules and Iolaus's friendship suffers a blow when an evil warrior princess named Xena comes between them.

In the ninth episode of *Hercules: The Legendary Journeys*, a character was introduced that would eventually change the face of television. This episode is one of the most romanticized in the Xenaverse: everyone who saw it when it first aired knows where they were when they first saw . . . her. But is it as good as they say?

Xena first appears when she's testing the fighting skills of her men. Wearing a peasant dress and sporting curls in her hair, she hardly looks like a fierce warrior woman, but that's part of her plan. Despite watching her single-handedly beat up her entire army, we can't help but think that she is shy and not quite as cunning as she later turns out to be. This is a woman who uses her sexuality to trick and deceive men — Iolaus, Theodorus, and Estragon — a trick she learned from her own arch-enemy, Julius Caesar (see *X:WP* "Destiny").

Going back to watch this episode when *X:WP* is in its third season can be a disorienting experience because this Xena isn't like the later Xena; despite the fact she is on the side of evil, the good Xena is far more intimidating. There are many inconsistencies with this character and what we are later told she was like at this time. Lucy doesn't have the Xena voice perfected yet, and she lacks the haughty confidence of a warrior princess. Even with her warriors, she tends to seem more like she's saying her memorized lines rather than getting into the character. However, what can we expect? First of all, Lucy has had absolutely no time to develop this character. Secondly, she's an actor who is guest-starring in someone else's show, rather than being the title character with all the focus.

It's interesting to see certain tricks used for the first time. The chakram, for instance, is first used in this episode when she kills one of her own men for not following her "code." That code, which she still boasts in the third

MCA TV / SHOOTING STAR

season, is that she will be loyal to whoever is fighting on her side, and she expects the same from her warriors. She will never surrender, but will fight to the death.

The bath scene with Iolaus, in which Xena seduces Iolaus and convinces him that Hercules thinks Iolaus is second best, is the best part of the episode. The look on her face when she knows she's tarnished the friendship speaks louder than any words in this episode. "The Warrior Princess" ends with Xena shouting "You haven't heard the last of me, Hercules!" the classic call of the sequel seeker. No, we definitely haven't heard the last of her.

YAXI: Xena says her three brothers and father were killed in battle which is either an inconsistency or a lie to garner Iolaus's sympathy. Her father was not killed in battle, and at this point she believes he's just abandoned the family. Xena has only two brothers to our knowledge, Toris and Lyceus. (Steven Sears has mentioned that we might get an explanation for the third brother in a later episode.) Also, why haven't Hercules and Iolaus heard of her? The one problem she faces throughout the first season is having to overcome a reputation as an evil murderer that precedes her wherever she goes.

112 The Gauntlet

ORIGINAL AIR DATE: May 1, 1995
WRITTEN BY: Rob Bielak
DIRECTED BY: Jack Perez
GUEST CAST: Lucy Lawless as Xena
Robert Trebor as Salmoneus
Matthew Chamberlain as Darphus

When Xena's army mutinies against her, she must decide whether she wants to try to win them back or if she should reconsider her life as a warrior princess.

Now *this* is the Xena that should have premiered on *H:TLJ*. "The Gauntlet" is a fantastic episode that is leagues away from "The Warrior Princess." Having played Xena once, Lucy falls quickly into character for this episode, and is far more confident, evil, and appealing. Of the episodes in the *H:TLJ* Xena trilogy, this is the best, and the one that is integral to the Xenaverse; this is where Xena turns from her evil ways.

The episode opens with Xena dressed in that amazing warrior outfit that was shown far too briefly in "The Warrior Princess." Complete with menacing breastplates, silver claws on her shoulders, and the long black and silver cape (she has much better hair in this one, too!), this Xena fights with two swords, while the "good" Xena will only use one. It's amazing how much younger she looks here, too.

Certain aspects don't add up, though. It's not only Lucy's acting that has become more confident, but the character has been written to be more so as well. In "The Warrior Princess," Xena's army was a bunch of inept men who lost every battle they were in, but in a matter of weeks she has managed to conjure up a new army of accomplished and fierce warriors. We will later discover that one of Xena's many skills is building victorious armies in a snap. Darphus, her lieutenant, is a cold, blood-thirsty killer who will be the key to her downfall as a warrior and her rebirth as a warrior who fights to protect people.

The first hints that Xena isn't a thoughtless warlord is her treatment of Salmoneus. She says he amuses her and lets him babble on about how she needs some good publicity and a theme song. Salmoneus believes in her inherent goodness and will later try to convince Hercules that Xena's not the same woman who tried to destroy his friendship with Iolaus.

Although *X:WP* is three seasons past these initial episodes, the gauntlet scene is still one of the most powerful Xena scenes ever. As Xena makes her way through a gauntlet that is flanked by men from her own army, she is literally beaten into seeing the error of her ways, although it takes Salmoneus to bring Xena and Hercules together. The scene is powerfully filmed in slow motion, forcing the audience to endure every grimace, every blow, every betrayal. As Xena desperately crawls towards the finish line, her body beaten and broken, Salmoneus's face says it all: if no one has ever survived the gauntlet, how could Xena possibly do it? However, everyone is wrong, and as she slowly stands up in weary defiance, a new hero is born. We know that despite her later bid to win back her army, deep down she knows she'll never lead them again and she's better off for it. This is a beautiful and powerful episode — the true introduction to the Warrior Princess.

113 Unchained Heart

ORIGINAL AIR DATE: May 8, 1995
WRITTEN BY: John Schulian
DIRECTED BY: Bruce Seth Green
GUEST CAST: Lucy Lawless as Xena
Robert Trebor as Salmoneus
Matthew Chamberlain as Darphus

Xena begins her new life as a warrior-turned-good by joining with Hercules, Salmoneus, and Iolaus to prevent Darphus from destroying the world.

Although this episode wasn't as interesting or powerful as "The Gauntlet," it was essential to resolve the conflict between Xena and Iolaus and to convince the audience that Xena had, in fact, changed her ways. There are important changes in her character in this episode: she feels remorse for what she'd done to Iolaus; she works alongside the trio, rather than leading or following them; and she trusts Hercules enough to fall in love with him.

Unfortunately, we can't help but think that Iolaus must be devastated that the two have fallen for each other. In "The Warrior Princess" Iolaus resents Hercules for thinking Iolaus is second best, something that Hercules insists is not true. However, Xena tricks Iolaus into falling in love with her so she can get to Hercules (albeit to kill him) whereas here she really does fall for Herc. If you were Iolaus, wouldn't you feel like you were second best once again? In fact, wouldn't you feel some doubt as to the sincerity of Xena's feeling towards Herc? After all, when she tells Hercules that holding up the rock in the cave was the most courageous thing she'd ever seen, it has undeniable echoes of Xena telling Iolaus that he was the most courageous warrior she'd ever seen. It is only when Xena saves Iolaus's life in battle that he trusts her and reluctantly forgives her.

The feminist tones that will later dominate *X:WP* have their early roots in this episode. As Xena goes outside of the campsite to scout for marauders, she leaves Hercules and Salmoneus to cook dinner. While she's out, she takes on an army single-handedly and walks away without a scratch.

The ending of this episode leaves the doors wide open for Xena's own adventures. Eschewing a life with Hercules to devote her life to atoning for her sins, Xena sets out on a journey that isn't only physical, but will involve some of the deepest soul-searching and emotional turmoil that has ever been shown on television. Hold on to your seats — the Warrior Princess is coming.

XENA: WARRIOR PRINCESS

SEASON ONE (1995–96)

PRODUCTION STAFF:
> Music Composer: Joseph LoDuca
> Developer: R.J. Stewart
> Co-Producer: Liz Friedman
> Producer: Eric Gruendemann
> Supervising Producer: Babs Greyhosky
> Supervising Producer: Steven L. Sears
> Co-Executive Producer: R.J. Stewart
> Executive Producer: Sam Raimi
> Executive Producer: Robert Tapert
> Creators: John Schulian and Robert Tapert

STARRING:
> Lucy Lawless as Xena
> Reneé O'Connor as Gabrielle

101 Sins of the Past

ORIGINAL AIR DATE: September 4, 1995
TELEPLAY BY: R.J. Stewart
STORY BY: Robert Tapert
DIRECTED BY: Doug Lefler
GUEST CAST: Jay Laga'aia as Draco

Darien Takle as Cyrene
Stephen Hall as Hector
Linda Jones as Hecuba
Willa O'Neill as Lila
Geoff Snell as Herodotus
Anton Bentley as Perdicas
David Perrett as Gar
Patrick Wilson as Cyclops
Wally Green as Old Man
Roydon Muir as Kastor
Huntly Eliott as First Citizen
Winston Harris as Boy

Xena returns to her home village of Amphipolis but is shunned for her evil deeds.
She and Draco are locked in a battle to the death for the safety of the village.

In this first episode of *Xena: Warrior Princess*, Lucy plays a prodigal daughter.
Coincidentally, her first acting role ever was as the person who stole the
prodigal son's money. It seems her acting career had come full circle.

Although Xena had eventually turned to the side of good in the three-
episode arc in *Hercules: The Legendary Journeys*, we realize in the first episode
of *X:WP* that the process to convince others that she has changed will be a
long and arduous one. We learn vital information about Xena's past — why
she turned to evil, how she started fighting — while also learning about
her family. Her deceased brother, Lyceus, and how he died, will become
important information in later episodes.

We also meet Gabrielle, who will become Xena's trusty sidekick. It is
strange for fans now to look back on these first episodes of *X:WP*, because
Gabrielle is annoying, naive, and treats Xena like an idol. Xena rolls her
eyes whenever she sees her, obviously wishing to be alone. Only in later
episodes will Gabrielle prove her worth and her talkative nature will be a
lovable asset, not an annoying trait. Gabrielle will teach Xena to love and
respect others, something Hercules and Iolaus could never have taught her.
Not only do we learn of Xena's family, but we see Gabrielle's as well.
For some strange reason, Gabrielle's parents are named Herodotus and
Hecuba. The historical Herodotus (c. 485–425 BC) was called the father
of history by Cicero, as he recorded in lengthy books the Greek wars
beginning with Croesus's conquest of the Greek colonies in Asia Minor
and ending with the Persian wars. Because Gabrielle will become a bard,
it makes sense that her father should be named after such a great man.
However, Hecuba was the often pathetic and luckless mother of Paris, and
it is said that she had a dream before he was born that she would give birth
to a torch that would burn Troy. Hecuba was also the mother of Cassandra,
who was cursed by being able to see the future but no one would believe
her prophecies. Because Gabrielle was originally supposed to be a character with second sight, it is fitting in this sense that her mother's name should
be Hecuba. Otherwise, it's a strange choice of moniker.

Xena and Draco in "Sins of the Past."

MCA TV / SHOOTING STAR

"Sins of the Past" is a great pilot because it contains so many elements that properly introduce the series. Xena uses the neck pinch to obtain important information from her opponents; we see the hateful reaction most people have when they see her, and so understand the difficulties she will soon encounter; we are made familiar with the villages of Poteidaia and Amphipolis. Everything is introduced to us so that by the second show we already feel as if we've got a strong grasp of what these people are all about. The final fight between Draco and Xena is one of the most bizarre things ever shown on television and sets the stage for even campier battle scenes.

We are also given a clue about what the show will stand for when Gabrielle meets the cart driver. As she begins her Bardic tale about Oedipus, she's immediately informed that Oedipus wasn't tragic, he was foolish. The cart driver begins his story and immediately the stage for historical revision is set.

Could there have been a mighty warrior princess? Why are we told that all the bards are men when obviously Gabrielle is just as capable as anyone else of telling a good story? The basis and reasons behind both these questions are complex. Unlike the Hebrews, whose world was unambiguously patriarchal, gender in the Greek myth was full of contradictions, and also changed over time. In early pre-Hellenic times, for instance, succession was matrilineal. When the Dorians arrived toward the close of the second millennium, they brought patrilineal systems. Festivals of Male Kinship replaced Festivals of Female Kinship, although their rites still consisted of sacrifices to the Mother Goddess, which men were not allowed to attend. The Olympians were originally a meld of pre-Hellenic and Hellenic views — a compromise of earth-Goddess and sky-God concepts, balanced in gender. There were six gods (Zeus, Poseidon, Hephaestus, Ares, Apollo, Hermes) and six goddesses (Hestia, Hera, Athena, Aphrodite, Artemis, Demeter), who ruled in a Babylonian-style co-sovereignty. Although the subsequent myths are a strong mix of matriarchal and patriarchal power, they embody conflicting theological dogmas. Their players were male and female, all-powerful and gifted, and also quarrelsome and humorous — concepts of the divine that were utterly foreign to the serious Hebrews. In turn, the Greek myths are not solemn, like Bible stories; although the trend over time was toward a Biblical-style patriarchy.

Gabrielle's ambition as a storyteller is fraught with mythic ambiguity. The Bards were instructed by the Muses and the goddess Aphrodite, female voices that possessed men as their instruments through their vulnerability to the love of priestesses and prophetesses. In Jungian terms, the Bard's male anima (a female element) could comprehend the female voices of the Muses, but would also be helplessly entrapped to the Muses by his masculine libido (although that term is now out of favor in modern psychology). The classical poets are said to have claimed to be the goddess's master, the Muses existing under their protection. In either case, the informing voices were female. The poets and Bards themselves were effectively accessories. The goddess often discarded her Bards when their usefulness to her was spent, after which they would turn to Apollo for a modest livelihood.

So Gabrielle might have been capable of telling a better story, but in legend the goddess and Muses didn't possess women. They adopted men, whom they dominated and controlled. To hear the voices of the Muses as a Bard in the manner of legend, Gabrielle would probably have had to be an anima-informed lesbian with a masculine libido, if the claims of the classical poets are true.

As to the likelihood of a mighty warrior princess, in mythic terms this was not only probable, but central — even essential — to the Olympian world-view.

TIME: About 50 years after Oedipus was king.

GABRIELLE'S FIGHTING SKILLS: Gabrielle fights the men trying to take the villagers, but other than that, she hides. She has a long way to go, and her subtle development of fighting skills is one of the more notable accomplishments of the writers this season.

YAXI: Xena says to Argo, "C'mon, boy" but we now know that Argo is female, and Gabrielle's betrothed, Perdicas, is not played by the same actor as the one in "Beware Greeks Bearing Gifts" and "Return of Callisto."

102 Chariots of War

ORIGINAL AIR DATE: September 11, 1995
TELEPLAY BY: Adam Armus & Nora Kay Foster
STORY BY: Josh Becker & Jack Perez
DIRECTED BY: Harley Cokeliss
GUEST CAST: Nick Kokotakis as Darius
Jeff Thomas as Cycnus
Stuart Turner as Sphaerus
Morgan Palmer Hubbard as Argolis
Patrick Morrison as Lykus
Ruth Morrison as Sarita
Robert Harte as Ugly Ruffian
Nigel Godfrey as Tynus
Dane Jerro as Homesteader

When a warlord's army attacks a small village, Xena must try to turn them to the side of good or defeat them.

This episode does not have as much happening as "Sins of the Past," but that is to be expected. The writers of this one draw an interesting connection between Xena and the father-son relationship: where Cycnus believes in all-out war to achieve certain ends and Sphaerus refuses to slaughter innocent people, Xena finds herself caught between the two ideals. The father represents her past (and her present) and the son is a metaphor for her present and future. Her act at the end of this episode is the only thing she could have done to move on and become more like the son, although she struggles with that decision.

Another connection is between Xena and Darius, the carpenter who is raising a family alone. His insistence on leaving when the going gets tough hearkens back to Xena's initial choice a decade before, when her village had been attacked. By choosing not to run away, she turned to a life of corruption and evil, yet now she urges Darius to stay. The scene with Darius removing the arrow from her side is one of the most vivid of the season, and considering how rarely she is hit, a unique one as well. This is one tough woman!

Gabrielle as the Bardic storyteller is developed, as well as her quick wits and her feminism, as she tells stories in the tavern. Her 1990s attitude shines through when she insists she doesn't want to get married and have children and sacrifice her future. If we take the history books as correct, Gabrielle wouldn't have had a future other than that. Again, while this episode wasn't as good as "Sins of the Past," it shows the potential of history re-written.

GABRIELLE'S FIGHTING SKILLS: She clumsily flies through the water on a horse and is very hesitant when Xena tells her to jump; she doesn't fight.

YAXI: Darius is a Trojan refugee, but later in the season, Xena will fight in the Trojan war. Hmm . . .

OOPS: In the final chariot scene, watch Xena's horses: they switch sides of the chariot partway through the scene.

103 **Dreamworker**

ORIGINAL AIR DATE: September 18, 1995
WRITTEN BY: Steven L. Sears
DIRECTED BY: Bruce Seth Green
GUEST CAST: Nathaniel Lees as Manus
Desmond Kelly as Elkton
Sydney Jackson as Storekeeper
Colin Francis as Swordsmith
John Palmer as Baruch
Bruce Hopkins as Termin
Matthew Jeffs as Gothos
Michael Daly as Mesmer
Peter Phillips as 1st Xena Warrior
Grant Boucher as 2nd Xena Warrior
Lawrence Wharerau as Mystic Warrior
Patrick Smith as Dolas
Polly Baigent as Doppelganger

Gabrielle is forced to undergo various tests to become Morpheus's bride, while Xena gets trapped in her own dreamscape and must fight the demons of her past in order to save Gabrielle.

Where "Chariots of War" veered away from the issue of Xena's past, this excellent episode forces her to confront it head-on. Also, Gabrielle picks up a staff for the first time and we see the beginnings of her fighting skills.

This is the first time the issue of fighting has been raised between the two women and Xena's advice to always run — while seeming contradictory to her own actions — proves most important to Gabrielle when she's captured by Morpheus's people.

In Greek legend little is known of Hypnus, the personification of sleep. He was the son of night and in one Greek legend (the only one of which he was a subject) he fell in love with Endymion, a beautiful shepherd, who chose the gift of eternal sleep and eternal youth. Hypnus granted him an additional gift of sleeping with his eyes open, so Hypnus could always see them. Although sleep never really advanced beyond an intangible idea, Hypnus was the father of Morpheus. Morpheus's name derives from the Greek word for form — hence the word metamorphosis — and Morpheus would take the form of human beings and appear to them in their dreams. As a winged creature, Morpheus was able to travel from one end of the earth to the other, which is how he can appear to so many people in their dreams at night.

In "Dreamworker," Morpheus is referred to as the god of dreams, and he forces Xena to become a victim of her own nightmares, which invariably involve the atrocities of her past. Until now Xena has been battling with her conscience, but now her conscience becomes concrete and she must battle it as she has so many of her enemies: to the death. The scene of Xena fighting "Dark Xena" is very effective, and the reason Xena's struggle with her old self is such a difficult one is because she is not altogether past it. At the beginning of this episode the indifference with which she kills the highwayman is in contrast to Gabrielle's "blood innocence." Even after she forces her way out of her dream and into Gabrielle's reality, she mercilessly kills at least five warriors.

This episode is important not only for showing the difficulties that will haunt Xena's new life, but in showing Gabrielle's intelligence in a fighting situation, her use of wits over strength, her choice of the staff over a sword, and her acceptance of Xena's advice as her own moral code. The scene at the end with Gabrielle and Xena sitting by the lake is one of the most poignant and poetic of the early episodes, a perfect analogy of Xena's inner war. Interestingly, this is the first episode in which we discover how important Gabrielle has become to Xena. Xena's desperation at Gabrielle's disappearance opens up a whole new arena for the show. Let the subtext begin!

104 Cradle of Hope

ORIGINAL AIR DATE: September 25, 1995
WRITTEN BY: Terence Winter
DIRECTED BY: Michael Levine
GUEST CAST: Mary Elizabeth McGlynn as Pandora
Edward Newborn as King Gregor
Simon Prast as Nemos

Kirstie O'Sullivan as Ophelia
Beryl Te Wiata as Cynara
Christine Bartlett as Philana
Tony Bishop as Weasel
Paul Minifie as Innkeeper
Latham Gaines as Kastor
Alan De Malmanche as Old Man
Carl Straker as Young Man
Susan Winter as Woman
Paul Norell as Street Vendor

Gabrielle and Xena find a baby that has been sentenced to death and Xena must try to convince King Gregor that the baby is not a threat to his throne. Along the way, they meet up with Pandora.

This episode melds Greek and Judeo-Christian stories: Pandora is the main character, while elements of the stories of Christ and of Moses form the plot. King Gregor sentences to death a baby boy whom he believes will usurp him as king, much as Herod sentenced Jesus to death upon hearing He would become King of the Jews (Matthew 2: 1–18). When the servant in this episode places the baby in a basket in the river, we move to the Old Testament, where Exodus chronicles the plight of the Israelites, whose newborn boys were thrown into the Nile to stop the Israelites' numbers from growing. One woman hid her baby in a basket in the river and the baby's sister watched as the king's daughter found it. She then approached her and offered to find a Hebrew woman to suckle the baby — the baby's real mother. Eventually, the baby Moses is adopted by the king's daughter and he leads the Israelites out of Egypt to the Promised Land.

Pandora's legend is a more complicated one. There is more than one Pandora in Greek mythology, but the one who concerns this episode was the first woman, created by the gods and goddesses. She was fashioned out of clay by Hephaestus, given life and clothes by Athena, beauty by Aphrodite, and taught guile and treachery by Hermes. She was also granted the gift of music (hence Pandora singing to the baby in this episode). Epimetheus had been warned by his brother, Prometheus, never to accept gifts from Zeus: he didn't listen. When he married Pandora, a gift from Zeus, he neglected to tell her about his earthenware pot which contained all evils and one good — hope. Immediately after marrying, Pandora opened the lid and let all the evils which now plague mankind out into the world, and was able to trap only Hope inside. Despite the cries of Hope to be let out to alleviate their woes, men and women were left to suffer and labor all their lives. Another version of the story states that all good things were in the pot, which belonged to Prometheus, and Pandora let them out — thereby lost to mankind forever — and she returned to the heavens. Another says that Hope escaped after all of the evils, but only to keep people working at their unhappy labors, to prevent them from succumbing to despair. Whichever way, Pandora was sent to Earth by Zeus for the torment of mankind.

Director Michael Levine at WarriorCon '97

JOAN STANCO

   The Pandora in "Cradle of Hope" is supposed to be the granddaughter of the legendary Pandora. This is an interesting and intriguing episode. Xena shows no maternal instincts, seems repulsed by the thought of having the baby, and cries, "The boy should be with its mother!" Perhaps the writers didn't have "Orphan of War" in mind at this point, or this comment could be taken as her own sense of guilt coming through.

   Gabrielle is downright annoying in this episode. All the respect that she earned in "Dreamworker" vanishes in "Cradle of Hope." When Xena and Gabrielle rescue Pandora from a group of thugs, Gabrielle practically orders Pandora to thank them. Later, after specifically being told to be careful with the box, she drops it and snaps back that she was just trying to help. What happened to the girl with the heart of gold?

   The box itself is beautiful, and the writers add a new chapter to the legend: it may have been a woman who let the evil into the world, but this episode reminds us that it was also a woman who kept it in. They do alter the meaning of the legend, however, in suggesting that Hope *should* have been trapped in the box/pot, not that she was trapped there accidentally.

There is very little in this episode that has to do with Xena's past, although we see a touch of the old Xena when she indifferently knocks out King Gregor during an otherwise touching moment. The belly dancing scene is fantastic as we discover that Xena is indeed a woman of many skills! This is also the first episode in which we see Xena's fire trick, where she takes a swig of alcohol and blows it on a torch or candle, creating a blowtorch. The casting agents for *X:WP* deserve a round of applause for *never* casting Simon Prast in another episode. Prast — who plays King Gregor's chief officer, Nemos — overacts his way through this episode in a way that suggests he majored in melodrama at his acting school. Does anyone else think this guy reminded them of the Newman character on *Seinfeld*? The difference is, Newman is *supposed* to act that way. Nevertheless, Nemos is important because he is one of the few opponents ever to disarm Xena, and he does so twice.

The scene with the baby being used as a football is very funny, if you take it as suggesting that in ancient Greece a single mother could still fend for herself while taking care of her baby. This scene sparked the first of the infamous disclaimers which appear at the end of many episodes. Watch for a similar fight scene in Season Two's "Warrior . . . Princess . . . Tramp." The very end raises some interesting ethical questions: could hope really be a concrete object that exists outside of us? Did Gabrielle and Xena make the right decision about not telling Pandora what they had discovered?

TIME: Two generations after the first woman was created.

DISCLAIMER: "No babies were harmed during the production of this motion picture."

105 The Path Not Taken

ORIGINAL AIR DATE: October 2, 1995
WRITTEN BY: Julie Sherman
DIRECTED BY: Stephen L. Posey
GUEST CAST: Bobby Hosea as Marcus
                Stephen Tozer as Mezentius
                Nicola Cliff as Jana
                Jimi Liversidge as Agranon
                John O'Leary as Antonius
                Iain Rea as Brisus
                Crawford Thomson as Dictys
                Peter Saena-Brown as Soldier #1

A man asks Xena to save his kidnapped fiancée, and Xena meets her old love, Marcus, who is still involved in the evil actions that Xena used to pursue.

Xena shows a completely different side of herself in this touching episode. Marcus is a man she loves deeply, but she can joke with him and is generally very comfortable around him. Marcus has a good heart, yet he still kills and kidnaps, as Xena used to do, which shows that she is inherently a good person, like Marcus, and that something was needed to bring that side of her to the foreground. Mezentius, on the other hand, represents completely what Xena used to stand for.

The opening scene in the bar is worth the entire episode. Xena is not a woman most people would want to mess with in a bar and this scene shows what happens when men do. The look on Lucy's face as she moves through this scene is perfect: steady, unwavering, and smug. Gabrielle doesn't have much of a role in this episode. As usual, Xena leaves her behind because she hasn't yet learned to fight, and she's stuck with the fiancé of the missing girl.

The intriguing aspect of this episode involves Xena and Marcus. We may look at Xena as being responsible for his death, but considering what we already know about her, we can understand why she couldn't trust him. Her army mutinied and even her own mother turned against her. It was unfortunate, though, that Xena and Marcus's life together had to be sacrificed for an annoyingly ineffectual couple.

This is the first funeral we see on the show and the funeral dirge that accompanies it is written and performed by Lucy herself. The end of this episode, when Xena repeats over and over to Gabrielle that Marcus had been her friend, is very poignant as we realize that other than Gabrielle (and perhaps M'Lila and Lao Ma), he's probably the only true friend she's ever had.

NITPICK: We see at Marcus's and in future funerals on the show that the dead are cremated. If this is a sacred ceremony, which it undoubtedly is, then why does Xena visit her brother's tomb? Why was Lyceus not cremated? Or Xena's mother? Or Xena, for that matter?

106 The Reckoning

ORIGINAL AIR DATE: October 16, 1995
WRITTEN BY: Peter Allan Fields
DIRECTED BY: Charles Siebert
GUEST CAST: Kevin Smith as Ares
Bill Johnson as Benitar
Christopher Mayer as Peranis
Danny Lineham as Grathios
Christian Hodge as Teracles
Phaedra Hurst as Teresia
Meryl Main as Areolis' Widow
Sam Holland as Teen Son
Ross Harper as Polinios

Xena is accused of murder while she is trying to save some dying men. When she discovers that Ares is the murderer, he tempts her to be his queen and to return to her old way of life.

So far we've seen that Xena can defeat any opponent, but what happens when that opponent disappears? This episode features the *X:WP* debut of Ares, god of war. Ares was the son of Zeus and Hera, and is one of the twelve major deities. He is generally represented by the helmet and sword, was taller than most humans, and had a fierce battle cry (the producers of this show have taken some liberties with these characteristics). Although he was the god of war, he did not always fight on the victorious side. Many of the Greek stories featuring Ares have him outwitted by other warriors, a thread that Peter Allan Fields continues here (see "Ties That Bind"). One of the deities who often tricked Ares was Athena, and Xena appears to be based on many of her characteristics.

When Zeus seduced Metis, who was his aunt and a Titaness, she became pregnant and Zeus was told that if she had a son he would take over his kingdom but if he had a daughter she would be remarkably wise. So Zeus swallowed Metis and when it came time to give birth he ordered Hephaestus (or Prometheus, by some accounts) to split open his head with an axe. From Zeus's brow sprang Athena, fully grown and dressed in armor. As she leapt forth she shrieked a battle cry that was heard throughout the heavens and the earth (perhaps ALALALALALA), and it was she who would later outwit Ares on the battlefield time and again. It is also said the story was a fabrication that Zeus invented because Poseidon had claimed Athena as his daughter by Libya, the African goddess, after she was found wandering as a child by the shores of an African lake. But Athena thought that Poseidon was exceedingly stupid, and she thus allowed Zeus to pretend she'd been hewn from his skull.

Athena forged many trails that Xena follows on the show: in various legends, she helped Heracles in his battle with the giants (in this guide I'll be referring to the Heracles in Greek mythology by his Greek name, not his Roman one, to be consistent); she helped Odysseus (Ulysses) return to Ithaca; she oversaw the building of the largest ship ever built to that point coincidentally named the Argo; she outwitted Poseidon; she became the protector of towns. Her name is strikingly like "Xena," and the producers once said they named the character so because children would remember the "X." Athena also had a darker side: when Paris did not choose her as the most beautiful goddess, she became very hostile to the Trojans and contributed to the devastation during the war. According to some authors, Athena was the daughter of Pallas, and when he tried to rape her she killed him and wore his skin as a breastplate. Of course, Xena was (we think) born of mortals, so she is only loosely based on the warrior goddess. However, it's safe to say that there were warrior princesses in existence at the time.

In "The Reckoning," Gabrielle is redeemed once again as she becomes the world's first defence attorney. Although these scenes were a little too

L.A. Law in some respects, Gabrielle is very clever and we know she's working hard because she cares for Xena. There is a genuine look of pain on her face when she first sees Xena in chains, making the scene where Xena lashes out at her all the more devastating. Our hearts go out to Gabrielle upon her return and we realize that she is Xena's true friend and probably the most understanding person Xena's ever met. Xena realizes this as well, and for the first time refers to Gabrielle as her best friend.

Why doesn't Xena tell Gabrielle that she knows who the hooded man is? Probably because Ares' offer is so tempting, and she's ashamed to admit she has seriously considered it. Xena still has the evil streak in her, although we gradually see her hiding it as the season progresses. The fact that she can calmly smirk as the villagers say in effect, "Oops, sorry about that" at the end of the episode is a testament to how far she's come in just one day. Her trick played on Ares was foreshadowed in "The Path Not Taken," where Xena tells Marcus, "You said I could have anything. I was just calling your bluff."

GABRIELLE'S FIGHTING SKILLS: She doesn't fight physically, but her battle of wits in the court room is one of her best fights yet.

107 The Titans

ORIGINAL AIR DATE: October 30, 1995
WRITTEN BY: R.J. Stewart
DIRECTED BY: Eric Brevig
GUEST CAST: Mark Raffety as Hyperion
  Amanda Tollemache as Theia
  Edward Campbell as Crius
  Andy Anderson as Hesiod
  Paolo Rotondo as Phyleus
  Syd Mannion as Calchas
  David Mackie as Rhodos
  Jack Dacey as Creon
  Sian Hughes as Young Woman
  Peter Morgan as Barkeep
  Maggie Tarver as Villager #1
  Simon Cameron as Villager #2
  Tania Anderson as First Woman
  Julianne Evans as Second Woman

Gabrielle inadvertently awakens three of the Titans and when they resist being made her slaves, Xena and Gabrielle must prevent them from destroying the human race.

After all that Gabrielle does for Xena in the last episode, Xena's attitude after her battle in the opening scene is completely uncalled for. This battle contains the gravity-defying Xena running around in a circle (while her body is parallel to the ground) kicking people in the face — without a doubt the most campy and over-the-top battle move of the show.

This episode is one of the least-liked episodes among fans. Neither Xena nor Gabrielle have motivation for any of their actions, and even the Greek mythology is way off-course. Why would Xena treat Gabrielle the way she does in the beginning? Why would Gabrielle try to enslave the Titans?

The Titans were the six sons of Uranus (the Sky) and Gaia (the Earth), consisting of Oceanus, Coeus, Hyperion, Crius, Iapetus, and Cronus (although some authors wrote that there were seven, one in charge of each day of the week). Gaia had created Uranus to cover her completely and she created him without the help of a male. The Titanides, or Titanesses, were the six daughters, Tethys, Rhea, Themis, Phoebe, Mnemosyne, and Theia (or Thia). Gaia and Uranus also produced the Cyclopes and the Hecatonchieres, and Gaia convinced Cronus to castrate his father because she didn't want any other children. According to some versions of the myth, when the testicles fell to the earth the Meliae, Aphrodite, and the Furies were born. As with many Greek myths, incest plays a large part. All of the Titans coupled with their sisters to produce other deities, including Atlas, Prometheus, Helios, the Oceanids, Poseidon, Hades, Hera, and Zeus. The Olympians were descended from Cronus.

In "The Titans," the three giants are Theia, Hyperion, and Crius. Crius is not featured in many legends, other than being the father of Pallas by his sister Eurybia (who was not a Titan but the daughter of Gaia and Pontus) which is probably why he is killed so quickly in this episode. Hyperion and Theia coupled and produced the Sun (Helios), the Moon (Selene), and the Dawn (Eos). Often Hyperion and Helios are identified as the same character, with Hyperion referred to as the sun god. Gaia put Theia in charge of the sun, and legends state that Hyperion was blinded by his enemies every night and restored to sight in the morning, hence the sunshine.

Cronus had heard that one of his sons would dethrone him, so he swallowed his children as they were born. However, Rhea couldn't bear this cruelty, so she hid her last son, Zeus, in a cave. When Zeus came of age he freed his brothers and they waged war against the Titans, expelling them from the heavens and condemning them to Tartarus, where they were imprisoned behind bronze doors. It is unclear in Greek myth if life was better when the Titans were in charge or when the Olympians became the gods; because the Titans were so ancient they were not worshipped by mortals. In this episode, the writers have them encased in rock on earth. There were twelve Titans and Titanides in total, yet here there are hundreds of Titans in the rock that Hyperion wants released, a rather liberal use of poetic license. The writers have also invented the story of a virgin goddess releasing them, a clever way of revealing an important aspect of Gabrielle's character: we already know of her blood innocence and now we know she is chaste (although Gabrielle doesn't appear to be too thrilled about it).

Gabrielle's treatment of the Titans is completely out of character. If all life — in heaven, Tartarus, and Earth — descended from the Titans, and some little bossy virgin turned them into slaves, it's no wonder they have a severe dislike for humans. The writers had to have Hyperion stab Crius, or else we wouldn't exactly feel right about them being evil.

Although Gabrielle still must hide in the bushes while Xena fights at the beginning of this episode, by the end Xena needs Gabrielle and she acknowledges that. Only Gabrielle can destroy the Titans — and she tricks them momentarily into making them believe she is no longer a virgin. Speaking of which, when Xena finds Gabrielle in bed with a man the look on her face is a complicated one. Disapproval? Surprise? Jealousy? We'll leave that one for the subtexters to fight about.

GABRIELLE'S FIGHTING SKILLS: She and Xena must work together, using Gabrielle's brains and Xena's brawn.

NITPICK: The size ratio of Titans to humans keeps changing. Sometimes the humans are the size of the Titans' feet, while at other times the humans appear to come up to their knees.

108 Prometheus

ORIGINAL AIR DATE: November 6, 1995
WRITTEN BY: R.J. Stewart
DIRECTED BY: Stephen L. Posey
GUEST CAST: Michael Hurst as Iolaus
Kevin Sorbo as Hercules
John Freeman as Prometheus
Jodie Dorday as Io
Paul Norell as Statius
Russell Gowers as Demophon
Sara Wiseman as Young Woman
David Mitchell as Innkeeper

Hera binds Prometheus to a rock with the chains of Hephaestus, thereby causing mankind to gradually lose the gifts that he'd given them, including fire and the ability to heal. Xena and Gabrielle join Hercules and Iolaus to try to free him.

In the eighth episode of the first season, the producers attempt a time-honored trick: "the crossover." By putting Herc and Iolaus in an episode of *X:WP*, they are reassured that the *Herc* fans who haven't yet been won over to Xena will tune in to at least one episode. And what an episode — this one is clearly more *H:TLJ* than *X:WP*, right down to the settings, the dialogues, and those darn monsters. When the earliest episodes of *X:WP* aired for the first time, an encore presentation of "The Warrior Princess" was aired between "The Path Not Taken" and "The Reckoning," while an encore of "The Unchained Heart" ran between "The Reckoning" and "The Titans." So now was the time to bring Hercules back. Ironically, in the second and third seasons Xena would appear on *H:TLJ* several times, perhaps indicating that viewers had moved to *X:WP* and needed to be won back.

Prometheus was the son of Iapetus, a Titan, and was thus Zeus's cousin. During Zeus's war with the Titans, Prometheus remained neutral and was therefore spared and permitted to live at Olympus, although other sources say that Prometheus warned the Titans that Zeus's victory was secured and that he fought on Zeus's side against Cronus. In either case, he despised Zeus for destroying his race and turned his love toward mankind. Prometheus is said by some to have fashioned the first man out of clay, and was no doubt the one who provoked Zeus's dislike of humans. When man demanded to be able to eat meat, Prometheus devised a test whereby Zeus would choose what part of the animal the gods would receive during a sacrifice, the remainder being left for man. He split a bull in half and divided it into two piles — the flesh and the intestines were hidden under the stomach, and the bones were hidden under the fat. He then told Zeus to choose a pile and he would give the remaining pile to mankind. Zeus chose the fat, thinking that the best parts would be cleverly hidden in the more unsavoury pile, and was enraged to discover he'd been tricked into choosing the bones. From then on sacrifices to the gods consisted of fat and bones, while man was able to keep the rest of the animal to eat. In Zeus's rage he decided to withhold fire from mankind, but Prometheus nevertheless brought it to man as a coal stolen from Hestia's hearth.

Writer, developer, and co-executive producer R.J. Stewart

CATHERINE M. WILSON

As punishment, Zeus sent Pandora (see "Cradle of Hope") to bring ruin on mankind. Prometheus was then chained to a rock and a large bird — an eagle or a vulture, depending on the account — was sent down to devour his liver. His liver would then regenerate, only to be devoured again each day. Heracles freed Prometheus after he had endured the punishment for 30,000 years, but Zeus condemned him to wear a chain attached to a rock. Prometheus became immortalized after taking the burden of immortality from the dying centaur, Chiron, and Zeus forgave Prometheus his deeds when Prometheus told Zeus of an oracle which said the son of Zeus and Thetis would overthrow his father.

In "Prometheus," we see how important he was to the humans, who don't truly appreciate his gifts until they're gone. Both Xena and Hercules battle (for altruistic reasons) over who will sacrifice themselves by breaking Prometheus's chains, while Gabrielle learns that she's not the only sidekick who feels left out. The scene where Gabrielle is stuck with the salesman, who is also a recognizable face from *Hercules*, is very funny and a complete jab at modern-day tacky souvenirs, although it would have been a perfect role for Salmoneus. The cave of Hephaestus — the god of transforming fire and so an enemy of Prometheus — looks exactly like the cave of "The Titans" (can you say: limited sets?) and it is strange that Xena would be able to successfully get through the cave while the guards — who presumably know the cave — are all tricked. The final scene with Prometheus is very trying to one's suspension of disbelief. The egg men jumping out of their styrofoam prisons reek of *Spinal Tap*, while the giant bird is too far-fetched. There have been some incredibly brilliant moments with computer animation on *X:WP* and *H:TLJ*, but this is not one of them.

The "relationships" between Gabrielle/Iolaus and Hercules/Xena are far too clichéd as well. If Gabrielle truly believes Iolaus is the other half of her soul, why is she so quick to fall for Talus in the next episode? And what about that guy in "The Titans?" Hmm . . . It is touching, however, that Xena's last thought as she goes to make the ultimate sacrifice is that Gabrielle attend the Academy for Bards, foreshadowing Episode 113.

GABRIELLE'S FIGHTING SKILLS: Poor Gabrielle is stuck hiding in the corner while the other three fight, but she does pick up tips by watching them, and realizes that a sidekick can fight, too.

DISCLAIMER: "Iolaus was harmed during the production of this motion picture. However, the Green Egg men went on to live long and prosperous lives."

109 Death in Chains

ORIGINAL AIR DATE: November 13, 1995
TELEPLAY BY: Adam Armus & Nora Kay Foster
STORY BY: Babs Greyhosky, Adam Armus & Nora Kay Foster
DIRECTED BY: Charles Siebert

GUEST CAST: Kate Hodge as Celesta
Ray Henwood as Sisyphus
Leslie Wing as Karas
Kieren Hutchison as Talus
Erik Thomson as Hades
Chris Graham as Toxeus
Gordon Hatfield as Seerus
Paul McLaren as Streptus
Kelly Greene as Guard
Beryl Te Wiata as Old Woman
Wayne England as Wounded Man
Allan Wilkins as Thug

Sisyphus captures Death and Xena must try to free her before her candle burns out, thereby condemning all humans to eternal suffering without the relief of death.

The writers have altered a myth for this episode, for death was always represented by a winged male spirit named Thanatos (the root of thanatology, the study of death). Hades was the son of Cronus and Rhea, and thus the brother of Zeus and Poseidon. His sisters were Hera, Hestia, and Demeter, and he was the uncle of Persephone (Demeter's daughter, who in another famous story Hades carried off to be his wife), Ares, Athena, and Triton, among others (see "Mortal Beloved").

Thanatos was the angel of death, who would cut off a lock of hair from the dead to give to Hades and then carry the spirit away. The only myth where Thanatos appears in any important way is the one acted out in "Death in Chains." The writers have chosen to personify death as a female named Celesta for this episode, giving her a more benevolent duty. Sisyphus was known for his cunning: when Autolycus (see "The Royal Couple of Thieves") stole Sisyphus's cattle, Sisyphus came to recover them, and he slept with Autolycus's daughter, Anticleia, on the eve of her marriage to Laertes. Because she gave birth to Odysseus nine months later, Odysseus is sometimes considered to be the son of Sisyphus.

In another story, Sisyphus witnessed Zeus kidnapping Aegina, the daughter of the river god Asopus. Sisyphus told Asopus who the kidnapper was, thereby incurring the wrath of the gods. Zeus sent Thanatos down to capture Sisyphus and condemn him to the underworld, but Sisyphus captured Thanatos in chains, as he does Celesta in this episode. According to legend, Zeus freed Thanatos by sending Ares (although we know better). Sisyphus was taken to the Underworld, but he told his wife not to perform any of the funeral rites for him. When he arrived in the Underworld, he complained to Hades that his wife was not religious enough to perform the ceremony, and he asked to be returned temporarily to earth to punish her. It was another of Sisyphus's tricks, however, and once back on earth he stayed there and lived until a very old age, continuing his cunning ways (see "Ten Little Warlords"). Other writers say that Hades, hearing Sisyphus's laughter, sent Hermes the very next day to bring him back, after the Fates snipped Sisyphus's thread of life in Hermes' presence.

However, the gods were not going to be tricked again, and when he died naturally and returned to the Underworld, they gave him the task of rolling a large stone uphill, only to have it roll back down, for all eternity. This way, he'd always be too busy to escape again. Oddly, a detail that has never been mentioned on *X:WP* is that Sisyphus was in fact the brother of Salmoneus (see "The Black Wolf").

"Death in Chains" seemed a somewhat confusing episode when it first aired, because it was aired out of the order in which it was filmed. "Hooves and Harlots" was made first but aired later. Gabrielle is wearing Terreis's necklace in this episode, which was given to her later, and the outfit she's wearing here is derived from the Amazonian outfit she'll wear in the next episode. Oops.

Lucy Lawless recalls this episode as one of the most memorable of the first season because of the scene with the rats, which scratched her and got caught in her hair: "It was so vile. I had to get a tetanus shot." And we thought Xena's outfit looked painful!

Gabrielle falls in love with Talus (quickly forgetting her "soulmate," Iolaus) and Reneé delivers a very moving performance at the end of this episode. The uncomfortable look on Xena's face when Gabrielle sobs on her shoulder, although she does attempt to comfort her, shows us that Xena still has far to go in expressing her emotions. This is an interesting and well-acted episode.

NITPICK: If no death means men will suffer eternally and still feel their wounds, why is the band of thugs roaming around with stab wounds not affected by them? Also, simple physics would dictate that Xena's chakram couldn't be used as a free-standing power saw. However, as we know in the Xenaverse, *nothing* obeys the laws of physics.

DISCLAIMER: "No Jumbo Sized Cocktail Rats were harmed during the production of this motion picture."

110 Hooves and Harlots

ORIGINAL AIR DATE: November 20, 1995
WRITTEN BY: Steven L. Sears
DIRECTED BY: Jace Alexander
GUEST CAST: Danielle Cormack as Ephiny
David Aston as Tyldus
Alison Bruce as Melosa
Mark Ferguson as Krykus
Rebekah Mercer as Terreis
Colin Moy as Phantes
Chris Bailey as Celano
Antony Starr as Mesas

John Watson as Arben
Aurora Philips as Magdelus
Tanya Dignan as Eponin
Andrew Kovacevich as Tor

When an Amazon is killed, apparently by a centaur, she passes on her right of caste to Gabrielle, making her an Amazon princess. Meanwhile, Xena must find out who the real murderer is to prevent a war between the centaurs and the Amazons.

Because some scholars insist on the actual existence of the Amazons while others believe they are mythic, there are far more conflicting stories about them than you find with mythic characters. Hippolyta, the queen of the Amazons, was Ares' daughter. A group of fierce warriors, the Amazons allowed male visitors into their camps once a year to mate, but would kill or enslave any male children. The root of the name Amazon comes from one of two possibilities. The first suggests the root is *maza* (barley), meaning they did not make bread because they were hunters. The second and much more common translation is "without breasts," leading to the widespread belief that a girl's right breast was cut off and cauterized to allow easier use of a bow and arrow (guess there were no southpaw Amazons?). One tribe fought against the Greeks in the Trojan war, and they are generally seen negatively in Greek mythology. Heracles and Theseus were able to slaughter the tribe when Heracles killed their queen, Hippolyta, for her girdle. Herodotus records that some Amazons married Scythians and founded a new nation. There are many actual names of Amazons that were recorded, among them, Melousa and Valasca. The Amazons are still important today for their feminist implications, although sometimes the aspects of feminism are a little over-simplified in both *X:WP* and *H:TLJ*. The Amazons worshipped Artemis, the goddess of the hunt and the moon.

The centaurs were always depicted as monstrous and bestial creatures, who became violent and out of control under the influence of wine. By many accounts, they worshipped Dionysus (see "Girls Just Wanna Have Fun"). The centaurs were either descended from Ixion (see "Orphan of War") or Centaurus, or both. Two centaurs, Chiron and Pholus, came from different parentage, and they were both generous and kind.

In one story, the centaurs are invited to the wedding of King Pirithous of the Lapiths, also descended from Ixion. The centaurs became very drunk and rowdy at the wedding, and one centaur — Eurytion — tried to rape Hippodamia, the bride. The centaurs were driven out of Thessaly after a battle broke out. In another story, Heracles was visiting Chiron and asked for some wine. Chiron told him the wine belonged to all the centaurs and had been given to them from Dionysus on the basis that they only open it when Heracles visits. Considering the condition fulfilled, Heracles insisted and Chiron opened the wine, but when the other centaurs detected the scent they came down from the mountain and began fighting. Heracles accidentally shot Chiron with a poisoned dart, and in his agony Chiron cried out to be released from the burden of immortality, which Prometheus took upon himself. The centaurs did get revenge, however, by some accounts. Heracles died when he wore a tunic drenched in the poisoned blood of the centaur, Nessus.

In "Hooves and Harlots," Xena's initial response to the Amazons is respect and understanding, but she literally turns her nose up in disgust when she hears of the centaurs. However, unlike the rest of the people, Xena believes in the ultimate innocence of Phantes. We'll find out why in the opener of Season Two, "Orphan of War." "Hooves and Harlots" is an intriguing episode and the fan response led to the Amazons reappearing in later episodes, not surprising for the overall theme of the show. The irony that the blood-innocent Gabrielle should become an Amazon princess will be dealt with later as well, and this episode is crucial to Gabrielle's fighting skills. Her choice of the staff as her weapon is appropriate, as Gabrielle prefers to fight without killing (although crushing skulls and probably inflicting permanent brain damage doesn't seem to be outside her moral code). The scenes of her learning to use the staff and trying to do the Amazon dance are very funny, and demonstrate Reneé O'Connor's genuine comedic skills.

Again, this episode explains where she got the necklace that mysteriously appears in "Death in Chains." The viewer can tell these are out of sequence because of her outfit at the beginning — the *Little House on the Prairie* get-up she'd been wearing all season to this point. Oops again. The fight scene with Melosa is amazing, and it's a real disappointment that the producers don't use Alison Bruce more often. This episode is very complex and very well-executed.

YAXI: The Amazons make a big deal about giving Gabrielle Ephiny's staff, yet it's gone in the next episode, or at least all the ornamentation is gone.

NITPICK: Melosa attacks Krykus and almost kills him, but isn't Gabrielle supposed to do so? How does she get off the hook for this revenge murder? Also, why is he given a fair trial when Phantes was denied one?

DISCLAIMER: "No males, Centaurs, or Amazons were harmed during the production of this motion picture."

111 **The Black Wolf**

ORIGINAL AIR DATE: January 8, 1996
WRITTEN BY: Alan Jay Glueckman
DIRECTED BY: Mario Di Leo
GUEST CAST: Robert Trebor as Salmoneus
Kevin J. Wilson as Xerxes
Nigel Harbrow as Koulos
Emma Turner as Flora
Ian Hughes as Diomedes
Maggie Tarver as Hermia
Ross Duncan as Parnassus
John Dybvig as Brigand (Ox)

Jonathan Bell-Booth as Chief Guard
John Pemberton as Arresting Guard
Tim Hosking as Blacksmith
Colin Francis as The Grump
Adam Middleton as Black Wolf Sympathizer
Jimmy Rawdon as Father

A band of rebels led by the Black Wolf is captured and put into Xerxes' dungeon. Because Xena has a personal attachment to one of them, she must try to get them out by discovering which one is the Black Wolf.

"The Black Wolf" begs one very important question: why isn't Salmoneus featured in more episodes? Robert Trebor is the funniest actor on this show and should be featured more often. As mentioned earlier, the Salmoneus of Greek legend was the brother of Sisyphus. However, he was such a minor figure in Greek mythology that the writers have been able to shape him into the lovable character played by Robert Trebor (the best palindrome in show business).

Salmoneus was the son of Aeolus — who was the grandson of Deucalion and Pyrrha — and Aenarete. He moved away from Thessaly, his birthplace, and founded a city called Salmone, with himself as the king. He married Alcidice, producing a daughter, Tyro. Tyro would be involved in the ongoing war between Sisyphus and Salmoneus: when an oracle informed Sisyphus that the only revenge on Salmoneus would be to have children by his niece, Sisyphus did so, and Tyro gave birth to twins. Tyro heard of the oracle and killed her children. She would also have children by Poseidon — disguised as the river god, Enipeus — who would become the corrupt twins, Pelias and Neleus. After Alcidice died, Salmoneus married Sidero. She was an evil stepmother who abused Tyro, and who would later be killed by Pelias, with Hera's assistance.

Salmoneus has found his place in Greek myth because of his arrogance. Thinking he could impersonate Zeus, he constructed a bronze roadway and drove a chariot that dragged chains to imitate the sound of thunder. Because he couldn't produce lightning bolts, he threw burning torches from the chariot on the road and at his own people, and ordered them to bring sacrifices to him. Zeus was so enraged he killed Salmoneus by sending down a real thunderbolt, which also destroyed Salmone and its inhabitants.

Although the not-so-brilliant idea of impersonating Zeus may be along the lines of the Salmoneus on *X:WP*, the writers have altered his character to make him less arrogant. Here he's back to being a travelling salesman, selling Black Wolf merchandise, obviously playing on the Nike ad campaign: "Just cry wolf!" Gabrielle comes into her own in this episode as well, as she cleverly makes a chakram hat and whip belt and gets herself thrown into the dungeon. Xena still acts as Gabrielle's protector; note the murderous look she flashes Salmoneus when Gabrielle utters the now-infamous line, "You wouldn't be in here in the first place if you'd kept your hands off my tomatoes." However, Gabrielle fights pretty well in the final scene, and Xena isn't always looking over her shoulder to check on her.

We discover more details of Xena's past as another of her devotees, Flora, recalls her childhood with Xena. We realize there was another Gabrielle figure in Xena's past, whom she regarded as a sister. Flora (named after the Greek nymph who gave vegetation its ability to blossom and grow) is tested here as Xena makes Flora discover for herself why Xena never helped her into the tree.

The followers of the Black Wolf exercise a ritual whereby each member steps forward to proclaim that he or she is the Black Wolf. This throws off the enemy and keeps the identity secret. This trick was used in the 1960 epic, Spartacus, which is given a nod in "Athens City Academy of The Performing Bards." And who is the Black Wolf? You'll have to watch this episode and find out.

112 Beware Greeks Bearing Gifts

ORIGINAL AIR DATE: January 15, 1996
TELEPLAY BY: Adam Armus & Nora Kay Foster
STORY BY: Roy Thomas & Janis Hendler
DIRECTED BY: T.J. Scott
GUEST CAST: Galyn Görg as Helen
                Scott Garrison as Perdicas
                Cameron Rhodes as Deiphobus
                Warren Carl as Paris
                Ken Blackburn as King Menelaus
                Adrian Keeling as Miltiades
                Aidan MacBride Stewart as Greek Soldier
                John Manning as Greek Scout
                Matthew Jeffs as Trojan Soldier #1
                Peter Ford as Trojan Soldier #2
                Geoffrey Knight as Trojan Guard

Xena and Gabrielle are summoned to Troy by Helen, who fears that something awful is about to happen. At Troy, they encounter the Trojan Horse and Gabrielle is reunited with her once-betrothed, Perdicas.

Helen was the daughter of Zeus and Leda, although by some accounts she was the daughter of Zeus and Nemesis, and raised by Leda. When Tyndareus, Helen's earth father, decided it was time to marry her, men from all over Greece appeared as her suitors, as she was known as the world's most beautiful woman. Because many of them were princes or warriors, Tyndareus was worried that the spurned men would start a war against the victor, so he made them all agree to support the decision and stand behind the chosen man, fighting anyone who would try to take Helen from him. The man chosen — either by Helen or Tyndareus — was Menelaus.

Menelaus was the brother of Agamemnon — who married Helen's sister Clytemnestra — and the son of Atreus, although they were both the foster sons of Tyndareus. He was known for his relative gentleness, compared to his more violent kinsmen. With Helen he had at least one child, Hermione.

When Hermione was nine, Menelaus travelled to Crete to attend the funeral of his grandfather, Catreus. While he was gone, Helen took his place as the host of their guests: among those guests was Paris. Paris was the son of Hecuba and Priam, but because of a dream that told her Paris would set fire to Troy, Hecuba abandoned him on a hillside, and he was raised by shepherds. Paris eventually returned to Troy to take part in the Trojan funeral games, held, ironically, in his own honour as the son of Priam who died at an early age. When his sister Cassandra and brother Deiphobus recognized him, he was welcomed back into the family.

The next major episode that involves Paris was that of the judgement. At the wedding of Peleus and Thetis, Ares' daughter, Strife, threw a golden apple onto a table to be given to the most beautiful of three goddesses: Aphrodite, Athena, and Hera. No one wanted to decide who was the most beautiful, and Paris was forced to choose. Hera offered him the kingdom of Asia, Athena wisdom and victory in battle, and Aphrodite the love of the most beautiful woman in the world. He chose Aphrodite and the Trojan War was imminent.

There are many different versions of the meeting of Paris and Helen: according to some, he seduced her with his own beauty, or his gifts. In others, Aphrodite disguised him as Menelaus. And in others Helen was forced unwillingly, and taken as a prize back to Troy. While agreeing with the popular consensus that Helen went willingly, the writers of this episode of *X:WP* alter the story to show that she eventually changed her mind and fell out of love with him. When Menelaus heard what happened, he called all the Greek leaders — who had been sworn to support him earlier — to fight with him against Troy. The Trojan war continued for ten years, and Helen was hated by the Trojan people. Paris was eventually killed by one of Philoctetes' arrows, and Helen married Deiphobus. Deiphobus was one of Paris's brothers, and he was chosen by Helen after defeating his brother Helenus in a competition to win her.

In the final trick at Troy — the Trojan Horse — Menelaus was one of the warriors inside the horse. According to one legend, he spotted Helen inside Troy, and as he ran at her with a raised sword, she turned and he was halted by her beauty. They made peace, and she returned with him to Sparta after he killed Deiphobus. There are many variations of this story. In some of the more tragic versions, Helen was kidnapped by Hera and Paris ran away with an image of Helen — thus, the Trojan War was fought over an apparition.

In the *X:WP* version of the story, everything happens against Helen's will. The "face that launched a thousand ships" has been blamed for a bloody war, but we discover that there was a possibility that she was used as a pawn for a bunch of warriors' machismo. In a poignant moment when Xena asks Helen what she wants, Helen turns to her and admits, "No one's ever asked me that before." Paris is the first sexist male in a prominent role on this show, and his attitude toward Helen is beyond offensive. He tells her to get her beauty sleep, for her beauty is what he's fighting for. As usual, he doesn't attribute to Helen any intelligence or wit. In a brilliant job of casting, Helen is not played by a blonde and blue-eyed actress, as is usually the case, but one with dark hair and dark skin — probably a more accurate depiction of what she would have looked like.

An interesting subplot to this episode is the relationship between Gabrielle and her previously betrothed, Perdicas. Reversing the traditional gender roles, Gabrielle completely emasculates Perdicas, telling him he'll hurt himself as a soldier and to go back to his farming. Interestingly, he doesn't say the same to her, yet on a daily basis she is in dangerous situations herself. At one point he tells Gabrielle, "You can't tell me what to do anymore," implying that Gabrielle probably treated him more like a child than an adult. Throughout this episode, Gabrielle treats Perdicas as if he were (and always was) a lovesick klutz, yet he hides her and protects her at the end (although she could have taken care of herself). In a continuation of the gender role-reversal, when Perdicas tells Xena about Captain Deiphobus, she immediately assumes the captain is a woman, the opposite to what would be assumed today. It is as if the whole society were the opposite of ours: women fight and rule, and Paris is the "masculinist" who must shout out that anything women can do men can do just as well.

"Beware Greeks Bearing Gifts," besides having the most tongue-in-cheek title of the season, was an intriguing revision of the Trojan War, although it severely simplified the war itself. However, unless they had spun this episode off into a six-hour miniseries, it would have been difficult to do the war justice. The idea of the Trojan Horse as a collector's item was very clever though.

TIME: c. 1250 BC, the estimated time of the fall of Troy.

GABRIELLE'S FIGHTING SKILLS: Xena and Gabrielle fight as a team, often with one setting the victim up while the other clobbers him.

OOPS: When Xena and Deiphobus are fighting, he throws her against a rock that not only moves, but appears to cave in. Twice!

DISCLAIMER: "No Oversized Polynesian-Style Bamboo Horses were harmed during the production of this motion picture. However, many wicker lawn chairs gave their lives."

113 Athens City Academy of The Performing Bards

ORIGINAL AIR DATE: January 22, 1996
WRITTEN BY: R.J. Stewart & Steven L. Sears
DIRECTED BY: Jace Alexander
GUEST CAST: Dean O'Gorman as Orion
Grahame Moore as Polonius

Andrew Thurtell as Twickenham
Joseph Manning as Euripedes
Patrick Brunton as Stallonus   —
Alan De Malmanche as Docenius
Lori Dungey as Kellos
David Weatherley as Gastacius
Bernard Moody as Drunk

Gabrielle enters a contest to win one of four spots in the Athens Academy of The Performing Bards. Through flashbacks of previous X:WP episodes, we see her various methods of storytelling.

Halfway through the first season, the writers of *X:WP* have already decided to give us a flashback episode, probably to fill in those viewers who have just started watching the show. The producers put the episode together to stretch the budget a little further, and filmed it while Lucy was in the U.S. Although this episode is an interesting one, it's fraught with inconsistencies (according to our world, that is; but there is no normal timeline in the Xenaverse). At the academy, Gabrielle meets Euripedes, who lived c. 485–406 BC. Yet Gabrielle has just witnessed the destruction of Troy, which happened almost 800 years before.

Euripedes was one of the greatest of tragic poets, or at the very least, held in the highest regard. Soldiers would recite his lines on the battlefields to keep their spirits up. He was often mocked for making his characters' speeches too wordy and clever to be accurate portrayals, and the writers of this episode exaggerate his tendencies to make them laughable. He was laughed at by his contemporaries, and this author of the great tragedies, *Hippolytus, Alcestis,* and *The Bacchae,* was killed when dogs were set on him by the king of Macedonia.

To add to the inconsistencies, also attending the school is Homer, whose dates are about as stable as *X:WP*'s. His principal works were *The Iliad* and *The Odyssey*, and he remains one of the world's greatest poets. He was originally thought to have lived around the time of the events he described, but it is now generally believed that he composed his poems around 850 BC — 400 years before Euripedes. He recounted important events in Mycenaean history, and it is his version of the Trojan War that is still the most vivid and adhered-to version. Homer was known as the blind poet, but because that is the only detail we know of him, the reference could be to his powers of insight, not to a physical handicap.

In this episode of *X:WP*, Homer's blindness is attributed to the fact that he keeps his eyes closed while reciting, so that he can picture the scene. In a daring move of revisionist history, the writers suggest that Homer made it into the academy because a woman refused to go. (Virginia Woolf would have loved this.) The relationship between Gabrielle and Orion is interesting for being her first relationship with a male where she doesn't immediately fall in love with him. Reneé chose to play the part platonically on purpose, and later said, "I thought it would be a great way to show that men and women could have relationships, be friendly, and compete with each other on an equal basis, so that created another aspect to Gabrielle."

The friendship between Xena and Gabrielle is very touching at the beginning of this episode, and Xena acknowledges how important Gabrielle is to her when they are about to be separated. We also witness a moment where Xena talks about her childhood — a very rare moment indeed. While a flashback episode is usually a cheap and fast way of churning out an episode for any show, this one isn't bad.

TIME: Somewhere between 850 and 450 BC.

NITPICKS: Bards are different from writers in that they never wrote their stories down — at least that was the definition in the Greek era. Yet Gabrielle records her stories on scrolls.

DISCLAIMER: "The producers would like to acknowledge and pay tribute to Stanley Kubrick, Kirk Douglas and all those who were involved with the making of the film classic *Spartacus*. Additional thanks to Steve Reeves."

114 A Fistful of Dinars

ORIGINAL AIR DATE: January 29, 1996
WRITTEN BY: Steven L. Sears & R.J. Stewart
DIRECTED BY: Josh Becker
GUEST CAST: Jeremy Roberts as Thersites
Peter Daube as Petracles
Richard Foulkes Jr. as Lycus
Huntly Eliott as Calicus
Merv Smith as Head Villager
John Smith as Marleus
Lawrence Wharerau as Klonig

Xena and Gabrielle join Xena's enemies Petracles and Thersites to find the lost treasure of the Sumerians. Xena knows that in that treasure is the key to ambrosia, the food of the gods.

Ambrosia is referred to by different names in different cultures. In India the equivalent is Soma, an intoxicating beverage that the gods drink to remain immortal and was drunk from a bowl that would replenish itself. It was made from the juice of the soma plant, which is now unknown, and may have also been hallucinogenic. In Persia this drink was called haoma, but it also led to drunkenness and was condemned by Zoroaster, the Persian/Iranian prophet.

In *X:WP*, ambrosia can make a mortal a god, which is a very interesting twist that will be used in later episodes (see "A Necessary Evil"). Ambrosia is not a drink, however, but a gelatin substance. The gods on Mt. Olympus feasted on ambrosia and drank nectar.

Thersites was the grandson of Portaon, who was the ruler of Pleuron and Calydon. He was an ugly and cowardly Greek who fought at Troy. He was hunched over and limped when he walked and had very little hair.

Thersites is the only low-born Greek depicted in *The Iliad*. At Troy — as mentioned in *The Iliad* — Agamemnon tested his army by telling them to end the siege. Thersites immediately accepted and led the revolt against the leaders, for which he was beaten. The other soldiers looked on and laughed.

Thersites died as cowardly as he lived. Penthesilea was an Amazon who came with her army to Troy to assist Priam. She was killed by Achilles, but as she fell she looked at him and he immediately fell in love with her. Devastated by what he had done, he stood over her corpse, stricken, but Thersites mocked him for his love, and gouged out Penthesilea's eyes. Enraged, Achilles turned on Thersites and beat him to death with his fists. Achilles then had to travel to Lesbos to be purified of the murder.

Although Thersites was killed at Troy and should technically be dead before this episode, the writers of *X:WP* have stayed true to his nature. He uses Gabrielle as a ladder to get to the treasure, and is willing to kill everyone to make himself a god. This episode wasn't particularly exciting, and didn't further Xena or Gabrielle's characters at all.

NITPICK: If Xena realizes that Petracles was good before he died, why doesn't she put some ambrosia into his mouth to save him (see "The Quest")?

OOPS: The producers have gone really cheap on this episode by re-using footage of a skeleton on the wooden rack and spiders coming out of a skull first shown in "Beware Greeks Bearing Gifts." Such vivid footage is not easily forgotten, and to replay it only two episodes later is a foolish mistake.

DISCLAIMER: "No Ambrosia was Spilled, Spoiled or in any way harmed during the making of this motion picture. (Thanks to the indefinite shelf life of marshmallows.)"

115 Warrior . . . Princess

ORIGINAL AIR DATE: February 5, 1996
WRITTEN BY: Brenda Lilly
DIRECTED BY: Michael Levine
GUEST CAST: Iain Rea as Philemon
Norman Forsey as King Lias
Latham Gaines as Minius
Patrick Smith as Glauce
Michelle Huirama as Tesa
Jason Hoyte as Timus
Jonathon Acorn as Mirus
Ian Miller as Low Life
Chris Bohm as Guard
Mia Koning as Waif

Xena must switch places with Princess Diana, her coincidentally identical twin, in order to save her from being assassinated.

Hilarious! Lucy shines in this episode as for the first time all of her years as a comedic actress can be displayed on *X:WP*. Lucy is completely put to the test acting like Xena and Diana, as well as Xena as Diana and Diana as Xena. And she pulls it off superbly. Even when Xena is dressed as Diana, we are always aware that she is Xena. However, because Lucy Lawless has been playing this character for so long, it would have been easier for her to identify with Xena and still be able to give Xena's quirks away, even when Xena was disguised as someone else. (Everyone follow me so far?)

The real difficulty for Lucy is when she plays Diana playing Xena. This character is a new one, yet she's running around in Xena's costume. Lucy creates a new voice for her, whimpering away to Gabrielle that she wants to go home. Her reference to the chakram as the "round killing thing" is especially funny, and we discover what happens when someone other than Xena throws the weapon.

Although the writers of this show have some fun with the names of the characters — Diana was the fierce goddess of the hunt — it is not based on any Greek myth, but instead borrows from Mark Twain's 1881 novel, *The Prince and the Pauper*. Prince Edward trades places with a remarkably similar-looking pauper, Tom Canty, and through his experience he learns the injustice of the law and the shocking level of poverty in his kingdom. Tom Canty, on the other hand, initially relishes the luxuries of the castle, but ultimately discovers how difficult it is to govern a kingdom. When Edward becomes king, he is able to govern more democratically, and Canty is happy with his improved life outside the walls of the castle.

While the premise of "Warrior . . . Princess" is different from the book, Diana does see the degradation of her kingdom, and the viewer realizes how difficult day-to-day life probably is for Gabrielle and Xena, as well. "Warrior . . . Princess" is superbly acted, well-written, and the most fun to watch of this season.

GABRIELLE'S FIGHTING SKILLS: When Diana first appears but can't fight, Gabrielle must fight off the thief herself. Quick thinking on her part, considering she can't understand why "Xena" isn't fighting with her.

DISCLAIMER: "Neither Xena nor her remarkably coincidental identical twin, Diana, were harmed during the production of this motion picture."

116 Mortal Beloved

ORIGINAL AIR DATE: February 12, 1996
WRITTEN BY: R.J. Stewart
DIRECTED BY: Garth Maxwell
GUEST CAST: Bobby Hosea as Marcus
Paul Willis as Atyminius
Erik Thomson as Hades
Michael Hurst as Charon

Chris Graham as Toxeus
John Palmer as Traveler
Michelle Armstrong as Young Woman
Geoff Clendon as Bride's Father
Chantelle Brownlee as Bride

Marcus's ghost appears to Xena to ask for her help in undoing the chaos in the Underworld. Xena travels to the Underworld and back again to recover Hades' helmet and in doing so she must face the guilt she feels over Marcus's death.

The best episode of the season. As the season has progressed, we've witnessed the actors becoming comfortable in their roles, but in this episode especially, we see Lucy and Reneé expanding their characters beyond mythic heroes and fleshing them out into human beings. The acting has become more understated, and the ending of this episode will bring a tear to the most composed *X:WP* viewer.

Unlike the Christian idea of Heaven being above and Hell being below, in the Greek view of the world the gods inhabited the sky and the mountains, the people lived on earth, and the dead were in the Underworld, or Tartarus. The Underworld is usually described as being in three sections: the Elysian Fields, or Elysium, an orchard paradise for those who died a heroic death; the Asphodel Fields, a cheerless place where most (those neither very good nor very bad) were sent to wander; and Erebus, or Punishment Ground, inhabited by the cruellest sinners — and often by Zeus's enemies, whether cruel or not. Beyond the Asphodel Fields was the tall cold palace of Hades and Persephone, to one side of which was a cypress tree marking Lethe, the Pool of Forgetfulness, where the dead went to drink before entering Asphodel. This made their time there quite dull, it was said, because having forgotten everything of their lives they had nothing to talk about. (There was also Mnemosyne, the Pool of Memory, marked by a white poplar, for the select few given a secret password by Orpheus.) On their arrival, mortals faced the three Judges of the Dead: Minos, Rhadamanthys, and Aeacus.

When mortals died they were ordered by Hermes to follow him through the air to the main entrance in the Underworld, and the souls were ferried across the river Styx by Charon, who steered the boat while the souls of the dead rowed. The riverbank was protected by Hades' enormous three-headed dog, Cerberus, who let no ghosts escape and prevented any live mortal from entering (he was conspicuously absent from this episode). Charon was abusive and cruel, and the dead had to pay him to cross — hence the Greek tradition of placing a coin in the corpse's mouth. Ghosts who had no money either shivered forever on the riverbank, or had to find their way back to Greece and take a side entrance at Taenarus, where admission might be free. Charon was once beaten into taking a living person to the Underworld — Heracles — and was punished by the gods for doing so. In "Mortal Beloved," Charon is transformed into a sardonic, wise-cracking comedian who wants to be paid but never is. On first viewing, I thought the actor was great and should definitely be used again, only to discover Charon was played by Michael Hurst, who appears weekly on *H:TLJ* as Iolaus.

Hades makes his second appearance on *X:WP* (see "Death in Chains") but not his last. As the god of the dead, Hades had participated in the fight against the Titans, and the Cyclopes gave him the helmet of invisibility — hence the name Hades, which means invisible. Unlike the Hades of *X:WP*, Hades took no pity on any of his subjects and he never granted anyone their life back. Hades fell in love with Persephone, Demeter's daughter (and therefore his niece), but Demeter refused him. So Hades kidnapped Persephone and brought her to the Underworld. Although Zeus had a mute involvement in the abduction, soon after he sent Hermes with a message saying if Hades did not release her, Demeter's vengeant curse on the land — forbidding trees to bear fruit and cattle to eat — would ruin them all, and because Persephone hadn't eaten the food of the dead, Hades could not hold her. Hades then took sympathy on her, seeing that she was unhappy, and offered to send her back, but she had picked and eaten seven pomegranate seeds from the fruit of the Underworld, and anyone who eats the food of the Underworld cannot be restored to Earth. The eventual compromise was that Persephone would spend more than half of the year with Hades (seven months represented by the seven seeds) and the other part with her mother. As queen of the Underworld, she was as ruthless as Hades. Hades was also known as Pluto, because it was unwise for mortals to say his real name out loud.

In *X:WP*, Hades' power compared to the other gods is diminished. In "Death in Chains," he must ask for Xena's help to get his sister back; couldn't he have entered Sisyphus's room invisibly and saved her? Here, without his helmet, he's absolutely powerless. Instead Atyminius gains a lot of Hades' power just by having the helmet, and he sets the harpies at Hades' castle.

The harpies were winged creatures, portrayed as winged women and as birds with women's heads. They were the daughters of Thaumus, who was the son of Gaia, and Electra, who was the daughter of Oceanus. Although Hesiod only mentions two harpies, there were in fact three — Aeollo, Ocypete, and Celaeno, or Pordage (not Fee, Fie and Fofum!). They would carry off children and the souls of the dead, and they are featured in a legend of King Phineus. Phineus was cursed so that everything that was handed to him would be snatched by the harpies (hence their name, meaning the Snatchers). To end the curse, the Argonauts chased the Harpies, but Iris intervened and pleaded for their lives. The Harpies agreed to leave Phineus alone and hid in a cave in Crete. In *X:WP* and *H:TLJ*, the harpies are a group of monsters that are constantly attacking, not three fixed (and named) beings. Xena discovers they aren't especially fond of fire, and the special effects to create the harpies are quite amazing.

"Mortal Beloved" is the first episode where we see Xena cry. In a reversal of the Orpheus/Eurydice myth — where Orpheus travels to the Underworld to bring his wife back to the living — the writers show a deeper side of Xena. She has always looked uncomfortable in emotional scenes, but here she unselfconsciously shows Marcus how much she loves him. Not only is Xena's love for Marcus touching, but Gabrielle's undying loyalty as she twice waits for Xena's return shows what a faithful friend she is. Whenever Xena and Marcus kiss in this episode, you can hear the strains of Lucy's funeral song, "Burial," foreshadowing Marcus's short time on Earth. This episode is a must-see.

GABRIELLE'S FIGHTING SKILLS: Because she is alone for most of the episode, Gabrielle must learn to fight without relying on Xena, and she draws blood (that we see) for the first time by giving Atyminius a bloody nose.

NITPICK: Xena says to Hades that he can see all and thus knows of Marcus's generosity. Why, then, didn't he know where the helmet was hidden?

DISCLAIMER: "No Winged Harpies were harmed or sent to a fiery grave during the production of this motion picture."

117 The Royal Couple Of Thieves

ORIGINAL AIR DATE: February 19, 1996
WRITTEN BY: Steven L. Sears
DIRECTED BY: John Cameron
GUEST CAST: Bruce Campbell as Autolycus
Mark Raffety as Arkel
Grant Bridger as Sinteres
Crawford Thomson as Prognese
Arch Goodfellow as Kelton
Patrick Khutze as Belart
Ian Harrop as Magmar
David Telford as Malthus

Xena joins Autolycus, the self-proclaimed king of thieves, to try to steal back a box that is very important to some friends of hers.

"The Royal Couple of Thieves" was an important event for many Raimi/ Tapert fans, for it was the *X:WP* debut of Bruce Campbell as Autolycus. Bruce Campbell is best known for his work in the Raimi Tapert *Evil Dead* films — *Evil Dead*, *Evil Dead 2: Dead by Dawn*, and *Army of Darkness* — and he has a huge cult-like fan following. In 1979, with Raimi and Tapert, Campbell raised the $350,000 needed to make *Evil Dead*, and after four years of production, it was hailed by Stephen King as "the most ferociously original horror film of the year" and became England's biggest-selling video of 1983. Campbell has also appeared in Coen brothers' films, *Ellen*, and various other films and television shows. As Autolycus, a role he developed on *H:TLJ*, Campbell delivers some of the best *X:WP* lines to date.

Autolycus was the son of Hermes, and thus the grandson of Zeus. In turn, he was the grandfather of Odysseus by his daughter Anticleia (see

"Death in Chains"). From Hermes, Autolycus learned the ability to steal without being caught. However, he was caught by Sisyphus when he tried to steal his cattle. One legend states that Sisyphus had his own name engraved into his cattle's hooves, while another reads that, anticipating what Autolycus would do, Sisyphus had "stolen by Autolycus" engraved in the hooves.

Generally, though, Autolycus was a successful thief. He stole a helmet to give to Achilles, who wore it at Troy. He would often steal animals — as his father had done — and would dye the skins of the animals so their owners wouldn't recognize them. By some accounts, Autolycus was one of the Argonauts in search of the Golden Fleece. According to other writers, Autolycus taught Heracles how to fight and had the ability to transform himself.

This episode is a comic one, although a viewer can't help but wince when Autolycus introduces Xena as his concubine. Is this guy suicidal? Xena's dance of the three veils is a condensed version of Salomé's dance of the seven veils, perhaps indicating that Xena wanted Autolycus's head on a platter, as Salomé had requested of John the Baptist.

The writers seem to have borrowed some ideas from *Raiders of the Lost Ark* for this one, which is obviously a favorite among the *X:WP* scribes (see "The Xena Scrolls" for more direct borrowing). For inconsistencies regarding the appearance of the casket and what it was supposed to look like, see Exodus 25: 10–22.

Sinteres is a character this episode could have done without. This guy is so annoying and he holds his fingers in the most over-exaggerated way in every scene as if actor has seen *The Karate Kid* one too many times. Campbell, on the other hand, does a great job here, and it's reassuring to know that he'll be back for more episodes on *X:WP* and *H:TLJ*.

oops: Autolycus lowers the casket back to its original spot and immediately escapes, but when Arkel discovers it, all the ropes have mysteriously vanished.

disclaimer: "No Ancient and Inflexible Rules governing moral behaviour were harmed during the production of this motion picture."

118 The Prodigal

original air date: March 4, 1996
written by: Chris Manheim
directed by: John T. Kretchmer
guest cast: Tim Thomerson as Meleager
Willa O'Neill as Lila
Alan Palmer as Pharis
Steve Hall as Damon
Kelly Greene as Derq

Anton Bentley as Athol
Barry Te Hira as Head Highwayman
Wally Green as Elderly Driver
Ashley Stansfield as Sentry
Stephen Walker as Peasant
Margaret Conquest as Villager

When Gabrielle returns home to do some soul-searching, she discovers that Damon's army has been attacking Poteidaia, and the villagers have hired Meleager the Mighty to save them. When Gabrielle discovers he's an alcoholic who's lost his nerve, she must become the warrior and save the village herself.

Meleager the Mighty is named after the warrior of Greek legend. By some accounts, Meleager was the son of Althaea, a sister of Leda, and King

An energetic Tim Thomerson, Meleager
the Mighty, at WarriorCon '97

JOAN STANCO

Oeneus of Calydon; by others his father was Ares. In *The Iliad*, one story of Meleager is told by Phoenix. King Oeneus made regular sacrifices to the gods, but always neglected Artemis. To show her anger, she sent a wild boar to Calydon, and it was Meleager who stopped it. Still angry, Artemis began a war between the Aeotelians — Meleager's tribe — and the Curetes. When Meleager killed his two uncles, his mother cursed him and brought the wrath of the gods against him. Shunned, Meleager retreated to his house with his wife, Idas's daughter Cleopatra, and refused to continue fighting in the war. His countrymen came to him one-by-one pleading that he help, but it took Cleopatra to convince him. He returned to battle and helped his people win, but he was killed.

In another version, after Althaea gave birth to Meleager she was visited by the three Fates, one of whom told her that Meleager's life would end when a particular log on Althaea's fireplace would be consumed. Althaea quickly removed the log from the fire and placed it in a chest. When Meleager was older, he organized a group of brave warriors to rid Calydon of the wild boar. One of those warriors was Atalanta, with whom he was having an affair. Atalanta was the first to wound the boar, but Meleager killed it. He offered the spoils to Atalanta, but his mother's two brothers argued they should get them. Meleager fought and killed both of them, and, upon hearing the news, Althaea threw the log onto the fire. Meleager was engaged in a battle when he felt his energy drain and he fell. Althaea soon realized what she had done and committed suicide.

By all accounts, Meleager did not live to a very old age, so, despite being a great warrior named Meleager the character in *X:WP* may not actually be based on the character of Greek legend. Tim Thomerson is wonderful as Meleager, the warrior who has turned to drink to hide his fears. Through Meleager, Gabrielle discovers that if you have the heart of a warrior, you can overcome your fears.

This episode is full of the hilarious twentieth-century language that is so prominent in the Herc/Xenaverse. Phrases like "stuck between a rock and a hard place" and "rock and roll" are used, and Gabrielle refers to roadkill and the difficulty of folding up road maps. Gabrielle comes into her own in this episode. Separated from Xena, she's forced to fight alone and even form an army of people who are just like she used to be. In a great role reversal, Gabrielle becomes like Xena to her sister, Lila, and when she tells her to stay put, Lila does what Gabrielle always does — runs away to help anyway. Gabrielle recognizes that she no longer has to completely rely on Xena, and that she can now be an asset to her. In an ironic twist, Meleager tells Gabrielle and Lila to stand back and let the men fight, a comment that seems completely out of place on *X:WP*. Ironically, Meleager and Damon's sword fight is by the book, and lacks the zeal of any of Xena's fights.

Like "Athens City Academy of The Performing Bards," this episode features Gabrielle while Xena is elsewhere, showing the confidence the writers and producers had in Reneé's character even then. However, it also leaves us with some mildly disturbing questions. When Gabrielle leaves Xena to go to Poteidaia, why doesn't she hug her or say good-bye, considering her intent is to leave for good? Xena looks far more distraught than Gabrielle in this scene. Also, Gabrielle says she needs her family. After all they've been through, she needs her family now? It would seem that an issue like losing one's nerve in battle would be more appropriately discussed with Xena. All in all, a fun episode. The producers are wise to bring back the Meleager character later.

TIME: Gabrielle quotes Sophocles, who lived from 496–406 BC, setting this episode some time after that.

GABRIELLE'S FIGHTING SKILLS: She not only stands up to an army, but leads one as well.

NITPICK: Where are Gabrielle's parents throughout this episode?

OOPS: In the final scene, when Gabrielle uses her staff as a pole vault over the cart, watch where she actually goes over it. A frame-by-frame advance reveals not only that the staff is missing, but the line where they've accidentally airbrushed it out.

INTERESTING FACT: Meleager's sister was Deianeira, the name of the character Reneé O'Connor played in *Hercules and the Lost World*. Also, that pole vault was actually completed by a male stuntperson. Nice midriff!

DISCLAIMER: "Meleager the Mighty, the generally Tipsy and Carousing warrior-for-Hire, was not harmed during the production of this motion picture."

119 Altared States

ORIGINAL AIR DATE: April 22, 1996
WRITTEN BY: Chris Manheim
DIRECTED BY: Michael Levine
GUEST CAST: David Ackroyd as Anteus
David de Lautour as Icus
Karl Urban as Maell
Teresa Woodham as Zora
Sean Ashton-Peach as Zealot #1
Graham Smith as Senior Zealot
Jack Dacey as Brawny Zealot
Peter Ford as Zealot Guard

When Xena learns that a boy is about to be sacrificed to "the one god" by his father, she attempts to find out what sort of father would kill his own son.

"Altared States" is the first episode that is entirely based on a biblical story. In the Old Testament, stories abound of God testing the faith of various followers. In Genesis, he tests Abraham. Abraham and Sarah could not have any children, so Sarah offered to him her slave girl, Hagar, with whom he might conceive a child. Hagar became pregnant and acted proudly, snubbing Sarah, who then treated her so cruelly she ran away. God appeared to Hagar and told her to return to Sarah, and that he'd grant her a son, whom she should name Ishmael, but that he would hate and be hated (Genesis 16: 1–16).

Thirteen years later, God appeared to Abraham and told him he'd grant Sarah a son, despite the fact they were both in their eighties (Genesis 18: 1–15). That son was Isaac. One day Sarah found Ishmael teasing Isaac, so she sent both Ishmael and his mother away, into the wilderness. Ishmael grew up to be a great hunter.

When Isaac was older, God called on Abraham to prove his love to Him by sacrificing Isaac on the altar. Abraham obeyed without question. Making Isaac carry the wood while he carried the knife, he shrugged off Isaac's questions about where the sacrificial lamb was. The Biblical story is very cold, for Abraham calmly puts his son on the altar and raises the knife, but God stops him, saying that Abraham has proven his fear of Him. In gratitude, Abraham slaughters a lamb and offers it to God (Genesis 22: 1–18).

In *X:WP*, the writers have altered the Hebrew names to make them sound Greek. Abraham becomes Anteus, Issac Icus, Ishmael Maell, and Sarah is Zora. Maell appears to be Zora's son, giving him a closer relationship to Icus. In this re-telling of the ancient myth, there is more emphasis placed on how difficult it must have been for the father to kill his own son. The story is also revised to take the blame off God and put it onto a mortal. In this re-telling, God is forgiving and benevolent, not malicious, and while in the Old Testament Ishmael was sent to the wilderness, this episode shows what may have happened if he had never left. With the Old Testament as our background to the story, his reaction is actually an understandable one.

Out of desperation, Zora returns to her old religion and worships Hestia. Hestia was the goddess of hearth and home. One of the 12 Olympians, she was the first of Cronus and Rhea's children, but the last to be disgorged — thus, she is considered the eldest by some writers and the youngest by others. She was wooed by both Apollo and Poseidon, but Zeus respected her choice to remain a virgin all her life. In return for not having a family, Zeus made her the goddess of the hearth, so that she would be the centre of every home and would receive bountiful sacrifices. Hestia did not participate in the shenanigans of the other Olympians, and instead quietly remained on Mt. Olympus as its moral centre. Hestia doesn't figure in the various dramas of Greek myth in the same way the other gods and goddesses of Olympus do.

This episode is an interesting one, but is more difficult for some viewers to accept; after all, this is no longer Greek myth they're playing with, but Judeo-Christian. To transform the Old Testament God from a vengeful, angry (Olympian-like) one to a benevolent one is interesting, but at the same time the Abraham character is played for a fool.

The opening of "Altared States" is excellent, for we not only hear the beginnings of the hinting subtext — "Come on Gabrielle, you've been wanting to do this for ages" — but we see Xena's complete unselfconsciousness about her own body. As she leaves the water, completely naked, and approaches the band of slack-jawed gawkers, she makes no attempt to cover herself. The scenes with a drugged Gabrielle in the cave are amusing (although we'll just ignore the fact that the soprano / alto / tenor / bass configuration hadn't been developed until the fifteenth century AD) and give Reneé O'Connor a great opportunity to let loose with her character.

The idea of one supreme being versus numerous gods will recur in later episodes, but it's unfortunate that the writers don't attempt a more serious historical approach to what would have been a very volatile situation. However, the point of this episode is to make modern-day Christian viewers rethink their own beliefs. After all, if they believe in a vengeful god, how different is He from the Olympians?

YAXI: If Xena can run across the clotheslines in "The Royal Couple of Thieves" with such agility, why does it take her so long to cross a bridge that has ropes to hold onto as well as the tightrope?

DISCLAIMER: "No Unrelenting or Severely Punishing Deities were harmed during the production of this motion picture."

120 Ties That Bind

ORIGINAL AIR DATE: April 29, 1996
WRITTEN BY Adam Armus & Nora Kay Foster
DIRECTED BY: Charles Siebert
GUEST CAST: Tom Atkins as Atrius
Kevin Smith as Ares
Stephen Lovatt as Kirilus
Sonia Gray as Rhea
Lutz Halbhubner as Tarkis
Jonathon Whittaker as Andrus
Nancy Broadbent as Areliesa
Heidi Anderson as Slave Girl
John Manning as Ranch Hand #1
Mark Perry as Warrior #1
Tony Williams as Warrior #2
James Marcum as Warrior #3
Robin Kora as Village Elder

Xena is tested when her father, who abandoned her family when she was very young, re-enters her life.

This episode is little more than an attempt to give us more of Xena's background and to show yet again that Xena still has that evil streak in her.

Despite its problems, however, it will be crucial to the third season episode, "The Furies."

As mentioned earlier, Ares had no scruples and was the most boastful and cruel of the gods. He never married, but had many children. Two of them, Deimos and Phobos (Fear and Terror) were produced with Aphrodite, and they accompanied him on the battlefield. Aphrodite was married to Hephaestus (see "For Him the Bell Tolls"), who, when he learned of the affair, constructed a huge net to drop on the sleeping lovers. Once they were caught in the net, the gods came down from Olympus to laugh at them, and Ares was humiliated. It certainly wouldn't be the last time.

It is important to note that as odious as Ares was, he had many children and he would avenge anything that happened to any of them. When Poseidon's son, Halirrhothios, raped Ares' daughter Alcippe, Ares killed him on the spot. Poseidon held a trial for Ares, but the other gods found him not guilty.

In "Ties That Bind," Ares refers to himself as a father-figure for Xena, yet it would be truer to say that Xena is like a daughter-figure to him. Skilled in battle and capable of becoming a vengeful murderer when any of her family is killed or hurt, she embodies everything that would make a daddy like Ares proud. However, Xena prefers to play with him, outwitting and humiliating him like the goddess Athena did, rather than respecting him and fighting in his name.

This episode is the closest Ares comes to tricking her, and he's very sly about it. The abandoned daughter story is a new one for us, but the plot itself isn't very interesting. Xena turns on Gabrielle so quickly in the village, and then tells her that friendship is thicker than blood, but it seems like too little, too late. Friendship wasn't so important to her five minutes earlier, when she was about to run Gabrielle through with a sword. Xena's anger in this episode and in the upcoming "Death Mask" will render her attitude to Callisto far more complex and hypocritical than if we just take "Callisto" on its own.

YAXI: In retrospect, we realize Ares tricked Xena by listening in on the story she'd just told Gabrielle about the horse and her father, then repeating the same story he'd just heard to earn her trust. However, if Xena is smart enough to know what the Trojan Horse really was before anyone else, why didn't she figure this one out?

NITPICK: Her father tells her he left the family because he was far too young, basically a child. Yet, judging by the actor, he must have been over 30 when he left!

OOPS: After Atrius runs the assassin through with his sword there isn't a single drop of blood on the weapon. Also, when Xena knocks Kirilus's head against the butt of her sword, she pulls his head down in front of the sword, clearly missing the sword by a mile.

DISCLAIMER: "No Fathers, Spiritual or Biological, were harmed during the production of this motion picture."

121 The Greater Good

ORIGINAL AIR DATE: May 6, 1996
WRITTEN BY: Steven L. Sears
DIRECTED BY: Gary Jones
GUEST CAST: Robert Trebor as Salmoneus
Peter McCauley as Talmadeus
Jonathon Hendry as Ness
Natalya Humphrey as Photis
Timothy James Adam as Kalus
David Mitchell as Gorney
Kenneth Prebble as Old Man

When Xena tries to save a village from Talmadeus's army, she is hit with a poison dart. As she slowly dies, Gabrielle must convince the army that Xena is fine.

What would happen to Gabrielle if Xena were to die? Would she go back to Poteidaia? Would she be killed? The answers to these questions are found in this episode, where Xena seems to die and Gabrielle is left to continue what Xena began. Reneé is given the chance to be in the spotlight, not as a bard or as a big sister (as in past Gabrielle episodes) but as Xena's protégé, the little-girl-turned-fighter who must say good-bye to her best friend and save a village from an army.

Salmoneus is back to add some levity to an otherwise bleak episode, and he is able to shine as well. As Lord Seltzer — the salesman who sold fizzy water to a village by calling it a magic elixir — he's much closer to the sly Salmoneus of Greek legend. In this episode he still delivers the classic Salmoneus lines, but when he discovers a lifeless Xena, his few words — "Proud Warrioress . . . I will miss you" — are deeply touching, and the scene shows Trebor's versatility as an actor.

Gabrielle dressed as Xena is amusing, although one would think the costume would be slightly bigger (and where did they get the hair dye?). When she returns to find Xena dead, however, the dye has been washed from her hair, symbolizing that no matter how agile a warrior she becomes, she'll always be Gabrielle in Xena's clothing. She'll never be Xena, but instead will accomplish things her way, talking her way out of a situation, rather than killing. The scene of her dealing with her grief by whacking a tree is Reneé's best acting of the season. This is also the episode where Gabrielle and Argo become friends. Gabrielle risks life and limb to take Xena's corpse back to Amphipolis, proving that Xena's dying wish is more important to her than her own life. And how does Xena get out of this one? Let's just say there are certain things you just can't give away in an episode guide.

GABRIELLE'S FIGHTING SKILLS: Gabrielle saves Xena for the first time — small step for Gabrielle, giant leap for sidekicks.

YAXI: We learn that Argo's a pretty good fighter, and can communicate to other horses. However, her fighting skills are inconsistent with previous episodes, where she gallops away when the going gets tough (in "Sins of the Past," for example).

OOPS: Xenites on the Internet spelled Xena's war cry "AYIYIYIYI" for a long time before Lucy announced during an appearance on *Live with Regis and Kathie Lee* that she was actually saying "ALALALALA." However, when Gabrielle tries to imitate Xena's yell in this episode, she pronounces it "AYIYIYIYI." No wonder fans were confused: apparently Reneé heard the same thing we did!

DISCLAIMER: "Excessive belching can cause brain damage and social ostracism. Kids, please don't give in to peer pressure. Play it safe."

122 Callisto

ORIGINAL AIR DATE: May 13, 1996
WRITTEN BY: R.J. Stewart
DIRECTED BY: T.J. Scott
GUEST CAST: Hudson Leick as Callisto
Ted Raimi as Joxer
David Te Rare as Theodorus
Ian Hughes as Melas
Kenneth McGregor as Akteon
Patricia Donovan as Old Woman
Toby Mills as Tall Man
Michael Hallows as Tall Villager
Henry Vaeoso as Fat Warrior

Xena finally meets her match, and her nemesis, in Callisto, the woman whose family was slaughtered by Xena's army when Callisto was young.

Callisto is the best secondary character on the show this season. She's fierce and ruthless, and far more appropriate than Ares as a mechanism by which Xena must come to terms with her past.

Callisto, derived from *Kalliste*, meaning "The Beautiful One," is named after the daughter of King Lycaon, who became such a skilled huntress that Artemis took notice of her. She made a vow to Artemis to remain a virgin all her life, and became Artemis's hunting companion. However, when Zeus saw her he immediately fell in love with her, and, appearing to her in the guise of Artemis, seduced her. A few months later, when Artemis invited some of her companions to swim with her, she saw that Callisto was pregnant. Artemis angrily asked who'd impregnated her, to which Callisto replied that Artemis herself had done so.

From here, there are many variations on the story. In some Callisto was shunned from Artemis's sight and went off to give birth to a son, Arcas. Then Hera transformed Callisto to a she-bear. In other accounts, Zeus changed her into a she-bear to protect her from Hera's wrath. By still

Hudson Leick performs the
Callisto yell in Detroit, 1997.

JENNIFER HALE

others, Artemis immediately changed her into a bear, and Callisto had to
give birth to her son when she was not in a human form. Arcas, who became
a great hunter, one day saw a bear in the woods. He gave chase, not realizing
it was his mother. Callisto had no way of telling him, so she ran into a cave.
As Arcas was about to kill her, Zeus transformed both of them into
constellations — the Great Bear and the Little Bear. (By some accounts,
Callisto was transformed into a constellation after Arcas had killed her.)
Hera still had her revenge, though, and convinced the Ocean not to allow
the bears to drink from her, thereby forcing Callisto to constantly revolve
around the Pole Star.

The Callisto in *X:WP* bears a similarity with the Callisto of Greek legend
only in that she has been severely wronged. This Callisto is such a complex
character that it was necessary for her to reappear in the second and third

seasons. The viewers can't hate her, for she was a victim before she was the criminal. Xena turned to a life of evil because she lost a brother, while Callisto lost her entire family. Callisto is not only an important and vengeful remnant of Xena's past, but she is a named victim, a reminder that for many, the pain continued after Xena's army left the village. No matter how many lives Xena saves, Callisto is a reminder that she can never erase the memory of those she killed. Callisto becomes the physical embodiment of Xena's past, the reincarnation of the evil that Xena thought she'd quashed in "Dreamworker."

As much as Gabrielle has proven that she is an honourable character and a loyal friend to Xena, the trait that remains disturbing in her is a haughtiness toward some people. We must respect her for her moral code, but she tends to look down on those who don't agree with it, although she has never suffered as they have. In this episode she judges Callisto severely, despite having forgiven Xena for much worse. A distraught Melas, who has just lost his son, tells Gabrielle that she'd feel murderous revenge if she were in the same situation, but Gabrielle smugly replies, "No, I wouldn't," and looks condescendingly at him as she walks away. Getting onto her soapbox, she preaches that the cycle must end, and they must end it. Viewers should keep her words in mind while watching "Return of Callisto." Gabrielle has the best intentions, but it will be difficult for her to get people to listen and change unless she first tries to understand where they are coming from.

Another important character introduced here is Joxer, who has created the single biggest division among Xena fans (until the rift saga happens, of course). Joxer is the favorite character of many, while other fans hate him so much there is a "Shoot Joxer" web page on the Internet. Despite the claim that he is a sexist character — arising from his constant "Step aside, ladies" attitude — it's clear that he's a bumbling idiot. In my opinion, Joxer's creators are not sexist, because his claims of personal greatness are always invalid, rendering anything he says equally worthless. Ted Raimi is a great actor, and the warring chemistry which will develop between him and Gabrielle in the second season is one of the highlights of the show. Batman and Robin had Batgirl every once in a while, but she was effective. Reverse the gender roles, and the triangle no longer works, which is why Joxer's so funny: he is proof that women can be much stronger than men.

"Callisto" is an exciting episode full of fantastic new characters and has the single most suspenseful battle scene yet. Callisto's fortress is awesome and Joseph LoDuca's soundtrack for this episode is new and exciting. Definitely in the top five shows of the season.

GABRIELLE'S FIGHTING SKILLS: Well, we know she can take on Joxer with no problem. Now, whether that's an important accomplishment in her fighting development is another thing . . .

NITPICK: After discovering who Callisto is, why does Xena nonchalantly walk through the village, chatting it up with Melas and Gabrielle, while Callisto's army continues to sack the village in the background?

DISCLAIMER: "Joxer's nose was not harmed during the production of this motion picture. However, his crossbow was severely damaged."

123 Death Mask

ORIGINAL AIR DATE: June 3, 1996
WRITTEN BY: Peter Allan Fields
DIRECTED BY: Stewart Main
GUEST CAST: Joseph Kell as Toris
Michael Lawrence as Cortese
William Davis as Malik
Doug McCaulay as Aescalus
Elizabeth Skeen as Sera
Peter Needham as Village Elder

Xena is reunited with her older brother, Toris, and together they go after Cortese, the warrior who killed their younger brother Lyceus.

"Death Mask" was not an appropriate episode to have following "Callisto," unless it was the producer's intention to render Xena's judgement of Callisto completely hypocritical. Cortese's claim on Xena — "I created her" — echoes Callisto's "You created me" in the previous episode. Gabrielle's reference to a cycle of hatred is correct in this sense: who will Callisto create, for example? However, if we are to see Callisto as Xena's arch-enemy and as someone who should try to overcome her hatred, how do we explain Xena's immediate murderous reaction upon hearing Cortese's name?

Her brother Toris demonstrates that the brains Xena inherited from her parents weren't evenly distributed among the children. He has a tendency to speak out too much, to whine, and to undermine Xena's plans by giving them away. He wants the family revenge for himself, he hides behind the door as he's letting the army in the room to fight. (And didn't Rick Springfield have that haircut in 1982? Must have been his neo-Greek phase . . .)

Fortunately, Xena is won over by Gabrielle's rhetoric at the end and tosses the "gift" of revenge to her brother Toris, but we can't help but remember that she got a lot of revenge in over ten years as a warlord. Toris hasn't exactly been fighting long enough to get it out of his system, so his attitude isn't entirely without reason. As with "Ties That Bind," this episode gives us some of Xena's family background, but there's not a lot of substance beyond that.

GABRIELLE'S FIGHTING SKILLS: Xena teaches Gabrielle the warrior sense, where her body can feel an attack before it happens. Gabrielle immediately uses it in battle, showing her ability to learn quickly.

DISCLAIMER: "No messenger doves were harmed during the production of this motion picture. However, several are reportedly missing in action and search-and-rescue efforts are underway."

ORIGINAL AIR DATE: July 29, 1996

WRITTEN BY: Patricia Manney

DIRECTED BY: T.J. Scott

GUEST CAST: Ray Woolf as Marmax

Danielle Cormack as Ephiny

Andrew Binns as Hippocrates

Ron Smith as Galen

Simon Farthing as Democritus

Paul McLaren as POW Leader

Charles Pierard as Thessalian Guard

Tony Billy as Mitoan Warrior

Geoff Houtman as Gangrene Man

Deane Vipond as Head Wound Man

Harriet Crampton as Hysterical Woman

Adam Middleton as Blind Soldier

Edith as Runner

Caught in the middle of a war, Xena and Gabrielle enter a temple of healing, and by using her impressive medical skills, Xena saves many soldiers from both sides. When Gabrielle leaves the temple to save a child, even Xena's medical skills might not be enough to save her.

Often referred to as "*M*A*S*H* in Ancient Greece," this episode not only demonstrates Xena's skills as a surgeon, but exhibits Lucy's best acting to this point. The episode takes an issue that has been prominent for the last few centuries — science versus faith — and transfers it into ancient Greece, with science winning out. By showing that skilled techniques are more effective than praying to Asclepius, Xena convinces a young medical student named Hippocrates that her way is best, thereby forever changing the face of medicine.

There are many widely-varying accounts of Asclepius's genealogy, although it is unanimous that his father was Apollo. By some accounts, Asclepius's mother was Coronis, but when she fell in love with a mortal, Apollo killed her and ripped the child from her womb. In another, Apollo seduced the daughter of Phlegyas (a great thief) but she abandoned the baby in Epidaurus. A she-goat suckled the child and a shepherd found him, but Asclepius was surrounded by a golden light and the shepherd figured he was divine. Asclepius was thereafter worshipped in Epidaurus.

In any case, Apollo gave Asclepius to the centaur, Chiron, to raise, and Chiron taught him about medicine. Athena then gave Asclepius the good blood of Medusa — she used the evil blood to kill on the battlefield — and Asclepius discovered that he could use the blood to revive the dead. With this knowledge he resurrected many people, but when Zeus discovered what Asclepius could do he worried that man could become immortal through Asclepius's powers, and he struck and killed him with a thunderbolt. Asclepius continued to be worshipped in temples, and patients would sleep in them in the hopes of being healed. Among his symbols is the serpent wound around a staff, which is still a medical symbol today. The guild of physicians in ancient Greece — the Asclepiadae — worshipped him and said they were his descendants. Hippocrates was part of that guild.

Hippocrates, known as the "Father of Medicine," lived from 460 to 377 or 359 BC. He trained as a doctor on the island of Cos, located in the Icarian Sea, and he taught for money. As Xena does in this episode, Hippocrates wanted to distinguish medicine from ritual and occult, and he believed the four humors (phlegm, blood, yellow bile, and black bile) were the four seats of disease, a belief that persisted long after his death.

"Is There a Doctor in the House?" is rather idealistic and over the top, but a lot of fun to watch. This episode is Lucy's favorite from the first season and it shows. To film the episode, the cast and crew shot for five long, intense days. Originally the show was a lot more graphic — more blood and innards than we ultimately see — but advertisers threatened to pull out unless a lot of the gore was censored.

Ephiny is back for this episode, pregnant with Phantes' child, although Phantes has just been killed in the crossfire. Danielle Cormack is a wonderful actress for this role, and the birth scene is magnificent. The baby centaur must be the best special effect to date.

In this episode we see early forms of tracheotomies, amputations, splints, and a respirator (although the bladder looked more than a little plastic), and we are to assume that Hippocrates' writings are based on what Xena taught him. Near the end of the episode, where Xena loses Gabrielle, is phenomenal. Lucy gives this scene everything she's got, as if it were the last she has to play. The look on her face after she thumps Gabrielle's chest is priceless, and we know Xena is going to have a new respect for Gabrielle after this incident. A perfect way to end the season.

TIME: About 440 BC.

DISCLAIMER: "Being that War is Hell, lots of people were harmed during the production of this motion picture (but since television is a dramatic medium of make believe, all casualties removed their prosthetic make-up and went home unscathed)."

PRODUCTION STAFF:

> Music Composer: Joseph LoDuca
> Developer: R.J. Stewart
> Co-ordinating Producer: Bernadette Joyce
> Producer: Liz Friedman
> Producer: Eric Gruendemann
> Supervising Producer: Steven L. Sears
> Co-Executive Producer: R.J. Stewart
> Executive Producer: Sam Raimi
> Executive Producer: Robert Tapert
> Creators: John Schulian and Robert Tapert

201 Orphan of War

ORIGINAL AIR DATE: September 30, 1996
WRITTEN BY: Steven L. Sears
DIRECTED BY: Charles Siebert
GUEST CAST: Paul Gittins as Kaleipus
Mark Ferguson as Dagnine
David Taylor as Solan
Alexander Campbell as Miklan
Stephen Papps as See'er
Peter Tait as Daylon
Richard Adams as Warrior

Xena must prevent Dagnine, a member of her former army, from capturing the Ixion stone. By returning to the centaurs, she is reunited with her son, whom she gave up nine years earlier.

Ixion is often referred to as the Greek Cain. By various authors, he was the son of Phlegyas, Ares, Aeton, Antion, or Pision. His mother was Perimele, and when Ixion was older he became the Thessalian king and ruler of the Lapiths. When he married Dia, the daughter of King Deinonus (or Eionus), who was his kinsman, Ixion offered many bridal gifts to his new father-in-law. However, when Deinonus came to collect his presents, he fell into a pit lined with burning coals that Ixion had fashioned. Because this was the first known murder of one's kinsman (hence the Cain reference), Ixion could not find anyone to purify him of his crime. Taking pity on him, Zeus purified him and invited him to live on Olympus.

Escaping from his crime and living with the gods soon went to Ixion's head, and he began making amorous advances towards Hera. When Hera informed Zeus of what was going on, Zeus trapped Ixion by fashioning a cloud to look like Hera, with which Ixion committed adultery. The cloud, Nephelé, bore Centaurus, who begot the race of centaurs by mating with

Writer and Supervising Producer Steven L. Sears

CATHERINE M. WILSON

the mares of Mount Pelion. Enraged with Ixion's lack of gratitude, Zeus condemned him to Tartarus, where he was chained to a fiery wheel that rotated continuously. Because Zeus had given Ixion a drink to make him immortal, Ixion was forced to endure the punishment forever.

In "Orphan of War," Ixion is referred to as the father of the centaurs, although he was actually a grandfather to them. This episode is filled with new information about Xena's past, and it is more effective than "Ties That Bind" or "Death Mask." Xena's ex-lover, Borias, represents who she has become — an ex-warrior who fights for good. Borias gave his life to the centaur race, and Xena has risked her life for the centaurs and many others (for more on Borias, see "The Debt" and "The Debt II"). We also meet Xena's son by Borias, Solan, whose name means many things — "Sol" is French for "sun," which is often used as a homonym for "son" in poetry. (Viewers will notice the sun imagery they use with Solan in "The Bitter Suite.")

In retrospect this episode contains many elements that could be used in defence of the rift saga in Season Three. Gabrielle has been Xena's companion for a year, yet Xena hasn't told her about her son, and Gabrielle's pain at learning this information is obvious. Later, Xena tells Gabrielle that motherhood doesn't end with giving birth, but that the child continues to grow inside you. Viewers should remember this when watching "Gabrielle's Hope," and then ask themselves if Gabrielle's actions were skewed then. Despite all this turmoil, the special relationship between the characters prevails once again.

This episode features the debut of what fans lovingly call the BGSB, or Bilious Green Sports Bra, the green halter top that Gabrielle now wears. Gabrielle seems more confident with herself in this season, and throughout Season Two we will watch Reneé's talents mature into much more than a chattering, bardic sidekick. Reneé's name also appears during the opening credits now, and more scenes of her have been included in the final credits.

The image of Dagnine as Ixion at the end of this episode is amazing, and the makeup department has outdone themselves with this one. The directing at the very end is powerful; as Xena walks away from her son, the pace of the scene switches to slow motion, as if Xena is painfully dragging herself away from someone she loves. Lucy's acting is superb in this season, and this first episode is an indicator of what is to come.

NITPICK: If Xena and Borias both have black hair, why is Solan so fair?

DISCLAIMER: "No sleazy warlords who deem it necessary to drink elixirs that turn them into scary creatures were harmed during the production of this motion picture."

202 Remember Nothing

ORIGINAL AIR DATE: October 7, 1996
TELEPLAY BY: Chris Manheim
STORY BY: Steven L. Sears & Chris Manheim
DIRECTED BY: Anson Williams
GUEST CAST: Aaron Devitt as Lyceus
Robert Harte as Maphias
Stephen Tozer as Mezentius
Mark Ferguson as Krykus
Slade Leef as Caputius
Chris Graham as Slave Boss
Rebecca Kopacka as Clotho
Micaela Daniel as Lachesis
Elizabeth Pendergrast as Atropos
Mariao Hohaia as Minion
Geoff Barlow as Storekeeper
Andrew McMillan as Gate Guard

David Geary as Guard #2
Allan Wilkins as Head Guard
Daniel Chilton as Boy

The Fates give Xena a second chance at life, undoing all the destruction she has caused under one condition: if she draws blood in anger, all will return to the way it was.

The Fates, or the Moirae, their proper Greek name, were more abstract concepts than characters in their own legend. They appear every so often in other legends (see "The Prodigal"), but on their own they were seen as birth, life, and death goddesses. The Moirae consisted of three females: Clotho, Lachesis, and Atropos, who would spin and weave the fates of mankind. Clotho spun the wool when a person was born, Lachesis would measure out the length of their lives on the string, and Atropos would cut it, determining when their lives would end. Sometimes the Fates are personified as three women in different stages of their lives — the maiden, the mature woman, and the crone — and in other writings they are three elderly sisters. This latter representation is more in keeping with Hesiod, who called them the daughters of Zeus and Themis, but that view is not widely held. They were thought to be the oldest goddesses in existence, from well before the rise of the Olympians. After the clash with the Titans, Zeus is said to have given them lodging in the room behind the kitchen in the great hall at Olympus.

Many authors write that the Fates were more powerful than the gods because their decisions of destiny overrode all else, and because they also knew, but seldom revealed, the fates of the gods themselves. They were sometimes said to be the daughters of the great goddess Necessity, who was called "The Strong Fate." Many legends feature the gods consulting the Fates to find out the life cycle of someone they know, thus rendering the gods inferior to the powers of the three women. As with Hades, their names were not said aloud for fear of drawing their attention, or calling them out too soon; hence Xena's use of "the maiden, the mother, and the crone" rather than saying their names, which appear instead in the final written credits.

The plot for "Remember Nothing" is taken from Frank Capra's 1946 classic *It's a Wonderful Life*, where a man is given a chance to see how dreary the lives of his loved ones would have been had he not been born. In "Remember Nothing," it's the evil warrior princess who'd never been born, and Xena is returned to her life before she'd turned to evil. Xena is reunited with her beloved brother, Lyceus, who is a much more effective character than Toris. However, Xena discovers this alternate reality is just as painful as the one she's been living: her mother is dead, Gabrielle has been turned into a slave, and Xena is betrothed to someone she hardly knows and must fight off every natural instinct to fight. Mezentius, Krykus, and Cortese all live and rule because Xena wasn't around to quash them in one way or another. It may seem like everything that is terrible about this reality isn't worth getting her brother back, but the striking similarity in Xena and Lyceus's behavior demonstrates the close bond between the two of them. This episode is so effective because of the torture Xena is put through. She must endure Gabrielle's hateful, abused nature and Lyceus's bitter disappointment at her constant inaction. Interestingly, the alternate reality that Xena must consider is the one most history books portray — women as slaves and maids, or deferential family members; not warrior princesses. This has led to fan discussion that perhaps *X:WP* and *H:TLJ* take place in an alternate reality.

Lucy is wonderful in this episode, and she must display a whole range of emotions, from shock and delight at seeing Lyceus, to heartbreak when she recognizes Gabrielle, to despair when she is forced to choose a reality at the end. Reneé also shows that she can be someone other than the innocent sidekick she portrays in both *X:WP* and *Hercules and the Lost Kingdom*. When we see Gabrielle as a serious character whose soul has been blackened by the torment she has endured, we know that Xena's ultimate decision is the only one she could have made. Xena shows her deep love for her friend when she must let her brother go in order to save Gabrielle's pure soul.

YAXI: There could be many for this episode, such as why can people die if Xena wasn't there to save Celesta, or how are people able to use fire and heal their wounds if Xena couldn't save Prometheus, but perhaps we are to assume these deeds were accomplished by Ares and Hercules, who are attributed with them in the mythology books anyway.

INTERESTING FACT: Anson Williams, who directed this episode, played Potsie on *Happy Days*.

DISCLAIMER: "Xena's memory was not damaged or . . . What was I saying?"

203 The Giant Killer

ORIGINAL AIR DATE: October 14, 1996
WRITTEN BY: Terence Winter
DIRECTED BY: Gary Jones
GUEST CAST: Todd Rippon as Goliath
Antony Starr as David
Calvin Tuteao as Dagon
Dale Corlett as Jonathan
Dennis Hally as King Saul
Emma Brunette as Sarah
John Leonard as Soldier
Brad Homan as Head Archer

Xena meets an old friend, Goliath, who once saved her life, but when she discovers he's with the Philistines and bent on vengeance, she helps David try to kill him.

"Giant Killer" isn't a favorite among fans, mostly because it looks at Biblical rather than Greek mythology. Based on the story of David and Goliath from I Samuel in the Old Testament, "Giant Killer" sways from the original story in many ways.

When Saul became the king of the Israelites, he began to fight wars by using his gut feeling, instead of waiting to consult God. God became very angry at his repeated disobedience, and told Samuel to go and find another king to anoint. Meanwhile, King Saul was waging war against the Philistines, and won because of the heroic efforts of his son, Jonathan, who put his faith in God and sneaked into the Philistine camp unarmed. Samuel eventually found David and anointed him king, and God put his spirit into David and took it away from Saul. David went to live in Saul's castle as his harp player between the ages of 21 and 34, according to many Biblical scholars. One day a nine-foot tall Philistine began mocking the Israelite army and harassing the people. Saul offered his eldest daughter to whomever could kill the giant, named Goliath. David went to the king and asked for his blessing to try to kill him, which Saul granted. With God's spirit and a stone and slingshot, David killed Goliath, and received Saul's other daughter, Michal, as his reward. Saul hoped that Michal would trap David and have him killed by the Philistines, because Saul was jealous. Saul began persecuting David and tried to kill him with a javelin, and David had to flee with the help of Jonathan, who'd fallen deeply in love with him. David lived in exile for eight years with a band of outcasts.

When Saul died, David reigned in Hebron over the tribe of Judah, then became the ruler of Israel and the most beloved Israelite king ever. He made Jerusalem the centre of religion and politics, and built his palace on Zion, with the Ark of the Covenant below. He was succeeded by his son, Solomon. In "Giant Killer," David is portrayed as Saul's son and Jonathan's brother, and he's betrothed to a woman named Sarah, not Michal. One explanation for the new family connections is that David often referred to Jonathan as his brother in many songs, and Saul called David, "My Son."

In the tradition of many twentieth-century revisionist works where the monster is rewritten to have been wronged in some way, Goliath becomes a likable man to whom we owe Xena's very existence. However, he's also in the tradition of Melas, Xena, Toris, and Callisto, whose fantasy for revenge outweighs all else. This episode is a difficult one to watch, for Xena must kill someone she cares about a great deal — and someone who has lost everything for her — in order to crush the Philistines.

Gabrielle once again falls for a guy immediately after meeting him, although he turns out to be engaged to someone else. The relationship between Xena and Gabrielle is so strong and the chemistry so right that these relationships on the side have become unbelievable and shallow. Gabrielle has so much to offer as a character that these girl-meets-boy subplots are rendered almost offensive, and it's a relief when these relationships stop by the middle of this season.

The respect Xena shows for David's one god displays her lack of prejudice and her open mind. An important foreshadowing of episodes to come occurs when Gabrielle tells Xena that she hates it when Xena's so cryptic. It's Xena's enigmatic behavior that will get her into trouble later on (see "The Debt II").

TIME: Saul reigned from c. 1030 to c. 1010 BC, and David reigned from c. 1010 to c. 970 BC, setting this episode probably somewhere around 1025 to 1020 BC.

YAXI: Gabrielle says to Xena, "This one-god stuff is a new concept to me." Did the henbane in "Altared States" affect her mind so much that she forgot about the one-god concept that she was introduced to then?

NITPICK: Same as in "The Titans": the size ratio between humans and giants keeps changing. Also, David is presumed to have written Psalm 23 at the age of 35, while in exile, so he wouldn't have been able to read it to Gabrielle.

DISCLAIMER: "No Bible myths or stories were irreparably mangled during the production of this motion picture."

204 Girls Just Wanna Have Fun

ORIGINAL AIR DATE: October 21, 1996
WRITTEN BY: Adam Armus & Nora Kay Foster
DIRECTED BY: T.J. Scott
GUEST CAST: Ted Raimi as Joxer
          Matthew Chamberlain as Orpheus
          Anthony Ray Parker as Bacchus
          Kym Krystaly as Bacchae #1
          Daniel Parker as Thief #1
          David Goodwin as Thief #2

Xena's quest to kill Bacchus becomes personal when he captures Gabrielle and tries to make her one of his followers.

Greek myth meets Anne Rice in this very strange, subtext- and vampire-filled episode, which Lucy once referred to as a "rock-video-girlie-vampires-on-the-moon Halloween episode." The names Bacchus and Dionysus are usually used interchangeably, but Bacchus was solely the god of wine and ecstasy, while Dionysus was also a vegetation deity, which explains why the writers of this episode chose to refer to him as Bacchus. Dionysus was the son of Zeus and Semele, a mortal who was the daughter of Cadmus and Harmonia, who was the daughter of Ares and Aphrodite (in other words, Semele was not only Zeus's lover, but his great-granddaughter). When Hera learned of the affair between Zeus and Semele, she told Semele to ask Zeus to show himself to her. When he did so, the bright lightning

MCA TV / SHOOTING STAR

bolts which projected from his body were too powerful and Semele was burnt to ashes. Zeus knew she was pregnant, and he removed the baby Dionysus from her womb before she disintegrated and sewed him up in his own thigh until it was time for the baby to be born.

After Dionysus was born — the second time, from Zeus's leg — Zeus spent years trying to hide him from Hera by dressing him like a girl and transforming him into a kid to be raised by nymphs. When he became a man he discovered wine, but Hera found him once again and drove him mad. He wandered aimlessly through Egypt and Syria until he was cured of his condition, whereupon he inadvertently incurred the wrath of King Lycurgus of the River Strymon. To escape his hostility, Dionysus hid under the sea with Thetis the Neirad, but in the meantime Lycurgus captured the Bacchantes, women who were escorting him. The Bacchantes, or Bacchae, were women who had been thrown into an ecstatic frenzy by Dionysus' power. They could tear wild animals apart with their hands and were often depicted as holding wolf cubs in their arms. The Bacchantes imitated the Maenads, who were the divine followers of Dionysus. They, too, danced in a frenzied way, and followed behind him playing musical instruments. They would drink at water springs imagining that they were ingesting honey. In some myths, Maenads and Bacchantes are the same, in others they are differentiated between human and divine. Both represented a loss of self-control and debauchery in nature.

Eventually the Bacchantes were set free from Lycurgus and Dionysus moved on to India and Thrace, where he introduced the bacchanalia, revelries that threw entire villages — especially the women inhabitants — into an orgiastic fury. The people would roam the countryside in a crazed state, shrieking constantly and mooing like cattle. It was said some women ate their babies. Many kings and leaders denounced the bacchanalia and Dionysus drove them and their villagers mad. As late as 186 BC the bacchanalia were being forbidden, but it is believed by some that Julius Caesar reinstated it. One of the people who denied the bacchanalia was Orpheus.

Orpheus was the son of either Apollo or Oeagrus and Calliope, the Muse of epic poetry. He was a singer, musician, and poet who could sing so sweetly that wild beasts were tamed and plants bowed before him. He played the lyre and the cithara, which some say he invented. Orpheus was one of the Argonauts, but because he wasn't a strong fighter he learned to be useful in other areas: he could calm the waves, lull the Sirens and soothe the crew with his music.

The most famous story of Orpheus involves his wife, Eurydice. Eurydice was a dryad with whom he'd fallen in love, but after they married she was pursued by Aristaeus, who wanted to rape her, and she trod on a sleeping snake which bit her so that she died. Orpheus travelled to the Underworld to get her back, and charmed Charon and Cerberus and the Furies with his music. Hades and Persephone agreed to let Eurydice return to the world of the living under one condition: that she walk behind Orpheus and he not turn to look at her until they had left the Underworld. Orpheus complied, but at the last moment it occurred to him that Persephone, or some say Hades, may have played a trick on him. He turned and as his eyes met Eurydice's, she was dragged back to the Underworld.

Orpheus became inconsolable and he eschewed the company of women, turning to men instead. Some say he simply refused to recognize Dionysus as a god, and accused him of setting mortals a bad example by his wild behavior. Dionysus was furious and the Maenads, who had loved Orpheus, tore Orpheus apart and threw his head in the river. The head sang as it floated down the river to Lesbos, where his head and lyre were buried; others say fishermen buried his head on Lemnos and Zeus put his lyre in the sky as the constellation still called the "lyre." Another version has it that his body parts were collected and buried by the nine Muses at the base of Olympus, where the birds sang more sweetly. Orpheus travelled to the Elysian Fields where he sang to its inhabitants, and some say he returned to the living to tell them how to get into the Elysian Fields, making him an ancient predecessor to the Christ story.

"Girls Just Wanna Have Fun" delves into both of these myths, but makes some important alterations to make them fit the show. The directing of the opening scene is visually stunning, alternating between fast cuts of Joxer running through the woods with the wolves at his heels, and the wolves' point of view, which disorients the viewer.

We soon learn that Orpheus hates Xena and blames her for the death of Eurydice, who died in a battle between Bacchus's army and Xena's — a flagrant use of poetic license, considering the popularity of that myth. Also, if a disembodied head is going to be used in the show, the effect should be more believable. Some scenes are simply distracting because it is difficult to look past the fact, for example, that actor Matthew Chamberlain's body is hidden inside the rock that Joxer is sitting on. The dummy head they use later is really annoying, as it's a plastic model with a mouth that pops open and closed.

The scene that sticks in most people's minds from this episode is the one in which Gabrielle appears to be in an ancient Greek gay bar. Men are dancing with men and two women hit on Gabrielle, dancing erotically with her throughout the scene. The rave/rap music here and throughout the rest of the episode is fantastic, despite being about 2,500 years before its time.

The Bacchae in this episode do not resemble the Greek Maenads, but more so the vampires of nineteenth-century myth. They possess fangs, have white faces, slicked-back hair, and wear black capes like the Dracula of old movies. They suck blood from their victims' necks and can only be killed by a dryad bone through the heart (in vampire myth, a wooden or iron stake through the heart). The biggest departure from Greek myth is in the depiction of the dryads. Dryads were not the vicious harpy-like creatures that are portrayed here, but peaceful tree nymphs. Occasionally they are identified as hamadryads, but there is a significant difference between the two: hamadryads lived and died with the tree, rejoicing when it rained and crying when the tree lost its leaves. Dryads, on the other hand, lived in the tree. They lived a very long time — nearly a thousand years — but they were not immortal. Orpheus's wife, Eurydice, was a dryad, making the negative depiction in this episode even more baffling.

The fast-paced music-video-like atmosphere of this episode is unlike any other. "Girls Just Wanna Have Fun" is one of the campiest episodes yet, and the departures from Greek myth can be explained away by the fact that no single myth was respected in this episode, considering that Orpheus's body is restored at the end.

NITPICK: Orpheus was said to have lulled the Sirens with his beautiful voice, but Roseanne can sing better than this Orpheus. We know from a future episode that Xena can outsing the Sirens, so why can't *she* charm the Bacchae?

OOPS: When Joxer is being pulled under ground by a dryad, notice how the entire ground caves in, revealing it as probably styrofoam. Also, when Joxer notices the blood on Xena's neck, Gabrielle is holding the pole with Orpheus's head on it. After the commercial break, she's only holding her staff. Also, when Gabrielle first walks into the bar right before she starts dancing, look to the bottom lefthand corner of the screen. Looks like someone forgot to cover up those propane tanks they use to keep the torches lit.

INTERESTING FACT: Believe it or not, the actor playing Orpheus also played Darphus in the Xena trilogy on *H:TLJ*.

DISCLAIMER: "No Bloodsucking Bacchae were harmed during the making of this motion picture. However, several Dryads lost their heads."

205 Return of Callisto

ORIGINAL AIR DATE: October 28, 1996
WRITTEN BY: R.J. Stewart
DIRECTED BY: T.J. Scott
GUEST CAST: Hudson Leick as Callisto
Ted Raimi as Joxer
Scott Garrison as Perdicus
David Te Rare as Theodorus
Alex Moffat as First Guard
David Scordino as Second Guard
Lance Cheshire as Half Starved Man
Puck Willis as Kid #1
Frederick Bedford as Village Priest

Callisto returns to terrorize Xena, and Gabrielle gets married to Perdicus. When Callisto kills Gabrielle's groom, Gabrielle turns into the vengeful type of person she has always abhorred.

Callisto is back in all of her evil, adorable glory! The opening scene — where this tiny warrior breaks out of the prison — sets a high standard of excellence that will continue throughout this episode. "Return of Callisto" is beautifully written and acted, and it is so multi-layered that many of the issues that are raised in this episode will recur later.

Perdicus is also back (for unknown reasons the Xenastaff has altered the spelling of his name) and Gabrielle falls in love with him when she realizes that he abhors killing as much as she does. In "Beware Greeks Bearing Gifts," Perdicus killed with the fervour of a soldier, which is probably why Gabrielle didn't fall as deeply for him then (that and perhaps the fact that he tells her in this episode that he was suicidal until he thought of her). At the wedding, the troubled look on Xena's face is much like the one in "The Prodigal," when Gabrielle was leaving her for a while, but here Xena knows she will wander alone from this point on. The subtexters are given a teaser when Xena closes her eyes to kiss Gabrielle, moving just to one side of her lips. The marriage itself raises some important questions, however. Does Gabrielle really love Perdicus as much as she thinks or does she marry him out of pity? Throughout the series, Gabrielle has fallen in love with just about every male that she and Xena have encountered, as if she were desperately seeking a male love interest in her life. Is this desperation what sparks her decision to marry Perdicus?

After this episode Gabrielle is no longer a virgin, but what seems to be held in greater esteem in this world is her blood innocence. When Callisto viciously kills Perdicus in cold blood, Gabrielle almost loses that, too. She becomes the hardened woman that she was in "Remember Nothing," and the suffering expression on Xena's face as Gabrielle screams at her to teach her how to use the sword speaks volumes. This scene — and the rest of the episode for that matter — is superbly acted by both women. Not only is Xena losing the innocence of her sidekick, the trait that keep herself in balance, but she is losing the light in Gabrielle's eyes for which she forfeited everything in "Remember Nothing." At the same time, we realize how similar Xena and Gabrielle are: the only reason Gabrielle hasn't lashed out in anger in the past is because she has led a relatively charmed life. Again, when we now look back on previous episodes where Gabrielle preaches to others about the wrongness of killing, we see how easy it was for her to do so. Her character reaches new depths when she is forced to undergo the same struggle that Xena has for so long. In fact, it is Xena's recognition of Gabrielle experiencing a similar struggle that strikes up her own fear of the consequences. However, Gabrielle was right: the cycle does have to end, and in a triumphant moment, Gabrielle does end the cycle with herself, refusing to kill Callisto when given the chance.

The final action scene between Callisto and Xena in the chariots is terrific. Callisto's chariot wheels have been fitted with the large knives that are often fabled to have been used at this time, but Xena perseveres, even with one wheel. The stunt scene through the sand is the stuff of a major motion picture, and viewers can only cringe at how much sand must have gotten trapped in that bustier.

The final scene is one that still resonates in the most recent episodes. When given the opportunity to pull Callisto out of the quicksand, Xena sits to one side and watches her sink, ignoring her screams. Why does she do it? In letting Callisto die, she forfeits the good deeds she has been performing for the past year and shows us there is a limit to whom she will save. Never before since turning good has Xena ignored the mercy cries of her victim. Does she do it because she knows Callisto will kill again? Or does she do it so Gabrielle won't have to? For whatever reason, Xena sacrifices her soul and conscience to save others, and the after-effects of her deed will haunt her in later episodes.

OOPS: In the scene where Xena swings through the air on a rope, there is a camera angle that appears to be shot from her waist, giving a bird's-eye view of the lair. Watch the ends of her boot as she hits the thug: they bend right back. Either these are fake legs attached to the sides of the camera, or Xena has the tiniest feet in Greece, and should seriously look into buying her footwear in a smaller size.

INTERESTING FACT: This episode was dedicated to Michelle Calvert, one of Hudson's stunt doubles, who was killed in an accident unrelated to the show.

DISCLAIMER: "Although Xena finally conquered her dark nemesis Callisto, it took her weeks to get the sand out of her leather unmentionables."

206 Warrior . . . Princess . . . Tramp

ORIGINAL AIR DATE: November 4, 1996
WRITTEN BY: R.J. Stewart
DIRECTED BY: Josh Becker
GUEST CAST: Ted Raimi as Joxer
Chris Bailey as Agis
Iain Rea as Philemon
Norman Forsey as King Lias
Simon Fa'Amoe as Alcibiades
Collette Pennington as Nurse
Tai Hadfield as Guard
Tim Faville as Barfly #1
Lawrence Wharerau as Barfly #2

Xena returns to Diana's castle because the king is dying, only to discover yet a third coincidentally identical twin, Meg.

Lucy Lawless's comedic talents shine once again as she now must play three characters who are all very different. Diana is the regal, solemn princess, Xena is the tough warrior woman, and Meg is the lower-class girl whose every move is dictated by an abusive man. Lucy once pointed out, however, that although they seem like very different characters, Meg and Diana are actually very important elements of Xena's personality. The warrior, the princess, and the tramp are the three roles that women play in the history books, the former being the least common.

This episode was the first one filmed for the second season, but it was actually supposed to air after "Intimate Stranger." After watching "Intimate

Stranger," it becomes immediately clear that "Warrior . . . Princess . . . Tramp" does not belong in between the two Callisto episodes. But outside forces — namely Lucy's riding accident — forced the writers to quickly rearrange the episodes to introduce a new story arc while Lucy was recovering (see "Intimate Stranger" for more explanation). Lucy particularly enjoyed filming this episode because of all the extra work she had to do. And this is definitely her best comedic work. The final scene where the three "Xenas" enter the room and two of them misname the chakram ("In the blink of an eye I can split the skull of anyone who moves with my trusty . . . shamrock!") is an instant classic.

Because Joxer has been introduced as a comic element in the series, this episode is perfect for him. After Meg has come onto him (and he thinks she's Xena), he constantly mistakes Xena and Diana for her, leading to some of the funniest Xena moments yet. When he pinches Xena's behind, the murderous look on her face is priceless. Once again, however, Joxer gives up a chance to sleep with "Xena" because he thinks it may hurt her reputation, a sacrifice if ever there was one. Gabrielle is also very funny in this episode (although it seems devastatingly out of place following her husband's death) after being locked in the dungeon apparently by her best friend.

Lucy referred to Meg as a "raunchy bar-hag" in one interview and Meg's utter disrespect for her superiors — calling the king "Kingie" or Agis "Aggie" — is what makes this character so comic. The scene of Meg, dressed as Diana, trying to get Diana's baby to sleep by ungracefully rocking the cradle with her feet while belting out "99 Bottles of Beer" is one of the most effective and hilarious uses of a twentieth-century reference on the show. However, Meg is also a sad character, as we discover near the end when she explains that she's worthless and will always be used by men. It is this stereotype of woman that this show tries to alter, and when we discover she has a talent for cooking — enticing the king with her culinary treats — we realize that even the most seemingly insignificant woman can become part of the royal household. Although this episode breaks up the continuity between "Return of Callisto" and "Intimate Stranger," it provides much-needed comic relief and is the perfect forum for showing Lucy's wide-ranging acting talents.

NITPICK: When Meg first imitates Xena, she's never met her: how does she know how she talks? Also, why do people still refer to Gabrielle as "that irritating blonde" when she's now a redhead? And finally, where do Meg, Xena, and Diana keep finding three of every outfit?

DISCLAIMER: "Neither Xena nor her remarkably coincidental twin, Diana, were harmed during the production of this motion picture. Meg, however, suffered minor injuries while preparing Aardvark nuggets for King Lias."

ORIGINAL AIR DATE: November 11, 1996
WRITTEN BY: Steven L. Sears
DIRECTED BY: Gary Jones
GUEST CAST: Hudson Leick as Callisto
Ted Raimi as Joxer
Kevin Smith as Ares
David Te Rare as Theodorus
Erik Thompson as Hades
Darien Takle as Cyrene
Lee-Jane Foreman as Arleia
Michael Cooper as Gressius

Ares switches Callisto and Xena's bodies, and Xena is given 24 hours to return to the world of the living (in Callisto's body) and try to get her life back.

When Lucy broke her pelvis in four places on October 8, 1996, *X:WP* was forced to make some adjustments quickly. The first block of episodes (including this one and "Destiny") had already been filmed, but they had to change some endings to prepare for less use of Lucy. "Intimate Stranger" originally ended with Xena getting her old body back, but after Lucy's accident they re-filmed the ending so that Hudson could play Xena's role for another episode.

The opening of this episode is a clear indicator that "Warrior . . . Princess . . . Tramp" was out of place. Xena is haunted by the fact she didn't try to save Callisto, and Gabrielle is still mourning the loss of her husband. The show opens with many dreams-within-dreams, setting the illusory tone that will dominate the show. Xena is dragged into Tartarus by Callisto through a dream-like state and as Callisto explains, "Dreams are the fine line between the real world and the Underworld." After the bodies have been switched, it's wonderful to watch Lucy give her Callisto impression and Hudson imitate Xena. Both actresses pick up on the traits of the other without turning the characters into caricatures. Hudson gives Xena's indifferent stare, while Lucy holds her face and mouth like Callisto, even holding her left hand like Callisto when she's sword fighting.

Many fans were troubled by the fact that Gabrielle doesn't recognize that Xena's not herself, despite a body trade probably not being the first thing to come to Gabrielle's mind. However, in "Return of Callisto," Xena was so sensitive about Perdicus's death and so against the thought of Gabrielle murdering Callisto that her abusive behavior in this episode should be more suspicious to Gabrielle than it is. After Xena's adamant refusal to teach Gabrielle how to use a sword, wouldn't her tying a dagger to Gabrielle's staff seem rather dubious?

Argo seems to know Xena better than Gabrielle does, and Xena's mother knows right away that the woman who appears to be Xena is not so. However, we must keep in mind that Gabrielle has just lost her husband,

and the very thought that she might also lose Xena must be unfathomable to her.

The scene with Argo is a particularly poignant one. Fans have come to see Argo as an essential part of the wandering trio, and to see her laying on the ground dying is almost worse than seeing Perdicus skewered on Callisto's sword. When Joxer mistakes Xena (in Callisto's body) for Callisto, the way he immediately puts his life on the line for Argo is very

MCA TV / SHOOTING STAR

noble and touching, but although Xena thanks him for it, she'll continue to ridicule him later.

Ares is back as well, and as usual Kevin Smith plays him with wicked, sly charm. Callisto outwits him near the end, showing that she and Xena are closer in nature than we may think. When Callisto and Xena return to the Underworld, Callisto is faced with a dreamscape much like Xena's in "Dreamworker." As Callisto's past victims and her own mother come at her, she must decide to listen to them and destroy her past, or ignore them and continue her evil ways. Xena acts as her judge, which is appropriate considering that Xena is the only other person who could possibly understand what Callisto is going through. Perhaps Callisto is too bent on revenge, or perhaps she doesn't have a Gabrielle to inspire her, but she remains unchanged.

Xena is saved, however, but remains in Callisto's body — a difficult challenge for Gabrielle. Xena is trapped inside the only body that has made Gabrielle want to kill, and Gabrielle must learn how to cope with this new intimate stranger.

NITPICK: As before, if Hades can see all, why didn't he know of Ares' scheme?

DISCLAIMER: "Argo was not harmed during the making of this motion picture. However, she is undergoing intensive psycho-therapy to help her work through her resentment and feelings of distrust towards Xena."

208 Ten Little Warlords

ORIGINAL AIR DATE: November 18, 1996
WRITTEN BY: Paul Robert Coyle
DIRECTED BY: Charles Siebert
GUEST CAST: Hudson Leick as Xena
Ted Raimi as Joxer
Charles Siebert as Sisyphus
Kevin Smith as Ares
Chris Ryan as Virgilius
Bruce Hopkins as Tegason
Marcel Kaima as Sadus
Jason Kennedy as Carus
John Smith as Boat Captain
Patricia Donovan as Old Woman
Tony Ward as Messenger

When Ares' sword is stolen, reducing him to a mortal, Xena must travel to an island — where Callisto has been invited — to try to get it back.

"Ten Little Warlords" — from the title to some of the main plot devices — is based loosely on Agatha Christie's *Ten Little Indians*. In this murder mystery, ten people meet at a dock, all having been invited to the island home of a judge they all knew in one capacity or another. When they arrive at his home, he is not there, but a note has been left saying he will return. As the people prepare for dinner, a voice comes over a loudspeaker, naming each person and telling them what their crime was. In each bedroom is the poem, "Ten Little Indians," which lists ten Indians who die in various ways, each leaving one less Indian standing. One character has ten Indian figurines on her bureau. Soon, the guests begin dying one by one, according to the poem, and each time someone dies, a figurine disappears from the bureau. When one person remains, the question is: did that person do it or is there an outside individual committing the crimes?

As said, this episode is only loosely based on the book, as the warlords kill each other, and the mystery isn't in who is killing whom, but what is this scheme all about? Sisyphus is back, after having tricked Hades into allowing him out of the Underworld (see "Death in Chains"). It's interesting that a director, Siebert, should play the part of Sisyphus, for Sisyphus directed others around him to do things but always got in trouble for doing so. As in the last episode, Hudson pulls off a great Xena impression (notice her hair has been straightened as well!).

Gabrielle and Joxer are very funny in this episode as their anger rises due to Ares' mortality, and Gabrielle in the bar trying to put Xena's neck pinch on the bartender is a personal favorite scene. Despite the Baracas being no more than a fan, Joxer "defeats" it, although his claim on Ares' sword is a shabby one. Xena (in Callisto's body) and Ares interact well also, and one wonders if they could have been romantically linked if only Ares had learned to 'be nice.'

This episode is fun, although Lucy's absence is noticeable. When she appears to Gabrielle in her real body at the end, the director has used old footage of Lucy and a stunt double in the walking-away scene (notice that Gabrielle and Xena are never shown face to face in the same shot). Considering the outside circumstances, this episode is a clever way of handling what could have been a disaster.

NITPICK: While Ares remains a mortal, it is said that peaceful people will become violent and warriors will gain more control. Gabrielle gradually loses all control, as should be expected, but Joxer remains somewhere in the middle. Is this an indication that he is, in fact, a warrior? Also, when Joxer and Gabrielle find the "monster," they refer to it as the Baracas. How do they know what it is called?

DISCLAIMER: "No one was harmed in the making of this motion picture. However, Xena's ability to recover her body was severely impeded by Lucy Lawless' unexpected mishap."

209 A Solstice Carol

ORIGINAL AIR DATE: December 9, 1996
WRITTEN BY: Chris Manheim
DIRECTED BY: John T. Kretchmer
GUEST CAST: Joe Berryman as Senticles
Peter Vere-Jones as King Silvus
Sheri Booth as Melana
Daniel James as Lynal
Gennieve Lucre as Orphan #1
Jamie Karie-Gatalli as Orphan #2
Nicko Vella as Orphan #3
Junior Chille as Orphan #4
Heme Rudolph as First Guard
Mike Howell as Guard #1
Lucas Young as Bearded Guard
Tony Bishop as Donkey Owner
Johnny Glass as Man
Karen Morgan as Woman

When a Scrooge-like king threatens to evict the inhabitants of an orphanage on Solstice Eve, Gabrielle and Xena must try to change his mind by discovering why he hates Winter Solstice.

"A Solstice Carol" is based on Charles Dickens' *A Christmas Carol*, which hardly needs a description. King Silvus resembles Ebenezer Scrooge (even his bed looks like the one commonly depicted in film adaptations of the story). However, there are no ghosts of Christmas (or Solstice) past, present and future, but instead Xena masquerading as the Three Fates (see "Remember Nothing"). Also, the show doesn't completely rely on this particular Christmas story, but instead delves into other traditional aspects of Christmas, suggesting a much earlier origin than the nineteenth century for these common elements.

It doesn't take a rocket scientist to figure out who Senticles is, although I'd love to find out where they got that pine tree in Greece! Santa Claus is a nineteenth-century version of Santa Claus, first described to the world in Clement C. Moore's "'Twas the Night Before Christmas," and based on the figure of St. Nicholas. The first Christmas was celebrated in 326 AD, the year that St. Nicholas died. Christmas trees (which originated in Germany) and Christmas cards were also customs which began in the nineteenth-century. The tongue-in-cheek attitude of this episode would suggest that the writers are only playing around with the Christmas legends, not actually suggesting they began in Ancient Greece.

Gabrielle is very funny in this episode. Her child-like glee as she remembers her toy sheep and when she finds Senticles's stash of homemade toys sets her apart from Xena, who as usual, couldn't care less about Solstice or any of its customs. (It's also appropriate that Gabrielle should be the first Christmas elf.) Unlike Xena, Gabrielle honors the Solstice as a time of rebirth.

The Solstice occurs twice a year, when the sun is directly pointing at points farthest from the equator. The summer solstice is generally on June 22, when the sun is directly over the Tropic of Cancer at noon. December 22 is the winter solstice, when the sun is overhead at noon over the Tropic of Capricorn. It is generally used as the indicator of the beginning of winter, and it contains the fewest daylight hours of the year. Thus, the solstice is perfect for Xena's intrusion of King Sylvus's room as the Three Fates.

Lucy is very funny as the Three Fates, especially because Xena playing around like that is so unlikely. She puts on a very strange voice and flutters her eyes a lot, and Gabrielle flying around on a rope as the ghost of a woman who's not actually dead adds a particular comic element to the episode. While Joxer seems to have been introduced into the series as a comic foil, Lucy and Reneé demonstrate here that they, too, can be funny on their own.

This episode contains all the common archetypes of a sentimental Christmas show — orphans, innocence, a miser, a hero. Yet the comic elements save it from falling into the trap of a sappy Christmas special. Sure, viewers may groan when Senticles comes down the chimney and shouts "HoHoHo" upon landing, or when Gabrielle stands between two soldiers banging their helmets to mysteriously produce "Jingle Bells," but these elements are performed with a wink at the audience. (Xena picks up a Hercules action marionette at one point, for Zeus's sake!) However, I'm not sure how comforting it is to think that the first Christmas toys may have been used as weapons.

Knowing what Christmas is really supposed to be about, though, the writers do allude to the Christ story, but very carefully. When Xena and Gabrielle encounter a man, woman, and baby on the road and Gabrielle gives them her new donkey, Tobias, the allusion is obvious, but not overdone. The woman's name is Dia — a root of "God" — and if she is holding baby Jesus, we are to assume they are returning from Bethlehem (which isn't exactly next door to Greece). The star of Bethlehem (now the star of Greece) is a bit much at the end, although Xena's little gift to Gabrielle along with her words is a show of emotion that is still very rare for the Warrior Princess. A successful "feel-good" Christmas episode.

TIME: If we do take the trio at the end to be Jesus, Mary, and Joseph, this episode would be set around 6 BC.

NITPICK: How old is Melana? She appears to be in her mid-40s at the very most, but that would have made her 15 when she left her husband. Also, when Xena is disguised as the Fates, she introduces herself by calling out their names, which would have been sacrilegious (see "Remember Nothing").

DISCLAIMER: "Senticles was not harmed during the making of this motion picture. However, several chimneys are in dire need of repair."

210 The Xena Scrolls

ORIGINAL AIR DATE: January 13, 1997
TELEPLAY BY: Adam Armus & Nora Kay Foster
STORY BY: Robert Sidney Mellette
DIRECTED BY: Charlie Haskell
GUEST CAST: Ted Raimi as Jacques S'er
Kevin Smith as Ares
Mark Ferguson as John Smythe
Ajay Vasisht as Nikos
Reza Nijad as Local
Campbell Rocsselle as Thug #1
Robert Tapert as Himself

In Macedonia in 1942, two archaeologists attempt to find the Xena scrolls to discover more about a legendary warrior princess, and they encounter Ares while doing so.

"The Xena Scrolls" perhaps takes the prize as the strangest of all *Xena* episodes. Lucy and Reneé play Mel Pappas and Janice Covington, two women on a quest for the scrolls (which were written by Gabrielle) who look remarkably like our favorite duo. Covington is a tough-looking, cigar-chomping woman who dresses like Indiana Jones (from the movies which this episode unabashedly rips off). Like Pappas, she lives in the shadow of her father, except that his line of work wasn't exactly honorable, while Pappas must overcome the enormous achievements of her father to prove that she, too, has something to contribute to the world of arch-aeology. Oh, and there's also Lt. Jacques S'er, of the French army. No explanation is needed for that one.

It's not clear why the personalities of Gabrielle and Xena have been switched, although Gabrielle was never as fearful as Mel Pappas is. Coving-ton is an annoying character played very over-the-top by O'Connor. And why is Mel such an idiot? When we discover they are the descendants of their Ancient Greek lookalikes, it's sad to think that Xena's descendant would be no more than a comic foil. Gabrielle's descendant has become more like Xena, but what is the message of this episode? That the reason women were deemed meek and "the weaker sex" is because they forgot their roots? A more interesting concept would have been to make them two strong, intelligent women who are made weak only by a society that wishes them so. Pappas is intelligent and learned — she can read ancient script — but she gives away the meaning of the script to a bunch of men who are working against them. The ending of the episode is interesting in that Mel and Janice decide to break out of their fathers' shadows, but Janice is now the leader and Mel the weak follower. It's upsetting to think that these friends will never be equal, no matter in which century they run into one another.

This episode only gets interesting when Xena's soul invades Mel's body to fight Ares, who is more exciting and evil in this episode than ever before.

Xena's soul appears to be embedded in the chakram; when the chakram becomes whole, Mel becomes Xena. Again, though, what does this mean? That Xena will never rest? That she was made a goddess? Or that she's trapped in some purgatory? Or that she would travel all these centuries to put some fire back into her descendant and some loving confidence into Gabrielle's? The disappointment Janice shows when she discovers she is the descendant of the "irritating blonde" (which at first she thinks must be Callisto) is only alleviated when Xena returns to tell her of the good deeds that Gabrielle performed. It would seem, then, that Gabrielle only wrote of Xena in the scrolls, only making mention of herself as a sidekick and not a hero, much like David only wrote of Jonathan's exploits in "The Giant Killer." This idea will be revisited in "The Quill Is Mightier . . . ."

The ending — where Robert Tapert makes his first on-screen appearance in the show — is not very satisfying. The guy pitching the show idea to him (Ted Raimi, who wants to call it "The Joxer Scrolls") tells him they could film it in a third world country "using the locals as extras" on a low budget. What do New Zealanders think of that comment? All in all, this is a confusing and confused episode, although the concept is great. And do the Xena Scrolls really exist? According to people affiliated with the show, they do. But then again, that claim wouldn't be the first publicity stunt they've pulled . . .

YAXI: When Ares becomes mortal in "Ten Little Warlords," he comments that he feels pain for the first time. In this episode then, why does he cringe when Xena shoves her chakram into his . . . family jewels?

NITPICK: If Ares remained locked in that cave for dozens of centuries, why does Covington blow it up at the end? Wouldn't that make it easier to escape? (He can't die, after all.)

INTERESTING FACT: In the script of "The Xena Scrolls," the writers indicated that it would be set in 1940, but the original airing of the episode flashed "Macedonia, 1942" at the beginning. However, "1940" continued to be indicated in the script, and in subsequent airings of the show the opening line was changed to read "Macedonia, 1940."

DISCLAIMER: "No Hollywood Producers were harmed during the making of this motion picture."

211 Here She Comes . . . Miss Amphipolis

ORIGINAL AIR DATE: January 20, 1996
WRITTEN BY: Chris Manheim
DIRECTED BY: Marina Sargenti
GUEST CAST: Karen Dior as Miss Artiphys
Robert Trebor as Salmoneus
John Sumner as Lord Claron
Calvin Tuteao as Dhoge of Mesini
Simone Russell as Miss Mesini

Stan Wolfgramm as Palantine of Parnassus
Jennifer Becker as Miss Parnassus
Timothy Lee as Regent of Skiros
Katherine Kennard as Miss Skiros
Brenda Kindall as Pageant Matron

Xena enters the Miss Known World beauty pageant when Salmoneus is worried about the contestants' safety.

The romp through the Raimi/Tapert world of camp continues in this strange and hilarious episode. The *X:WP* producers had to air the non-continuous episodes (which had been filmed before the accident) while they were re-shooting the "Destiny"/"Quest"/"Necessary Evil" trilogy to accommodate Lucy's accident. The idea of Xena as a contestant in a beauty pageant is completely absurd, which is why it's so perfect for this episode. Although this is probably the first Miss Known World pageant, it's clearly not the first beauty pageant; Gabrielle's outrage at the beauty pageant conventions shows that she's familiar with past ones. This entire episode is a parody of beauty pageants and the competition that goes on behind the scenes, but the real irony lies in the fact that Lucy herself has participated in the whole affair: she was Mrs. New Zealand in 1989.

The opening scene is a parody of one of the most sexist shows on television, *Baywatch*. The close-up shots of the contestants' chests as they run through the water in slow-motion is an obvious — and very funny — imitation. While on stage the women squeal and pat their "friends" on the back, backstage they're very open with their hostility, spying on and sabotaging one another. The warlords who are the sponsors of these women treat them like objects, although the women show later that they possess some very rare talents. Interestingly, two of the five finalists have dark skin, and technically, there are no blondes (the only fair-haired contestants are wearing wigs).

Salmoneus is especially hilarious as the annoying emcee of the competition, knocking over the podium when Xena walks on stage, announcing their hobbies, traits, and favorite gods, and singing the closing song to the winner: "A beauty so mythic/ Her figure's terrific!" Despite Salmoneus's upturned nose throughout the talent contest, the "talents" they exhibit are the usual ones in today's pageants. Miss Mesini plays a piece on the harp that sounds like it could have been written by Schoenberg, but the audience actually enjoys it.

Miss Artiphys (pronounced Artifice for obvious reasons) is an interesting touch, a drag queen in Ancient Greece who is trying to find an acceptable outlet for his desire to dress like a woman. *X:WP* prides itself on its revisionist tendencies, although ironically, homosexuality was far more acceptable in Ancient Greece than it is today. The part is played by Karen Dior, a drag queen extraordinaire who was recently inducted into the Adult Video News' porn star hall of fame. The thought that the first Miss Universe was actually a man is hysterical, although when he kisses Xena at the end, what is that look on Gabrielle's face? Shock? Jealousy?

The most subtle aspect of this episode is the way in which Xena becomes more and more feminine. Notice the sexy pose as she sits and discusses the warlord situation with Gabrielle, and how she holds the dagger like a nail file (the shot is very much like the famous scene in *The Graduate*). Could Xena actually enjoy preening herself?! A cleverly written tongue-in-cheek episode.

NITPICK: When did Gabrielle meet someone with a French accent whom she could imitate here? The song that Miss Artiphys dances to is actually Aram Khatchaturian's "Sabre Dance," first performed in 1942: it couldn't have been used at this competition. Finally, how do the contestants know the order in which their names will be called out, allowing them to bow out of the competition in the proper order?

INTERESTING FACT: The kiss was going to be edited out when Lucy said to leave it in. Dior suffers from AIDS, and she wanted to show that you can't get AIDS through a kiss.

DISCLAIMER: "No ribbons were harmed during the making of this motion picture. However, several experienced severe motion sickness."

212 **Destiny**

ORIGINAL AIR DATE: January 27, 1997
TELEPLAY BY: R.J. Stewart & Steven L. Sears
STORY BY: Robert Tapert
DIRECTED BY: Robert Tapert
GUEST CAST: Ebonie Smith as M'Lila
Karl Urban as Julius Caesar
Nathaniel Lees as Nicklio
Grant Triplow as Brutus
Mark Perry as Vicerius
Grant Boucher as Telos
Slade Leef as Sitacles
Dan Ryan as Roman #1
Rebecca McKinnon as Slave Girl
Rebecca Kopacka as Young Callisto

When Xena is seriously injured, Gabrielle must take her to the only healer who can save her — a healer from Xena's past. Meanwhile, only semi-conscious, Xena recalls a time ten years before when, through an act of betrayal, she was turned into an evil warrior princess.

This episode is a tour-de-force. The acting, music, costumes, dialogue, and setting are absolutely stunning. *Xena* fans are always clamouring for more information about Xena's past, and this episode offers it up like never before. As Xena's mind goes back in time, she recalls the man who betrayed her and destined her to a life of evil — Julius Caesar.

Karl Urban, Caesar, at WarriorCon '97.
Is it just me or is he wearing the wrong tag?

JOAN STANCO

Gaius Julius Caesar (100 or 102–44 BC) was a general and statesman, and is considered by many to be the best of both who ever lived. His conquests were numerous, and his battles were bloody, but through cunning he was able to advance the Roman empire into the west and northwest. At the age of 15 or 17 he was married, and he then travelled to Asia, fighting pirates (mentioned in this episode), and supporting Pompey. When the pirates captured him, he told them he was worth more money than they were asking, and after he was given back to his troops, he returned and crucified the pirates. The writers of this episode have altered this real-life event to include Xena and her army instead.

Caesar soon surpassed Pompey in popularity, and in 60 BC he was elected consul. That same year he entered into the First Triumvirate with Pompey, who supplied the army, and Crassus, who supplied the army and was a friend of Caesar's but a hated colleague of Pompey's. Caesar reconciled the two and gave his daughter in marriage to Pompey. For the next nine years Caesar left Rome to conduct conquests in the northwest, invading Brittany,

Normandy, and Britain. In 54 he crossed the Thames River and conquered the southeast part of the island. On his return, Caesar was defeated in northern Italy, but by 52 he had destroyed the two armies of the Gauls. A number of his victories were strategic masterpieces, and he was an active participant on the battlefield, keeping himself in outstanding physical condition throughout his life.

While Caesar was away, Crassus was killed and Pompey started to resent Caesar's fame. The Senate called on Caesar to disband his army, making Pompey the leader of the large powers. Caesar would have none of it, and his army went up against Pompey's; within three months, all of Italy was Caesar's. Pompey eventually fled to Egypt where he was murdered, and Caesar, after being appointed dictator for a year and consul for five, went to Egypt to fight in the Alexandrine Wars for Cleopatra. By 45, he had been victorious in Gaul, Egypt, Pontus, Africa, and had cut short an insurrection in Spain by Pompey's sons. He was made dictator for life, his face appeared on coins, his statue in temples, his figure was deemed sacred and he began making plans for libraries, laws, and new wars. But on March 15, 44 BC (the infamous Ides of March) he was assassinated by his friend Brutus and Brutus's cohorts. Caesar is thought by many to have known of the plot, but to have done nothing to undermine it. While some assert that he was one of the greatest leaders who ever lived, others believe his achievements were based on a bloodthirsty ambition.

This latter rendition is the underlying assumption of "Destiny," which tries to balance the final betrayal of Caesar — by his friend, Brutus — by suggesting that Caesar had betrayed, too. In a brilliant show of ironic casting, the evil Caesar is played by Karl Urban, who usually plays Cupid. Urban is superb as Caesar, with just the right amount of cunning to trick both Xena and the viewers. He walks around resolute in the idea that everything is based on destiny, his version of the Three Fates. He is a sexist character — perhaps gathered from the historical Caesar's political marriages — who plays on what he thinks is a woman's weakness: "Divide a woman's emotions from her sensibilities and you have her." The scene of Xena on a crucifix on the beach will be paralleled later in "The Deliverer," when Gabrielle suffers the same torture, and in "The Debt," when Xena imitates his line of bodies on stakes in a more gruesome fashion, using only heads.

M'Lila is also a wonderful character. All of Xena's mentors, friends, and influences seem to be women, and M'Lila is extraordinary. Watching her fight on the ship, we see a smaller version of Xena. She was obviously the one who taught Xena to fight the way she does, and she teaches her how to utilize pressure points.

Every aspect of this episode is beautiful. The faraway scenes of Caesar's boat on the water include gorgeous cloud formations over dark water (obviously a foreboding sign); the music is breathtaking (although it is a shame they make it diegetic music in the one scene, especially when the actress playing M'Lila isn't even remotely lip-synching the proper words);

the costumes are stunning, particularly Xena's dress in the seduction scene; the overall directing is the best to this point. The scene showing Xena's point of view as her crucifix is being raised is especially vivid.

Reneé O'Connor handles herself well in the final scene as well (although I couldn't help but wait for Nathaniel Lees to refer to her as "Innocent"). Originally, this episode ended with Xena coming back to life, but after her accident, they once again had to keep her out of her body, so the ending was re-filmed to leave her dead. The best episode of the season.

TIME: If it's set around the time that Caesar was fighting the pirates, it takes place around 75–74 BC. (Caesar was nowhere near Greece at the time!)

YAXI: Xena is a lot like herself in this episode, but compare this Xena to the one in "The Debt II." She speaks like Meg and isn't as clever as she is here.

INTERESTING FACT: Joseph LoDuca was nominated for an Emmy for the music in this episode.

DISCLAIMER: "Julius Caesar was not harmed during the production of this motion picture. However, the Producers deny responsibility of any unfortunate acts of betrayal occurring soon thereafter."

213 The Quest

ORIGINAL AIR DATE: February 3, 1997
TELEPLAY BY: Steven L. Sears
STORY BY: Chris Manheim, Steven L. Sears & R.J. Stewart
DIRECTED BY: Michael Levine
GUEST CAST: Bruce Campbell as Autolycus
Melinda Clarke as Velasca
Danielle Cormack as Ephiny
Michael Hurst as Iolaus
Jodie Dorday as Solari
Alexander Tant as Xenan
Kirstie O'Sullivan as Woman
Christian Hodge as Man
David Fitchew as Vendor
Michael Dwyer as Ruffian #1

As Gabrielle sets off to bury Xena's body faithfully in Amphipolis, she is sidetracked by the Amazons, who want to give Xena an Amazon funeral by fire. Meanwhile, Xena's spirit enters Autolycus's body to help him steal back her body so that she can be brought back to life.

This episode was filmed entirely after Lucy's accident, hence the lack of scenes with Xena in them. When Xena is shown — in her reflection in the water and at the end, sharpening her sword — there is almost no movement, and she actually looks somewhat uncomfortable. This episode tested how well the character of Gabrielle could do alone, and Reneé O'Connor is great! The scenes of her in mourning, the pained expression when she thinks Autolycus is stealing Xena's body, her choking sob when she sees Xena reappear, and her triumph when she becomes Queen of the Amazons show how many facets of one character she can perform in a single episode.

Autolycus is excellent, as usual. Again Campbell is given all the great lines, and instead of imitating Xena when she is in his body, as Hudson and Reneé had done, he caricatures her and has fun with it, speaking in a monotone and giving a blank stare. Campbell's talent for physical comedy is especially entertaining when he's fighting Xena inside him. The concept is borrowed from the 1984 Steve Martin film, *All of Me*, where Lily Tomlin has taken over half of Martin's body. Melinda Clarke makes a convincing villain as Velasca, the evil Amazon, although her performance is at times a little stiff. The final scene with Velasca battling Gabrielle is very fast-paced and suspenseful, although her return is made pretty obvious.

"The Quest" is often a number-one pick for subtext fans because of one thing — The Kiss. Now, there have been arguments for and against the subtext, but in my opinion, there is no doubt that Gabrielle kisses Xena, *not* Autolycus. The two women move forward to lock lips and the scene immediately cuts to Autolycus and Gabrielle, but Gabrielle's eyes are still closed. When she does open them she jumps back as if she thought she'd been kissing Xena. No doubt about it — that was more than just a friendly kiss.

Of the Xena-lite episodes, this one is the best.

NITPICK: Other than to extend the length of the episode, why does Xena choose Autolycus's body to inhabit? Why not enter Gabrielle's body once she has helped him steal the dagger of Helios?

DISCLAIMER: "Xena's body was not harmed during the production of this motion picture. However, it took weeks for Autolycus to get his swagger back."

214 A Necessary Evil

ORIGINAL AIR DATE: February 10, 1997
WRITTEN BY: Paul Robert Coyle
DIRECTED BY: Mark Beesley
GUEST CAST: Melinda Clarke as Velasca
             Hudson Leick as Callisto
             Danielle Cormack as Ephiny
             Jodie Dorday as Solari
             Mark Webley as Guard #1

Velasca returns as a goddess, having eaten some ambrosia, and to stop her Xena must enlist the help of her bitter enemy, Callisto.

To understand this episode completely, a viewer has to have seen the *H:TLJ* episode, "Surprise," a few weeks earlier. It immediately followed the story line of Callisto being condemned to Tartarus for good, but Hera gives her one day of reprieve in order to kill Hercules. Callisto drugs his family, forcing Hercules to try to obtain a golden apple at the tree of life, found in a cave at the end of the Labyrinth of the Gods. When they arrive at the cave, Callisto eats an apple and is made immortal, but Hercules traps her in the cave as he leaves and she has no way of escaping.

"Surprise" aired the same week as "Destiny" on *X:WP*, so viewers only had to wait two weeks to discover Callisto's fate. However, many questions arise from Xena's choice: why choose Callisto, an arch-enemy and a woman whom Gabrielle despises, and risk her becoming a goddess? When Gabrielle snaps at Xena, her anger is understandable. Xena must have known the emotional torment Callisto would force Gabrielle to undergo. Why doesn't Xena choose Ares (whom she could have easily outwitted, as usual) or call upon Artemis, whose temple Velasca has desecrated?

Artemis was the goddess of hunting and archery, but was also a protector of wild animals and the weak. She is characterised by her chosen virginity, and insisted that her attendants should remain so, punishing those who didn't. However, at the same time, she brought fertility to women and married couples. To modern readers she may seem like a walking contradiction. If any mortal saw her naked, she would change him into a stag and hunt him down. Her emblem was the she-bear.

Artemis was the daughter of Zeus and Leto (although some sources suggest her mother was Demeter). It is said that upon being born, she assisted in the delivery of her twin brother, Apollo. She was a vengeful goddess, and along with her brother would kill anyone who would violate her mother in any way. Once Niobe's children insulted Leto by suggesting that they were as good and strong as Leto's children, and Artemis and Apollo killed them all out of revenge. The two of them were often seen as a complementary pair: Apollo brought sudden yet natural death on men, while Artemis brought women an easy death. Apollo is often called the sun god, and Artemis was occasionally identified with the moon.

Artemis would punish mortals who did not observe her rites and give regular sacrifices to her; the boar at Calydon is an example of what would happen to those who did not worship her properly (see "The Prodigal"). Once Actaeon saw her bathing and she turned him into a stag, after which he suffered a horrible death by being devoured by his own hounds. She was a goddess who was worshipped in many regions for different reasons, hence her varied personality and traits. She was worshipped by the Amazons and was their protector because of their strength and hunting skills, and the fact that they didn't need men. Thus, it doesn't make sense that Velasca could destroy one of Artemis's temples and begin a rampage to end the Amazon race while Artemis just sits back and watches.

This episode was also filmed after Lucy's accident. Notice in the opening scene how she moves very little and is only shot from the shoulders up.

She shouts for Gabrielle to duck, then swings her arms as if she's about to dive behind something, but they immediately cut to a stunt double leaping through the air. The execution of these scenes is amazing — unless viewers knew about Lucy's accident, they would have no idea that Lucy wasn't actually moving around. In the opening scene Xena is hurled through the air, and when she stands there's a look of pain on her face which is probably real: just having to stand up must have been a real effort for her.

One of the most moving scenes in this episode occurs when Callisto forces Xena to stand in a village square and confess what she did at Cirra, Callisto's former home. This recalls the scene from the opening of "Destiny," where Xena returns to the ruins of Cirra and is haunted by the image of a young Callisto at the moment where her soul turned to evil. In "A Necessary Evil," Xena admits publicly that it was her fault that Callisto has become who she is, and Callisto looks visibly shaken. However, when Xena finishes she steps off the podium, says "Let's go," and walks away as if nothing has happened, leaving this viewer feeling uneasy about the sincerity of Xena's confession.

A particularly upsetting scene occurs when Gabrielle and Callisto play "Truth or Dare," as Callisto calls it. Why does Gabrielle trust Callisto enough to ask her about her past and trust that Callisto won't say something horrible about Perdicus, as she always gleefully does? Perhaps Xena accompanied Gabrielle while in Callisto's body long enough for Gabrielle to begin to trust Callisto's face. As Gabrielle walks away in disgust, Xena just asks, "What's wrong with her?" without going to find out. Knowing what Callisto has done to Gabrielle in the past, Xena should have shown a lot more compassion than she did.

As for Velasca, does she have a right to be angry? I think she does — after all, she was raised by Amazons, is trained in their ways and customs, while Gabrielle refuses to kill and isn't as strong in battle as the Amazons are. One of the great things about *X:WP* is the fact that even the worst villains are angry for somewhat valid reasons. Granted, Gabrielle is more desirable to these Amazons because she's more peaceful, and this is a more peaceful tribe. However, Velasca's gripe doesn't come out of nowhere.

The final scene with Callisto and Gabrielle and Xena all teamed up against Velasca is suspense-filled. The lava river adds an especially vivid effect that has the viewers on the edge of their seats. As the goddess of chaos, Velasca is truly evil, but has met her match in Callisto. Now what will *she* be? The goddess of revenge? Psychosis?

NITPICK: When Gabrielle is being sucked into Velasca's cyclone, why does Xena stand still and lamely scream out "Gabrielle!" every five seconds? For the first time Xena remains completely inactive until it's almost too late.

DISCLAIMER: "The reputation of the Amazon Nation was not harmed despite Velasca's overly radical adherence to an otherwise valid belief system."

ORIGINAL AIR DATE: February 10, 1997
WRITTEN BY: R.J. Stewart
DIRECTED BY: Michael Hurst
GUEST CAST: Murray Keane as Hower
Alison Wall as Minya
Willy De Wit as Zagreas
Tony Billy as Largo
Jim Ngaata as Gareth

This episode chronicles a day in the life of Xena and Gabrielle, where we see all those little daily activities that we usually just take for granted.

No matter where you are, if you ask a large group of *X:WP* fans what their favorite episode is, "A Day in the Life" will almost always come out on top. While Lucy was recovering, they needed an episode with as little fighting as possible. "A Day in the Life" is the perfect solution. For anyone who's ever wondered how they cook their meals, make a decision, relieve themselves without a bathroom, or whether they always get along, this episode is for you. Reneé O'Connor and Lucy Lawless are absolutely wonderful as they bicker, joke, play-fight, and work together to solve everyday problems (such as, where do you find a new frying pan when Xena uses yours as a chakram?).

Instead of just Gabrielle and Xena, we can actually see the real Reneé and Lucy through the characters. As they sit by the river and joke around, we see the charming humor of Lucy shining through Xena's tough exterior. We also see how Gabrielle could become easily frustrated with Xena — after the arduous task of compiling her list of pros and cons to decide which village they should defend, Xena flips a coin to decide. Why does Xena get to make the decision?

Minya and Hower are a delightful couple that they meet — a warrior princess wannabe and a guy who falls hopelessly in lust with the real warrior princess. The scene of Xena emerging from her bath in slow motion, flipping her long locks to try to dry them, sets her up as some sort of fashion model and parodies commercials and movies where the dainty female allures the men by acting sexy. Speaking of which, this episode contains the second most important scene to subtext fans — the hot tub scene. As Gabrielle and Xena wash each others' backs and hair (and Xena discovers that Gabrielle is sitting on the soap) fans of the lesbian innuendo shriek with delight (while non-subtext fans argue that with a shortage of hot water Xena and Gabrielle would have had to have taken a bath together). However, even Minya makes a parallel between her relationship and theirs by telling Xena that Hower belongs to her (Minya) and Xena has Gabrielle, and while Xena is fishing earlier in the episode, Gabrielle tells Hower that Xena won't get married because "she likes what I do."

This episode is directed by Michael Hurst, which is probably part of the reason why it's so damn funny. As Xena and Gabrielle enter Minya's village, Gabrielle makes a comment that all the villages look the same, apparently a direct comment on the limited set syndrome of *X:WP* and *H:TLJ*. The irony is that this village doesn't look the same as the others (though it will be used in later episodes)! Also, near the beginning of the episode Gabrielle places flowers on a fertility statue. After she and Xena have been travelling for a couple of hours, the statue appears again, which could mean one of three things: they've walked in a circle (not likely as their surroundings are different here), fertility statues by the side of the road were a common occurrence in Ancient Greece, or Hurst has put it in the scene as a joke.

The only serious part of the episode is Xena's fight with Gareth as revenge on behalf of Goliath. Although she kills him with a trick that Benjamin Franklin would "invent" centuries later (a belt buckle on a piece of "flying parchment" during a thunderstorm), his death is meant to be taken seriously.

Zagreus, on the other hand, is a neurotic nitwit. Looking more like a pro wrestler than a warlord, this idiot drives himself into a frenzy of anger by whacking himself in the head and challenging everyone to a fight. What kind of warlord is that?! This guy is hilarious!

This episode earns its title as fan favorite because it's got everything: subtext, humor, fight scenes, close interaction between Gabrielle and Xena. From Xena using Gabrielle's precious scrolls as toilet paper to the two of them commenting that the constellations look remarkably like water dippers and bears, this episode shows sides of Xena and Gabrielle that we hope to one day see again.

INTERESTING FACT: The scene where Xena conquers Gareth was originally shot for "Giant Killer," but the show was too long and this scene was cut.

DISCLAIMER: "No Slimy Eels were harmed during the production of this motion picture despite their reputation as a fine delicacy in select cultures of the known world."

216 For Him The Bell Tolls

ORIGINAL AIR DATE: February 24, 1997
WRITTEN BY: Adam Armus & Nora Kay Foster
DIRECTED BY: Josh Becker
GUEST CAST: Ted Raimi as Joxer
Alexandra Tydings as Aphrodite
Karl Urban as Cupid
Craig Parker as Sarpedon
Mandie Gillette as Ileandra
Craig Walsh-Wrightson as King Lynaeus
Ross Jolly as King Barus

Rachale Davies as Aria
Tai Hadfield as Guard
Mark Jones as Messenger

When Aphrodite makes Joxer a victim of one of her love spells, he alternately transforms into a gallant swordsman and back to his old goofy self whenever he hears a bell ring.

We now move from the favorite episode to one that was disliked by many *X:WP* fans because Xena doesn't appear in it, except for the beginning and the end. Some disliked it for the prominence of Joxer, despite the fact that this was one of Ted Raimi's best performances. This was one of the first episodes filmed after Lucy's accident, and when Xena does appear at the beginning, they film her from the shoulders up when she's on Argo, an indication that Lucy's not actually not sitting on a horse. When the camera pulls away, the woman on the horse is a stunt double. At the very end of the show, as the trio are walking away again Xena never looks to her side, another hint that the woman walking down the road might be a body double.

This episode is the first time the characters of Aphrodite and Cupid cross over from *H:TLJ*. Both are hilarious representations of the original myths, Aphrodite being a knock-out blonde in a pink bikini covered with a pink sheer number, while Cupid is a bleach-blonde (whose dark roots are usually showing) with five o'clock shadow. Both talk like stereotypical Southern

Reneé and Ted at Valley Forge, 1997

WENDY SPARKS

California beach-types, using phrases like, "Get a grip!" "Dream on!" "Duh!" "Ex-squeeze me?" and "Way not fair!" (for more on Cupid, see "A Comedy of Eros").

Aphrodite was the goddess of love and the giver of beauty and sexual attraction, the Greek equivalent to the later Roman Venus. She was usually represented as smiling an ironic smile, as she often mocked the other gods. According to Homer she was the daughter of Zeus and Dione, while Hesiod writes that she was fully grown out of the sea, found in a scallop shell off the island of Cythera, identifying her closely with Venus. She may also have been the daughter of Amphitrite by a lesser god named Triton. She was the wife of Hephaestus (made so against her will by Zeus, to keep her out of mischief) and was unfaithful to him, preferring Ares. On *X:WP*, Ares is nothing more than her brother, though with Zeus traipsing around like he did, it's a wonder that anyone could keep their family ties straight. She had several children with Ares (see "Ties That Bind") but the most important one for the purposes of *X:WP* was Eros, or Cupid, although he occasionally claimed to have been self-generated.

Aphrodite also loved Adonis and Anchises, and she proved that as well as punishing them, she was able to help mortals fall in love, although the couplings often had disastrous effects: she helped Paris win Helen, Melanion win Atalanta, Jason get Medea, and Aeneas get Dido. She helped her son, Aeneas, escape from Troy and found Rome, hence her role as the protectress of Rome. As kind as she could be, though, she was also cruel, and was especially vindictive to those who claimed to be superior to her.

The Greeks saw Aphrodite as cruel and even ridiculous, while the Romans saw her as kind and generous. She was mostly worshipped by women, although the festivals in her name, the Aphrodisia, were celebrated by courtesans. From the opposing representations of her there rose the occasional belief that there were actually two Aphrodites, the sacred and the profane. The sacred is believed to have been born from the sea, while the profane is the daughter of Dione and Zeus. The Aphrodite of *X:WP* is clearly not a sacred or even serious rendering. In this episode she toys with mortals — risking Joxer's life — to try to save her temples. She cares more for the beautiful objects in the temples (her "brand-new antiques," as she calls them) than for their religious significance — "Temples are my kahunas!"

This episode borrows from the Pavlovian idea that a bell ringing will cause animals to act a certain way, if they've been conditioned to do so. Add one of Aphrodite's spells and you can skip the conditioning process. This gimmick has been used in other movies, cartoons, and television shows, although the writers of this episode attribute it to the 1956 Danny Kaye film, *The Court Jester*. In this film, Kaye plays Hawkins, part of a Robin Hood-like band of men who are trying to restore the rightful king (who happens to be a baby) to his throne. When Hawkins meets the court jester on the road he decides to dress up like him, intimate himself with the court, and eventually steal the key to a tunnel where they can sneak the baby in.

When Hawkins is involved in a jousting match he's given a poison pellet, which he must drop in the drink of his opponent: the tongue-twister used to help him remember which cup has the poison in it shows Kaye at his best. Eventually the king's daughter falls in love with him and everything is turned upside-down.

Raimi's sense of comic timing is very much like Kaye's and he places Kaye among his movie idols. The writers also use a sword-fighting trick from *The Princess Bride*, where the hero appears to be losing in the battle, only to reveal that he isn't fighting with his proper hand. Raimi is very funny in this episode, and we're given a more sympathetic rendering of Joxer, which will continue in "A Comedy of Eros" as he realizes that only under one of Aphrodite's spells can he be considered a swashbuckling hero. It's too bad that Gabrielle isn't featured a little more prominently, especially considering the evolution of Reneé's acting over this season. But all-in-all this is a satisfying episode, despite Xena's absence.

NITPICK: When Gabrielle first enters Aphrodite's temple, Cupid asks her what her name is. Shouldn't he already know that?

OOPS: In the execution scene, the same footage of the executioner's sword going up and coming back down slowly is shown twice.

DISCLAIMER: "The producers wish to acknowledge the inspiration of Danny Kaye and pay tribute to the classic motion picture *Court Jester*."

217 The Execution

ORIGINAL AIR DATE: April 7, 1997
WRITTEN BY: Paul Robert Coyle
DIRECTED BY: Garth Maxwell
GUEST CAST: Tim Thomerson as Meleager
Tony Blackett as Arbus
Douglas Kamo as Sullus
Ranald Hendriks as Elysha
Ann Baxter as Elderly Woman
Matthew Jeffs as Head Guard
Patrick Kuhtze as Other Guard
Dean Stewart as Executioner
Colin Francis as Hurried Villager
Alvin Fitisemanu as Hawker
Jonathon Acorn as Slim Man

Gabrielle's sense of loyalty clashes with Xena's sense of justice when Meleager the Mighty is condemned to death for murder.

In this episode we see Gabrielle actively working against Xena for the first time (if we accept that she was too emotional to think straight in "Return of Callisto"). There is a lot more action in this episode than in the last few, and Xena's ample movement suggests that this episode was probably one of the last filmed after the accident.

"The Execution" definitely plants the seeds for the disastrous rift saga that will occur in the third season. Although this episode contains Reneé's best acting to this point, other than the main plot there is very little else going on. It raises a lot of discussion among fans on the lack of communication between Xena and Gabrielle. Is Gabrielle too much of an optimist, compared to Xena's pragmatism, for their relationship ever to be built on absolute trust? Or is Xena correct when she accuses Gabrielle of putting people on pedestals? She has clearly put Xena on one, and when Meleager topples off of his she is emotionally crushed.

However, Gabrielle's sense of idealism is what allows their relationship to flourish. Gabrielle keeps Xena grounded and prevents her from turning to the dark side once again by simply being the loving person whom Xena lives for. Xena does try to give her the benefit of the doubt, though, despite her belief that Arbus is a just man.

Tim Thomerson was great once again as Meleager, who, although sober throughout this episode, has fallen off the wagon since Gabrielle last saw him. Like Xena, he's not perfect, and Gabrielle must understand that. The look on Gabrielle's face when her trust in Meleager shatters is heartbreaking — in fact you can tell the moment that *her* heart breaks just by watching how her face changes throughout the scene. Reneé is wonderful here.

This episode, which was the producers' homage to Westerns, reveals what Xena was up to when Gabrielle attended The Athens City Academy of the Performing Bards. Why didn't she mention the incident to Gabrielle earlier, though? Was she scared that she'd fall off her pedestal, too?

OOPS: A fan at the Detroit Hercules/Xena convention in August 1997 pointed this one out: in the opening fight, as Lucy grabs one of the villagers and braces to throw him over the barrels, you can hear her mutter, "Don't move," to him, because she needs the stunt man to be still before she can toss him.

DISCLAIMER: "By popular demand 'The Executioner' will bring back his comfortable lightweight cotton-flax blend robe in a variety of spring colors."

218 Blind Faith

ORIGINAL AIR DATE: April 14, 1997
WRITTEN BY: Adam Armus & Nora Kay Foster
DIRECTED BY: Josh Becker
GUEST CAST: Jeremy Callaghan as Palaemon
Chris Bailey as Apex
Sydney Jackson as Vidalus
Graham Lauder as Lagos
Ajay Vasisht as Vendor

*Xena is blinded when she gets sumac oil in her eyes, but she must rescue Gabrielle,
who's been kidnapped in a sordid takeover plot.*

Once again Xena risks everything to save Gabrielle, as she declines finding
the antidote to her blindness in order to help her friend. The writers touch
on the subtext in this episode many times. It opens with Gabrielle begging
Xena to go "haggling" with her, which would be the ancient equivalent
of visiting a shopping mall, but Xena declines, finding shopping boring,
and says she'll go to the local tavern instead. In other words, Gabrielle and
Xena are set up in twentieth-century stereotypical husband and wife roles,
with Xena taking the masculine role.

When Palaemon arrives, kidnapping Gabrielle and telling Xena he has
killed her, Xena knows immediately that he's lying. Notice the way she
fights without the furious vigour from "Ties That Bind" or "The Path Not
Taken," two other occasions when a loved one was killed. Instead she fights
him as she would anyone else, cackling as she does so, which proves she
isn't too concerned. However, a fight is all Palaemon wants, and he goads
her for one throughout the episode.

The best parts of this episode involve Gabrielle and her "lady-training."
Kidnapped for the purpose of marrying a king, she is berated by Vidalus,
a Salmoneus-like character who is absolutely hilarious as he mocks her
dishwasher hands, her too-muscular stomach, and the way she walks.
Especially funny is the way he plops the scrolls on her head to teach her
grace, rather than using the traditional books that are used in modern
modelling academies. Reneé is excellent as she stumbles about in her high
heels, trips when she should curtsy, and whacks Vidalus in the face as she
holds out her hand to be kissed.

Lucy, on the other hand, is not very convincing as a blind person. As she
and Palaemon walk down the road she never once veers into a ditch or
walks into a tree, and at one point she grabs Palaemon by the throat and
holds him up against a tree while she threatens him. How does she know
that tree was there? Playing the part of a blind person takes a lot more than
a motionless stare straight ahead, and Lucy doesn't convince the viewer
that Xena can't see. Perhaps some fans would argue that Xena can sense
things, as she senses an oncoming attack. However, as she has explained to
Gabrielle in past episodes, she can sense moving things, not things that are
still. Catching her chakram while blind is believable because we know she
can sense its movements. However, she seems to find every door, turn every
corner in that castle without slamming into a wall, and pull the coffin out
of the fire.

All in all, this isn't one of the best episodes of the season, but it has its
moments. The scenes with Gabrielle saved the episode.

NITPICK: More on Xena's blindness: if Xena can sense all movement, as
demonstrated with the chakram, why can't she sense the soldiers in the
hallway? Also, Gabrielle is told that King Solis has a penchant for blue-eyed
blondes, to which she replies that she's actually a redhead. Has she never
looked in a mirror to notice that her eyes are also an emerald-green color?

OOPS: As Xena is running to grab the coffin from the fire, she dodges one of the soldiers. Quite observant for a blind person.

DISCLAIMER: "Once again, Gabrielle's luck with men was harmed during the production of this motion picture."

219 Ulysses

ORIGINAL AIR DATE: April 21, 1997
WRITTEN BY: R.J. Stewart
DIRECTED BY: Michael Levine
GUEST CAST: John D'Aquino as Ulysses
Rachel Blakely as Penelope
Tim Raby as Meticles
Carl Bland as Layos
Donna Pivac as 1st Siren
Geoffrey Knight as 1st Pirate
Charles Siebert as Poseidon

Xena and Gabrielle meet up with Ulysses as he is making his way back to Ithaca after the Trojan War, and he and Xena fall in love with one another.

"Ulysses" is one of the least-favorite episodes because of the inaccuracies in the retelling of this well known story. Because the story of Ulysses is a long and involved one, for the purposes of this episode I shall only recount the main parts of his voyage home to Ithaca. Ulysses is the Roman name, and for this episode it might have been more appropriate to have called him by his Greek name — Odysseus, the subject of Homers' *The Odyssey*. Odysseus was the son of Laertes and Anticleia, and although he did not want to travel to Troy and tried to escape his obligations to Menelaus (see "Beware Greeks Bearing Gifts"), he was one of the greatest heroes at Troy. The idea of the Trojan Horse is attributed to him, and he killed almost twenty named men by himself.

When Odysseus set out for Ithaca, he met up with Maron on an island, who gave him twelve jugs of sweet wine. Odysseus moved on and eventually landed on the island of the Cyclopes, where he met Polyphemus. After the giant ate at least six of his men, Odysseus got him drunk on the wine, and told him his name — "Nobody." After Polyphemus passed out, Odysseus took a pointed stake he had fashioned earlier, put it in the fire and then gouged the Cyclops's eye. He and his remaining men escaped as the Cyclops began screaming, but when the other Cyclopes came to his aid, Polyphemus claimed that Nobody had tormented him, and thinking he had gone mad, the Cyclopes left him alone. Polyphemus called out to his father, Poseidon, to hinder Odysseus's voyage home, which explains Poseidon's hatred for Ulysses in this episode of *X:WP*.

During his travels Odysseus met with Aeolus, the Warden of the Winds, who gave him a favorable wind to carry him home, putting all the other winds in a sac for Odysseus to carry. As they approached Ithaca, Odysseus fell asleep and his men opened the sac, thinking it held gold, and the released winds blew the ship all the way back to Aeolus. Odysseus also landed on the isle of the Lotus-Eaters, who gave two of his men a lotus plant to eat, which made them forget about their home and wish to stay. He stopped at the isle of Circe, where his men were transformed into swine and he became Circe's lover. He encountered the Sirens, but resisted them by stopping his men's ears with wax and binding himself to the ship's mast, and he also encountered the sea-monsters Scylla and Charybdis. He then met Calypso and stayed on her island for a length of time between one and ten years, depending on which author was recounting the story.

Eventually he found his way to Ithaca when King Alcinous helped him get there, but upon arriving discovered that his wife, Penelope, had arranged suitors to compete for her hand in marriage. After all, Odysseus had been gone for twenty years, and she thought he was dead. Athena disguised Odysseus to look like an old peasant and he disclosed his identity only to his son, Telemachus. Upon arriving at the castle, the only one to recognize Odysseus was his dog Argus, who, at twenty years old, struggled to stand for his master and died from the effort.

Penelope's test involved stringing a bow and shooting an arrow through a group of rings. However, none of the suitors could string the bow. Odysseus stepped up, strung the bow and shot the arrow, then revealed who he was, and he and Telemachus slaughtered the suitors, with Athena acting as Mentor. Peace returned to Ithaca soon after, but various writers added stories about Odysseus's death, ranging from him being condemned to exile for slaughtering the suitors, to Calypso's son unwittingly fulfilling a prophecy that Odysseus's son would kill him.

In *X:WP*, a new spin is put on an old tale. Xena helps Ulysses get to Ithaca, not Athena or King Alcinous. She defeats the Sirens by attempting to bind Ulysses to a post, then out-sings them when he gets free. Now Xena's singing is appealing, but it doesn't have the allure of the Sirens and could hardly have held him back.

Like the harpies, the Sirens were half-woman, half-bird, usually depicted with the heads of women and the bodies of birds. According to various writers, there were two, three, or four of them. They lived on an island in the Mediterranean, where the shore was white with bleached bones of sailors. As ships would pass, the Sirens would sing so beautifully that the sailors would steer the ships towards the rocks near the Sirens' island, and inevitably be destroyed on them. The only two men to resist them were Orpheus, who out-sang them, and Odysseus. By different accounts the Sirens were the daughters of the Muse Melpomene (Muse of tragedy) and the river god Achelous, Achelous and Sterope, Achelous and the Muse Terpsichore (Muse of choral songs and the dance), or Phorcys, the sea-god. Some writers believed the Sirens' shape was their punishment for escorting

Persephone to the Underworld. Odysseus's escape from their allurements is usually interpreted as his escape from worldly temptations.

In *X:WP*, the Sirens have no bird-like features whatsoever and appear to be standing in front of a giant clam. Also, while LoDuca's Siren song is quite beautiful, he can't take the credit for it: it's a direct ripoff of the even more beautiful "Sirens," by Claude Debussy.

Because Ulysses' sexual conquests are well known, his attraction to Xena is a believable one. It was Xena's attraction to Ulysses that has viewers baffled. This Ulysses was nothing like the legendary hero. First of all, after being one of the most cunning soldiers in the Trojan War, he wouldn't have been stupid enough to leap in front of an arrow, knowing Xena had her chakram. Secondly, the Odysseus of legend resisted the Sirens himself — while here he needs Xena to tie him up. He can't bend the bow by himself, but needs Xena under the table to bend it while he strings it. Fans of Greek mythology often dislike the mythological inconsistencies in *X:WP* but this episode has been picked apart for its numerous errors.

However, how is an episode of *X:WP* any different from the various accounts of Greek scholars? Hesiod, Homer, Virgil, Euripedes, Aeschylus, and others all wrote of events in Ancient Greek history, but their accounts vary drastically in each story for political reasons. The Trojan War had many accounts of events — Paris was tricked; Menelaus was betrayed; Helen wanted to go with Paris; Helen despised Paris. The account depended on what side of the war the author was from or what his political leanings were. The politics of *X:WP* are clearly feminist, so the stories are written with that political leaning in mind. So Ulysses is a hero because Xena works in secret, never letting anyone know that she bends that bow or out-sings the Sirens. Perhaps we can just chalk up the writers as offering yet another account of what may have happened. After all, there's as much likelihood that R.J. Stewart actually saw the Trojan War as there is that Euripedes did.

Besides, the idea that Ulysses would decide not to stay with his wife, but instead go back out on adventures isn't a new one. See Tennyson's "Ulysses," where Ulysses returns home to an ageing wife and a land he doesn't know, hands his kingdom to his son, and decides he'd rather go back out and see the world than settle for early retirement. Perhaps the writers of this episode named the character Ulysses instead of Odysseus to signal that this poem would be an influence. However, for most fans — who have dubbed this episode, "Uselesses," the show just doesn't work.

TIME: c. 1240 BC, ten years after the Trojan War.

YAXI: Xena tells Ulysses that she learned a long time ago not to leave Gabrielle out of things. Since when?!

NITPICK: Having been the greatest Greek hero of the Trojan War, it's not bloody likely that after Xena tells him she'd fought on the Trojan side he'd shrug it off by saying that it was a stupid war anyway.

DISCLAIMER: "Despite Gabrielle's incessant hurling, Ulysses' ship was not harmed during the production of this motion picture."

220 The Price

ORIGINAL AIR DATE: April 28, 1997
WRITTEN BY: Steven L. Sears
DIRECTED BY: Oley Sassone
GUEST CAST: Paul Glover as Menticles
Charles Mesure as Mercer
Tamati Rice as Garel
Mark Perry as Galipan
Jason Hoyte as Athenian #1
Bob Johnson as Athenian #2
Brent Gilbert as Drowned Athenian
Phillip Jones as Wounded Athenian
Allen O'Halloran as Fatigued/Gashed Athenian
Justin Curry as G'Kug
Sam Williams as Hordemaster

Xena's dark side resurfaces when she leads the Athenians against the bloodthirsty Horde. Shocked at her friend's behavior, Gabrielle chooses instead to see both sides as being made up of human beings, and tends to the wounded rather than contribute to the carnage.

Although there isn't much blood and gore in this episode, it is one of the most violent episodes of *X:WP*, if not *the* most violent to this point. The Horde are made to look like natives, possibly Scythians or Maori, and stand for every group of people who were ever exploited and made out to be less than human. Although it is not suggested in the show that the Horde were the first peoples of Greece, the episode does insinuate that the show is a parable about the folly of a "Cowboys and Indians" way of thinking.

The episode is significant in that this is the first time Xena has been scared of any group of warriors. After telling Gabrielle that her army had fought them and they had tied her men up and skinned them, not only does Gabrielle look completely frightened, but the viewers are robbed of their confidence that Xena can get them out of the situation. Gabrielle relies on Xena's confidence, and when Xena begins running away from the enemy in complete terror, where does that leave Gabrielle?

Is it plausible to suggest that Xena would almost completely abandon her newfound ideals and turn into a ruthless warrior once again? Why now? For the second time since her army mutinied in "The Gauntlet," Xena has formed another army to lead. Perhaps the adrenaline rush she gets from the experience turns her into a fierce warrior whose only sense is to kill the enemy, but why would she turn on Gabrielle like that? Sure, sometimes Gabrielle's saint-like qualities can be a little grating, but the way Xena orders her around and brutally shoves her out of her way at one point is too distant from Xena's character. How can Gabrielle give Xena her absolute trust when she never knows when Xena will lose it and turn on her (think "The Reckoning," "Ties That Bind," and "The Bitter Suite")?

On the other hand, by showing Xena's dark side quietly lurking under the surface, we are reminded once again that she will probably be tormented by her past for the rest of her life — Xena is living in a purgatory that she created. Once again there's an insinuation that Xena has a split personality, referring in this episode to the Xena that we all know and love as a part of her that she no longer thinks she needs.

Eventually — as is always the case — Xena is won over by Gabrielle's strong feelings, and the subtexters are teased once again. As she joins Gabrielle in helping the wounded, she says to her, "You understand hatred but you don't give in to it. You don't know how much I love . . . that." Gabrielle takes the time to communicate with the warriors, realizing that *kaltaka* is not the name of an evil god which they are calling out to, but their word for "water." Xena has understood that the Horde have a code, just like she does, and by seeing herself in them she learns to recognize their similarities rather than their differences. This is a very powerful episode, and the most suspenseful to date.

OOPS: After Xena kills one of The Horde by catching his tomahawk with her whip and returning it to him via his chest, watch the warrior who grabs him and paddles away in a canoe. As he paddles forward the canoe moves in reverse away from the shore, and as he paddles backwards it moves forward.

DISCLAIMER: "To show sympathy for the Horde, 'kaltaka' was only served upon request during the production of this motion picture."

221 Lost Mariner

ORIGINAL AIR DATE: May 5, 1997
WRITTEN BY: Steven L. Sears
DIRECTED BY: Garth Maxwell
GUEST CAST: George Henare as Hidsim
Nigel Harbrow as Basculis
Tony Todd as Cecrops
Edward Campbell as Altrech
Frank Iwan, Jr. as Colfax
John Smith as Bloomer
Michael Hallows as Tig
Charles Siebert as Poseidon

Xena and Gabrielle end up on the ship of Cecrops, a man whose punishment for defying Poseidon is to be trapped on a ship forever, with no chance of ever touching dry land again.

Cecrops was one of the first mythical kings of Attica. A peaceful ruler, he had the body of a man and the tail of a snake, indicating he had come from the Earth. He taught people how to bury the dead and how to build cities and is often considered the inventor of writing and of the census. He was also the first to recognize Zeus as the supreme deity by offering him cakes instead of animal flesh as sacrifices. During his reign, both Poseidon and Athena wanted godly rule over Athens, as is explained in "Lost Mariner." To make his claim Poseidon came to Attica and by throwing his trident he made a spring of brackish water appear. Then Athena appeared and with Cecrops as her witness she planted an olive tree. When it came time for the judges to decide who should rule over Athens, they chose Athena because Cecrops had testified that she'd made the first olive tree appear on the rock of Acropolis. In his rage, Poseidon sent a flood to cover Attica.

In "Lost Mariner," Cecrops explains to Gabrielle the folly of storytellers ending the myth there. What they don't know, he says, is that Poseidon cursed him by putting him on a ship which he could never leave, for he'd be instantly killed if he touched land. Taking pity on him, Athena granted him immortality, which Cecrops saw as making the curse only worse. He then lured merchant sailors aboard his ship, and once they set foot on the ship they couldn't leave until they died. This story is wonderfully played out in the episode, and the writers have done a terrific job of weaving their own story into one of the Greek myths and making it seem like it was legendary.

Just as interesting is the characterization of the vengeful god, Poseidon, the Greek counterpart to the Roman sea-god, Neptune. Poseidon was the son of Cronus and Rhea, and the often rebellious brother of Zeus, because Poseidon resented Zeus for getting Olympus while Poseidon was relegated to the sea. Poseidon would punish towns that didn't worship him by drying up their rivers or flooding them, as he did with Attica. He was the sender of storms, including earthquakes, which Hades often feared would eventually make the Earth collapse into the Underworld. Poseidon was depicted riding in a chariot with a trident (a fishing spear) and his wife Amphitrite. Although he never had children with her, Poseidon had many love affairs that bore children.

Poseidon was hostile to the Trojans during the war because he wasn't given his proper payment for helping to build the walls around Troy. Besides losing Athens to Athena, he lost Argos to Hera, and he dried up all the rivers in the country. However, Poseidon could be good: he gave horses to all his favorites, and he changed Thessaly from a lake into dry land.

In *X:WP*, Poseidon is only depicted as being angry and vengeful. The special effect of Poseidon rising from the sea is stunning, as is the whirlpool imagery when Cecrops's ship almost gets sucked in. In the opening credits, the image of Xena holding her sword up to Poseidon is the only one that wasn't taken from one of the episodes, so it is good to see him appear here and earlier in "Ulysses."

Tony Todd is brilliant as Cecrops, and the episode ends in such a way that he could return. He is a fan favorite, so it would be a shame if the producers decide not to bring him back. The added element of a man pining for the woman he loved was interesting as well, as Cecrops gazes longingly on an emerald, which reminds him of the eyes of Tarae, the woman who must have died 250 years earlier.

Although this episode boasts some of the best special effects to date, it also features the most over-the-top gravity-defying act yet, when Xena somersaults through the air from a cliff to Cecrops's ship, about half a mile out to sea. And why does Gabrielle encourage Xena to do it? Does it occur to Gabrielle that she just might be condemning her friend to an eternity on Cecrops's ship?

Hidsim is a wonderful character — like Meleager, he's a father figure to Gabrielle. He also looks up to Cecrops, despite having been trapped on the doomed ship by him. Hidsim refers to Cecrops as Rama, which Cecrops believes may have been a hero where he came from. That would make Hidsim a native of India, or at least a pirate who passed through India and picked up their beliefs. Rama is the subject of the great Sanskrit epic, *Ramayana*, written around 300 BC. Rama bears similarities to Odysseus when he's the only one who can bend a bow belonging to the god Shiva, and Hercules with the Hydra, when he tries to kill the Ravana by cutting off its heads, causing more to spring up.

When Rama bent Shiva's bow, he won his wife Sita, whom he loved dearly, and who accompanied him when he was exiled. Sita was kidnapped and held in Ravana's palace in Sri Lanka, but when Rama rescued her and killed Ravana, he refused to touch her, thinking she had likely been defiled. She became suicidal and tried to burn herself on a funeral pyre, but the fire god wouldn't burn her. Rama took her back, saying he had believed her all along but wanted her purity to be demonstrated to the world. In a later addition, the people convinced Rama that his wife was impure and he sent her into exile for 16 years. She called on the earth mother to prove her innocence and the ground opened and swallowed her. Rama was left to mourn for his wife and grieve about being so mistaken, and he followed her by walking into the river Sarayu. In another version he was taken to Heaven and happily reunited with Sita.

Rama remained faithful to his wife, but he was flawed in never believing in her fidelity to him. Like Cecrops he was a great hero, but one who never looked inside himself to see the love he had for others until it was too late.

INTERESTING FACT: Reneé O'Connor revealed at the Valley Forge convention that in the scenes where Gabrielle was merrily chomping on raw squid, she was actually eating marinated octopus.

DISCLAIMER: "Cecrops' 'Joie de Vivre' was not harmed during the production of this motion picture."

222 A Comedy of Eros

ORIGINAL AIR DATE: May 12, 1997
WRITTEN BY: Chris Manheim
DIRECTED BY: Charles Siebert
GUEST CAST: Ted Raimi as Joxer

Jay Laga'aia as Draco
Karl Urban as Cupid
Cameron Russell as Bliss
Anthony Ray Parker as Pinullus
Barry Te Hira as Craigan
Catherine Boniface as Priestess
Vanessa Mateja as Virgin #1
Cherie Bray-Taylor as Virgin #2
Michael Holt as Draco Man #1
Zen Player as Draco Man #2
David Perrett as Farmer
Collette Pennington as Housewife
John Carr Watson as Merchant
Sean Grant as Teenage Boy
Eric Lynch as Best Buddy

When Cupid's infant son, Bliss, disappears with Daddy's arrows, the love triangles that ensue send the entire Xenaverse topsy-turvy.

Hey, kids! Let's play spot the subtext! This is a hilarious and campy episode where sexual euphemisms run rampant. The subtext is all over this episode, despite the fact that Xena and Gabrielle have both fallen in love with other people. Cupid is back, although he's got a much better dye job this time!

Cupid, or Eros in the Greek myth, has numerous genealogies — according to some authors he was born out of Chaos, by others he was born from the egg of Night, which split into Earth and Sky. He was also considered the son of Hermes and Artemis or Hermes and Aphrodite. There are many different Eros's mentioned, but the one who is depicted as a winged creature is generally attributed to Hermes and Artemis, not Aphrodite. This last incarnation is almost always depicted as a child, whereas Aphrodite's son is shown as a handsome youth (*X:WP* combines the myths by making Cupid a winged youth).

The most well known story about Eros/Cupid involves Psyche. One of three daughters of a king, Psyche possessed a remarkable beauty that intimidated most prospective suitors. (The people looked on Psyche's beauty with such awe that they stopped worshipping Aphrodite.) Psyche's father visited an oracle to ask who her husband would be, and was told to dress her as a bride and chain her to a rock where a monster would come to possess her. The king did so, and meanwhile Aphrodite sent Cupid down to find the ugliest creature possible to marry her. However, he saw Psyche and immediately fell in love with her. He sent a wind to carry her off the rock and into a valley where she awoke to find herself in a beautiful palace. Cupid came to her in the dark as her husband, telling her never to try to see his face, or she'd lose him forever. After a few weeks, Psyche asked to go see her sisters and Cupid reluctantly obliged. When her sisters saw how happy Psyche was, in their jealousy they began filling her mind with doubt, telling her that if she hadn't seen her husband there was probably something wrong with him. That night, when Cupid was asleep, Psyche came into his room and looked at him by the light of a lamp. When she saw how beautiful he was, her hand began shaking and a drop of oil landed on his cheek. He awoke and promptly flew away.

Devastated, Psyche searched the land for him, and found herself at Venus/Aphrodite's castle, where she was enslaved and forced to do impossible tasks. One of them was to travel to the Underworld to obtain a flask of the water of youth, which she was forbidden to open. However, she opened it nonetheless and fell into a deathly sleep. Meanwhile Cupid had been searching everywhere for Psyche, and when he found her he pricked her with an arrow and restored her to life. Zeus gave his permission for them to marry, and Psyche was reconciled with Aphrodite and made immortal. Cupid and Psyche had a daughter named Joy.

In "A Comedy of Eros," however, Joy is depicted as a naughty son named Bliss. This episode has some of the best lines yet, ranging from Xena's "Ain't love a bitch!" to Draco's "Corral those virgins!" Xena falls in love with Draco, and Gabrielle with Joxer, and Draco with Gabrielle, when Bliss's arrows start flying all over the place. Xena's love is more of a ravenous sexual hunger, Gabrielle's is more of an adoring puppy love, and Draco is a possessive monster.

The scene where Gabrielle is hit with the arrow is exciting, and speaks more overtly to the subtext fans. When someone gets hit with Cupid's arrow, they are filled with amorous desire, which they immediately transfer onto the first person they see. Gabrielle gets hit and she immediately calls out Xena's name (could it be that she only recognizes those amorous feelings as something she's felt for Xena?). The scene is shot in slow-motion, adding suspense for all those subtext fans who know that she has to turn around to see Xena, who is slowly coming up behind her. Inevitably, though, Joxer jumps between them and Gabrielle falls for him.

Oh, but the subtext doesn't end there. The writers play with those timeless fruit metaphors to show the true difference between Gabrielle and Xena. As Draco emerges from his bath completely in the buff, Xena quickly finishes off her banana, a suggestive fruit if ever there was one. When Draco sits beside her to discuss plans of combining their efforts as warriors, though, she starts popping cherries into her mouth. Xena is obviously a woman who likes all kinds of . . . fruit. Similarly, as Gabrielle tries to escape Draco's love-hungry clutches by convincing him she doesn't love him, she dives for the red fruit: "Cherries! I love cherries!" To which Draco seductively replies, "So do I."

Although Joxer steps between Gabrielle and Xena, this episode was not one that Joxer haters could use for their cause. In fact, it is the episode that changed the way some people feel about the bumbling "warrior." While everyone else is chasing one another through the streets, he alone loves without some sort of delusion. He protects Gabrielle and loves her, vowing it before everyone at the end of the episode. He will be the one who is crushed when Cupid reverses his son's deeds and leaves Gabrielle the way she used to be — not in love with Joxer. The season ends with Joxer sitting by the fire, looking like he'd been emotionally destroyed after Gabrielle laughs at the thought of them being in love. It is this image that viewers are left with to ponder over the summer, and when he returns in the third season, there are more cheers than jeers. This is a delightful episode.

NITPICK: At one point, Xena dresses Gabrielle up in her Amazon Princess gear, complete with feather headdress. Where on Argo's back do they store that outfit?

DISCLAIMER: "No Cherries were harmed during the production of this motion picture."

Karl Urban (Cupid) hams it up with Doug Wong,
the show's martial arts instructor

JOAN STANCO

SEASON THREE
(SEPTEMBER 1997–FEBRUARY 1998)

PRODUCTION STAFF:

Music Composer: Joseph LoDuca
Developer: R.J. Stewart
Co-ordinating Producer: Bernadette Joyce
New Zealand Producer: Chloe Smith
Producer: Liz Friedman
Producer: Eric Gruendemann
Supervising Producer: Steven L. Sears
Co-Executive Producer: R.J. Stewart
Executive Producer: Sam Raimi
Executive Producer: Robert Tapert
Creators: John Schulian and Robert Tapert

301 The Furies

ORIGINAL AIR DATE: September 29, 1997
WRITTEN BY: R.J. Stewart
DIRECTED BY: Gilbert Shilton
GUEST CAST: Kevin Smith as Ares
Darien Takle as Cyrene
Äsa Lindh as Alecto
Graciela Heredia as Megaera
Celi Foncesca as Tisiphone
Gordon Hatfield as Rufinus
Craig Walsh-Wrightson as Lysis
Reuben Purchase as Keeper
Steve Farac-Ciprian as Orestes

Ares convinces the Furies to punish Xena with persecution and madness, and the only way for Xena to regain her sanity is to kill the person who murdered her father: her mother, Cyrene.

The Furies were the demons of the Underworld, also referred to as the Erinyes. The Furies were violent female deities, often described as withered, coal-black women with burning eyes, faces like dogs, snakes for hair and wings like bats, carrying torches and whips. They obeyed the laws of no one but themselves. They were formed by the blood that fell to the earth when Uranus was castrated, and there are generally believed to have been three of them — Alecto, Tisiphone, and Megaera. The Furies lived in Erebus, or the Punishment Ground, the darkest place of the Underworld. Mortals never referred to them aloud as either the Furies or the Erinyes,

MCA TV / SHOOTING STAR

but rather as the Eumenides, which means "the kindly," which was an attempt to pacify them.

The Furies were the avengers of crimes. One of their main jobs was to hear complaints brought by mortals to Erebus, and to hound the culprits relentlessly. They handed out especially ruthless punishments, usually with their whips, for crimes against the family. In particular they'd punish cruelty to children, rude or unkind treatment of old people, guests, or visiting travellers, and they hounded to death anyone who treated their mother badly, no matter how wicked she had been to them. Often the Furies would strike murderers with madness, or force them to wander until purified.

One of those victims was Orestes, the son of Agamemnon and Clytemnestra. His story is one of the most involved and complicated in all of Greek mythology, so I will offer only a basic outline of the events here. When Agamemnon returned from the Trojan War, he was killed by his wife and her lover, Aegisthus, and when Orestes became a man, he was instructed by the oracle at Delphi to avenge Agamemnon's death by killing his murderers. Orestes came to Clytemnestra disguised as a traveller, telling her that Orestes had died and that he needed to know where to bury the ashes. Delighted that her son was now unable to avenge his father's death, Clytemnestra sent Aegisthus out to meet him, whereupon Orestes killed him. When Clytemnestra ran back, having heard Aegisthus's cry, she begged Orestes to have mercy on her, but he killed her because he believed the instructions he'd received from the oracle had come from Apollo.

Soon after, Orestes went mad, and the Furies began pursuing him everywhere. Although Apollo purified Orestes of his crime after forcing him to undergo various tortures, absolution from the wrath of the Furies could only come through a formal trial, where the Furies were the public prosecutrix and Apollo was Orestes' advocate. Although the judges were split on their decision, Orestes was honorably acquitted when Athena, who was presiding over the court, cast the deciding vote. Orestes was finally cured of his madness when he and his sister Iphegenia travelled to Attica to build a temple to Artemis.

"The Furies" was a disturbing episode because the writers swayed too far away from the myths, and Xena's character was inconsistent throughout. When she is first persecuted by madness, she immediately falls into a routine that is part Three Stooges, part Monty Python. (During the neck pinch scene, she asks, "What is the capital of Assyria?" a line from *Monty Python and the Holy Grail*.) As she refers to Gabrielle as Mavis and rides her horse backwards, Lucy is absolutely hilarious. However, when Xena appears entirely naked before a village of women and children in the middle of the night and begins threatening them, her insanity takes on a more serious tone. Xena is no longer just a crazy gal, she's a tortured individual whose madness makes her dangerous.

Reneé O'Connor is given the chance to shine as she plays the one person who realizes what is going on, and she is absolutely terrified for her friend. Even when the audience is laughing at the Three Stooges routine, Gabrielle appears deeply concerned.

Although "The Furies" was originally supposed to be aired in Season Two, what makes it an apt season opener is that we once again learn more about Xena's past, which is an important aspect of each season opener ("Sins of the Past," "Orphan of War"). It's a disturbing past — Cyrene killed Xena's father when he attempted to sacrifice Xena to Ares, whereas Xena had been led to believe that her father had abandoned the family when she was young. Xena alters the story, though, to suggest that Ares is her real father. However, to think that she could be as strong as she is simply because she's part god would remove much of her mystery. Yet, by the end of the episode, it would seem that she has outwitted Ares once again. Of course, to do so she performs one of the campiest and best fight scenes yet.

Despite the highlights of the show, the way the writers alter the myths for this episode is almost unforgivable. First of all, The Furies would *never* be ordered around by Ares or dance sensually for him while he sat on a throne, and to suggest that they could be swayed by his insinuation of sexual favors isn't revision, it's gross negligence of an important myth. If I were R.J. Stewart, I'd have trouble sleeping at night after defaming the Furies as such. Also, if the priest who kept up the temple of the Furies really was offering them rotten fruit as a sacrifice, he'd have received a far worse punishment than a dirty look from Alecto. Finally, the Furies punished those who murdered family members worse than anyone else, so they hardly would have stood by watching while Xena took her mother's life. As for Orestes, he didn't rot away in a prison, as mentioned, but for some reason Stewart decided to overlook Orestes's illustrious life after his madness and he rewrote *why* he actually killed Clytemnestra. And finally, the dryads are back in all their evil, which, as mentioned earlier (see "Girls Just Wanna Have Fun"), is an unfair characterization. Where in other episodes the writers take the myths and alter them for their own purposes, it would seem that R.J. Stewart didn't do a lot of reading into these particular characters. However, "The Furies" is an enjoyable episode if you don't know the myths already, and Lucy and Reneé are wonderful, considering they had to deal with such an inconsistent and inaccurate script.

NITPICK: When Cyrene tells Xena about killing her father, she turns so that the audience sees her and Xena cannot, and she noticeably smirks. Why would she be smiling at such a serious moment?

DISCLAIMER: "Xena's sanity was not harmed during the production of this motion picture. The Furies, however, will be opening their own lap-dancing variety show off-off-off Broadway soon."

302 Been There, Done That

ORIGINAL AIR DATE: October 6, 1997
WRITTEN BY: Hilary J. Bader
DIRECTED BY: Andrew Merrifield
GUEST CAST: Ted Raimi as Joxer
                Joseph Murray as Neron
                Deverik Williams as Tybelus
                Rebekah Davies as Hermia
                John McKee as Lord Menos
                Norman Fairley as Lord Lycost
                Marek Summich as Edos
                Norman Forsey as Casca
                Rodney Cooke as Man #1
                Campbell Rousselle as Man #2
                Neill Duncan as Perion
                John Glass as Tius
                Mary Woodward as Altara
                John Smythe as Apothecary

Xena's day keeps repeating itself over and over, and she is caught in this limbo until she can discover what she must do to be able to go on with her life.

Although this episode completely rips off the Bill Murray film, *Groundhog Day*, it's far more entertaining. Lucy is uproariously funny as she plays a warrior woman who slowly loses control as her day repeats itself over and over. Reneé and Ted Raimi are also very funny as they try to grasp the concept that Xena's day is repeating itself, while each day seems new to them (keep in mind that Gabrielle has just been dealing with a Xena who'd been driven insane by the Furies — wouldn't *you* begin to wonder if she'd really been cured?)

The underlying plot is similar to that of *Romeo and Juliet*, and even rewrites it to avert the tragedy. Perhaps Hilary J. Baden read the 1990 play by Canadian writer Ann-Marie MacDonald, *Goodnight Desdemona, Good Morning Juliet*, in which the central question is, What if there had been a comic foil in *Romeo and Juliet* and *Othello* who could have entered the play at the moment of disaster and averted the tragedy? Well, here that foil would be Xena, who must somehow figure out how to stop the Juliet character from taking the nightsbane and killing herself. The Juliet character is Hermia (the name of a character in Shakespeare's *A Midsummer Night's Dream*), Romeo is Neron, Tybelus is Tybalt, and various other characters become Mercutio. Joxer is the first as he gets skewered on a sword in the middle of a fight (and cries of joy were heard over the Internet . . .). However, if Gabrielle is so distraught over Joxer's death here, why does she just show bafflement on the eighth day when Xena buries her chakram in his chest? The tragedy of the one moment versus the comedy of the next was an unnerving inconsistency in Gabrielle's character. Despite Gabrielle's contradictory reactions, though, the fact that Xena is far more distraught over the death of Argo than she is the death of Joxer is perfectly in keeping with her character.

Altogether there are fourteen days, which is appropriate, for Xena becomes a god-like character who must recreate the world, in a sense, so that she can put the time continuum back in order. On the seventh day she runs around and apparently fixes everything, but then feels she's missing something. Because she's human, she can't set things right in a single week, as God did in Genesis, and it's only on the thirteenth day that things are put back in order.

Lucy is delightful in this role as Xena increasingly loses control over things, becomes more and more frustrated, waking up each morning screaming and cursing when she realizes she's still on the same day. Lucy is even funnier when Xena is completely frustrated and is going over everything that has happened. As Gabrielle and Joxer look on, she stands on her head, drums her fingers on her chin, punches hay, and is so unXena-like that this scene is brilliant (not to mention the scene where she goes to sleep sucking her thumb).

"Been There, Done That" was also a great episode for subtext. After Joxer's death (the first time), Gabrielle falls asleep in Xena's arms. Also, after Gabrielle's death, when she wakes up beside Xena the next morning, Xena's unfettered delight at discovering Gabrielle indicates that Gabby is much more than just a friend. Yet, the best moment is on the fourth day, when Xena, Gabrielle, and Joxer are walking down a street and Joxer points to Xena's neck, asking, "Is that a hickey?" Watch how Gabrielle immediately turns away and looks down sheepishly, appearing to be the guilty party. Probably the most overt subtext moment yet.

The most disappointing moment in this episode is where Xena first talks to Neron and he tells her how he arranged to have the day repeat itself. He tells her that he was waiting for someone to come and save him and he expected Hercules, "or even Sinbad," but that Xena would have to do. Now, in my memory this is the first time that Xena's skills have been questioned because she's a woman, which is definitely a low moment for this show.

Overall, this was a very entertaining episode, and features the greatest chakram throw ever (35 ricochets, counting the old man's hat).

GABRIELLE'S FIGHTING SKILLS: Now, I know this is a category that is more important to the first season, but Gabrielle's fighting skills when Xena takes her staff away are very impressive. With no weapons at all, Gabrielle has developed incredible defensive strategies, and she can avoid getting hurt until Xena throws her staff back. Also, it should be noted that for the first time Xena praises Gabrielle's fighting skills: "Good girl!" All right, Gabby!

OOPS: When Joxer and Gabrielle are watching Xena as she rambles on (this would be the eleventh day), notice the horse behind them moving in slow motion. They obviously had to slow the scene down to make them look more stupefied. Also, if we're supposed to believe that they haven't moved all day because they've continued to look on as Xena babbles before falling asleep (notice Joxer is still holding the eggs in his hat), then why is Gabrielle now sitting to his left, where before she'd been on his right?

DISCLAIMER: "The rooster was not harmed during the production of this motion picture, although his feathers were severely ruffled. However, a little gel and mousse straightened out the mess."

303 The Dirty Half Dozen

ORIGINAL AIR DATE: October 13, 1997
WRITTEN BY: Steven L. Sears
DIRECTED BY: Rick Jacobson
GUEST CAST: Kevin Smith as Ares
Charles Mesure as Darnelle
Katrina Hobbs as Glaphyra
Jon Brazier as Walsim
Jonathon Roberts as Agathon
Stephen Ure as Monlik
Peter Ford as Villager #1
Roy Snow as Athenian Captain

Adam Schlooz as Guard #1
Amron McCormack as Warrior #1
Campbell Roussell as Warrior #2

When Ares uses the metal of Hephaestus to create an unstoppable army, Xena must create her own army to try to prevent him from destroying the world.

Hephaestus was the son of Zeus and Hera (see "Cradle of Hope," "Prometheus," and "For Him The Bell Tolls"), and was god of the smith-fire and forge, and of artisans in metal — goldsmiths, jewellers, blacksmiths — and also masons and carpenters. Hephaestus was a crippled god, about which there are various explanations. According to one version, Zeus and Hera were fighting and Hephaestus took his mother's side. Zeus angrily grabbed Hephaestus by the leg and threw him off Mt. Olympus. Hephaestus had a great long fall, and when he landed he was crippled for life, having to wear a leg iron, which he made for himself in gold. Another version says he was born deformed, and to avoid being humiliated by the other gods Hera threw Hephaestus off of Olympus. Out of revenge he built a throne of gold and sent it to Hera. Anyone who sat in the throne would immediately be enveloped in chains that would never release them (much like Sisyphus's chair in "Death in Chains"). Without thinking Hera sat in the chair and was trapped. Dionysus went to Hephaestus to convince him to release her, and helped sway Hephaestus's judgement by getting him drunk. Hephaestus returned to Olympus and freed Hera.

Hephaestus was an inventor and craftsman of unparalleled ingenuity, creating just about anything he put his mind to, and he has been mentioned several times on both *X:WP* and *H:TLJ* (on the latter, Atalanta keeps a statue of Hephaestus in her home). He formed Pandora out of clay for Zeus, created the chains that bound Prometheus, and Xena's chakram is apparently made from the metal of Hephaestus. He was married to Aphrodite, by most accounts against her will, and was linked with other females such as Charis and Aglaea. By most other accounts, however, he was not a favorite with the ladies.

Despite his many mentions on *X:WP*, Hephaestus never materializes, although he has appeared in *H:TLJ* ("Love Takes a Holiday"). Instead he is mentioned by mortals and gods like Ares. "The Dirty Half Dozen" was a poor episode because of its predictability and tired dialogue. Also, they aired it out of order — "The Deliverer" was supposed to appear before "The Dirty Half Dozen" — adding to the feeling of disjointedness that permeates the third season episodes (see "The Deliverer" for more explanation). Watch how "The Deliverer" opens with Ares talking about a new metal Hephaestus has invented that will allow him to take over the world. Oops.

Until now the feminist aspects of the show have been subtle in the sense that Xena is tough and Gabrielle is intelligent, yet neither feel compelled to have to explain why. Yet now they include a character like Glaphyra who, while being an intriguing character at first, is a devout man-hater spewing pro-feminist, anti-chauvinist epithets that were too obvious to be

Oh, Ares! Kevin Smith at Burbank, 1998

AMY PUTNAM

put on this show. Whether the fact that she ends up falling for Darnelle is
meant to be ironic or whether it's meant to be a way of teaching her the
error of her ways is unclear: the entire concept was just far too annoying.

This episode did feature one highlight: the debut of Gabrielle's new
outfit, although the change was very subtle. The top got shorter, so instead

of being the "bilious green sports bra," it's more like a push-up bra. Again, this outfit was actually supposed to debut in "The Deliverer." The question is, what was the reasoning behind the change? Why did Gabrielle go from being scantily-dressed to even *more* scantily-dressed? Also, did anyone else notice that her bangs appear to have been cut by that blind Cyclops?

The plot line concerning the metal of Hephaestus was silly and inconsistent. Those soldiers looked more like Robocops than anything else, and had those suits really been made of solid metal, they wouldn't have been able to move, much less defeat an army of 6,000 men single-handedly. In medieval times, the reason knights tried to stay mounted on their horses was because they knew if they had to fight while standing, they'd be at a severe disadvantage. And as for Agathon, why did Ares choose such a wuss for the leader of his army?

The best part of this episode was the discussion between Xena and Gabrielle about how Xena creates evil within otherwise innocent people. Gabrielle asks if she is who she is because Xena made her that way, and Xena eventually concludes that no, Gabrielle made herself the bright, strong individual she is. Is Xena correct, or is she trying to get herself off the hook for possibly being responsible for the fact that Gabrielle inflicts irreversible brain damage on her victims week after week? Xena cares for Gabrielle more than anyone and it's clear that Gabrielle's question is a painful one. Is it too late for Gabrielle to turn away? I feel a rift coming on . . .

NITPICK: There was a severe inconsistency with the potency of the armor: somehow the armor breaks Xena's sword in half, yet it doesn't even mark Gabrielle's wooden staff.

OOPS: After Xena breaks her sword, it mysteriously reappears without being marked. Also, the explosion at the end wasn't very subtle. It was pretty obvious that those rocks in front of the castle doorway contained the explosives — I mean, who puts a huge pile of rocks in front of their door?

DISCLAIMER: "No Convicts were reformed during the production of this motion picture. Can't we all just get along?"

304 The Deliverer

ORIGINAL AIR DATE: October 20, 1997
WRITTEN BY: Steven L. Sears
DIRECTED BY: Oley Sassone
GUEST CAST: Kevin Smith as Ares
Jennifer Ward-Lealand as Boadicea
Marton Csokas as Khrafstar
Meighan Desmond as Discord
Karl Urban as Caesar
Catherine Boniface as Meridian

Anthony Ray Parker as Deliverer
Anton Bentley as Centurion
Patrick Kuhtze as Brit Guard
David Holton as Lieutenant
John Manning as Captain
Brad Homan as Jiela
Daniel Martin as Soldier
Andre Coppell as Squad Leader

Xena and Gabrielle travel to Britannia so that Xena can help Boadicea fight Caesar, and Gabrielle meets Khrafstar, the priest of the temple of the one god. Little does Gabrielle know, he will be her downfall.

Was it inevitable? Couldn't Gabrielle continue to be pure? "The Deliverer" is the first episode of what has been deemed "the Rift Saga," a series of episodes where Gabrielle and Xena systematically change personalities, betray one another, and break down the trust and devotion that has always bonded them together. Apparently the producers though this was something that had to happen.

While "The Deliverer" was a visually stunning episode directed by the ever-brilliant Oley Sassone, it crosses a line that didn't have to be broached on this show. Gabrielle is violated, both physically and emotionally, and when this happens, it causes a huge chasm to open between her and Xena. One explanation is that Dahak knows Xena is the only person who can stop him (M'Lila had told her earlier that now that she knows evil she can fight evil). Thus, by causing a chasm between Xena and Gabrielle, Dahak makes Xena vulnerable enough to let him slip into the world.

A pleasant surprise in this episode was the character of Boadicea, one of the fiercest and greatest woman warriors in history. It is believed that Boadicea's real name was Boudicca, or Boudica, the Queen of the Iceni in East Anglia. Now the name Boadicea is generally used to refer to the mythic woman, the character who was embellished in plays and poems beginning in the seventeenth century.

Boudica was married to Prasutagus, the King of the Iceni, a tribe that had descended from the Celts. Prasutagus was a very wealthy king, and he had formed an important alliance with Nero, the Roman emperor. The Romans had first invaded Iceni territory in about 55 BC when Julius Caesar crossed the Thames with his troops. In 43 AD, Emperor Claudius again invaded Britain and began what became a 400-year occupation of the territory. An alliance with Emperor Nero was a very shrewd move for Prasutagus, and one he thought would insure the Iceni a certain amount of independence.

When Prasutagus died in 60 AD, he left half of his wealth to Boudica, who would probably have been in her thirties, and their two young daughters. The other half was given to Nero, and a healthy alliance should have followed. Needless to say, it didn't. The Romans took all the wealth and the castle, flogged Boudica with stones and humiliated her and raped her two daughters. They were banished from the castle, and Boudica immediately went and formed an army of her own to wreak vengeance on the Romans for committing such injustices to her and her family (sound familiar?). By most accounts her army was 120,000 strong, and more than half of it was comprised of women. Together they took the Roman-occupied cities of Camulodunum (present-day Colchester), Condinium (London), and Verulamium (St. Albans). Boudica's forces destroyed most of the Roman settlements by fire, and killed roughly 70,000 people.

The commander of the Roman forces, Suetonius Paulinus, collected two legions from Rome to fight in what would be Boudica's last battle. Somewhere in the Midlands, the Britons came up against Suetonius's army to fight a battle that lasted the entire day. Each member of the Roman infantry had two 7-foot javelins, and the cavalry had lances. As the Britons attacked the Romans held their ground, then threw the javelins. The cavalry then stepped in to take care of what was left of the army.

It is estimated that 80,000 Britons died that day. Boudica was among the dead, but it is believed she did not die in battle, but by her own hand as she took poison and most likely administered it to her daughters. Because of her bravery she became a figure of legend as Boadicea, a warrior woman with flaming red hair and fierce eyes, who rode in a chariot.

The Boadicea in "The Deliverer" is much like this legend, and with the exception of Xena, is the most exciting female warrior on this show yet. Unlike some of the women portrayed on *X:WP*, Boadicea does not wear a size two set of armor, and she is believably fierce. The problem occurs when Xena steps in to take over the plans of attack. If this series is about historical revision and about suggesting that women had a larger role in wars than the history books suggest, why would they try to take away the glory of the one historical female used thus far and attribute her deeds to Xena? There is absolutely no logic behind this reasoning.

Also, the character of Boadicea is wasted in an episode that becomes completely centred on Gabrielle. Just as the Britons are about to attack the Romans, Xena realizes that Gabrielle is in trouble and she leaves Boadicea in the lurch as she runs away to rescue her friend. In "Maternal Instincts" we find out from Ephiny that Boadicea won the battle, when in fact this should have been the one she lost. Considering that Caesar had been dead for over a century when the battle occurred, though, we can give them this little inconsistency.

Once in the temple, what happens with Gabrielle is traumatic for both Xena and the viewer to watch. When Gabrielle kills to save Khrafstar, her blood innocence is gone. She has risked her life in numerous episode — "Dreamworker," "Return of Callisto," and "The Price" to name a few — to avoid killing others, yet she makes a fatal error and goes against everything she believes in. Reneé is fantastic in this scene as she stares at her bloody hands in shock-filled horror, and her scream is one that echoes for many episodes afterward.

Where losing her blood innocence would have been traumatic enough, the writers add to Gabrielle's woes by having her dragged by the flames of

Dahak over his altar, where she is enveloped, prodded, and seemingly molested by the flames, which is apparent by the look of pain on her face. The effects were amazing, but because this scene is suggestive of rape, this episode was not a safe one for children, which Lucy herself stated at a recent convention. Gabrielle was supposed to be a kind of proof that peacefulness can conquer violence, but her goodness is sacrificed in this scene. As we shall see in "The Bitter Suite," it is in Dahak's temple where Gabrielle gained the ability to hate.

"The Deliverer" had a lot of potential, and featured some awesome special effects. However, by including Boadicea, Caesar, Khrafstar, Dahak, the loss of Gabrielle's blood innocence, and possibly a rape, it featured far too many elements for one episode. Boadicea's battle should have concluded and Gabrielle had far too many horrifying things happen to her at once. This should have been a two-parter, and the writers should have come up with another way to bring Dahak into the world rather than sacrifice Gabrielle's very soul. Granted, without doing so, there would have been no rift saga.

TIME: 60 AD

NITPICK: How could Dahak's temple have become Stonehenge, when Stonehenge is one of the baffling megaliths that was probably erected somewhere between 4000 and 1500 BC?

DISCLAIMER: "Gabrielle was slightly well-done during the production of this motion picture. However, the producers would like to recommend a zesty barbecue sauce to bring out the full flavor of the episode."

305 Gabrielle's Hope

ORIGINAL AIR DATE: October 27, 1997
WRITTEN BY: R.J. Stewart
DIRECTED BY: Charles Siebert and Andrew Merrifield
GUEST CAST: Peter Feeney as Caswallawn
Mark Clare as Eochaid
Robert Harte as Goewin
Michelle Huirama as Banshee #1
Nicola Brown as Banshee #2
Catherine Boniface as Meridian
David Mitchell as Tavernkeeper
Bert Keiller as Cadbury
Ronald Fryer as Old Man
Summer Proben as Hope (Toddler)
Hannah Carr and Alyssa Carr as Hope (10 Months)

When Gabrielle learns she has been impregnated by Dahak, she is forced to choose between the baby and Xena, who wants it dead.

As if "The Deliverer" didn't desecrate Gabrielle's character enough, now she is carrying the child of evil and sees Xena as her number-one enemy. In an attempt to drive a wedge between the two friends, the writers resurrect the plot from *Rosemary's Baby* and have them run around Britannia with banshees and the precursors to King Arthur's knights. Despite the fact that Gabrielle and Xena are driven apart, however, the rift is cleverly handled, and the situation becomes so complicated that the viewer is forced to see both sides of the issue and sympathize with both women.

One of the more disturbing aspects of this episode was when Gabrielle turns to the banshees over Xena. The banshee is a Celtic spirit of the dead. Her wailing foretold a coming death, and it is said she would repeat over and over the name of the person who would die. If she saw the traveller before he saw her, it is believed he would die immediately. In "Gabrielle's Hope" this aspect of the myth is altered slightly to suggest that they alternate between physical and spiritual beings, so they can hit Xena, whereas she can't hit them back because they've become ethereal again. The banshee of folklore usually had white hair, hollow eye-sockets, and a flattened nose, and she was depicted with a flowing white robe that was often in tatters.

The knights of the round table are also an interesting element in this episode. These are not Arthur's knights, but rather their predecessors. When Gabrielle asks about the sword in the stone, they reply that the sword was placed there by a man who was king before the Romans came. According to legend, however, the sword was placed in the stone by King Uther of Pendragon, who was Arthur's father and, if he existed at all, probably reigned in the fifth century AD. Arthur pulled the sword from the stone and became king, then later broke the sword in battle. The Lady of the Lake then gave him another sword, which he called Excalibur. Arthur established the round table as a way of avoiding hierarchy among his knights; in the event of a dispute, no knight would be closer to the head of the table, and thus could not claim more authority than any other. According to Geoffrey of Monmouth, Arthur died in 542 AD at the battle of Camblan in Cornwall, after having been betrayed and defeated by his nephew Mordred. Xena pulling the sword from the stone here is a nice touch, and one of the more clever revisionist moments on the show.

The birth scene itself is spectacular. The music, the effects, the lighting, and the acting are amazing, and the pounding music coupled with the knights pounding their way into the stable creates a heart-stopping suspense. The similarities to Christ's birth are there — the baby is born in a stable, animals are watching, men have been sent to kill it — but made subtle enough that it doesn't overshadow this storyline. It's not clear why they keep zooming in on the ram intently watching the birth, other than perhaps that the ram looks uncannily like the Deliverer. Could he have returned to ensure that the birth would go as planned?

Both Gabrielle and Xena have good reasons for acting the way they do. Xena has seen everything that has happened and is convinced that Hope must be destroyed. After all, Gabrielle undergoes her entire pregnancy in a single day, and the baby is ten months old by the second day. The baby entered the world amidst lightning and darkness, and Xena watched Gabrielle as she was enveloped by the fire as Dahak's seed was being planted. Gabrielle, on the other hand, gave birth to the child; Hope was a part of her. Although the child was born during a storm, when she arrived all was light. Yes, she seems to be growing at a remarkable rate but that's because she is a demigod, as Gabrielle sees it. Gabrielle is entirely convinced that because Hope is a part of her, she cannot be pure evil, which is why the scenes of Xena chasing Hope around trying to kill her are so painful.

In the end, Gabrielle betrays Xena by lying to her. But what else could she have done? Xena refused to listen to Gabrielle's pleas because Xena thought what she was doing would benefit the greater good. The communication has completely broken down between the two women, and the friendship has definitely suffered a harsh blow. The question is, how could Gabrielle possibly stay with Xena after what has happened? As far as Gabrielle's concerned, Xena tried to kill an innocent baby — Gabrielle's baby — and that should have been unforgivable. Is what happens in the next episode Gabrielle's revenge?

NITPICK: How does Xena keep up with Gabrielle and Hope when the latter two are on a horse and Xena's on foot?

DISCLAIMER: "Despite witnessing the bizarre and somewhat disturbing birth of Gabrielle's Hope, no farm animals were harmed or traumatized during the production of this motion picture."

306 The Debt

ORIGINAL AIR DATE: November 3, 1997
TELEPLAY BY: R.J. Stewart
STORY BY: Robert Tapert & R.J. Stewart
DIRECTED BY: Oley Sassone
GUEST CAST: Jacqueline Kim as Lao Ma
Marton Csokas as Borias
Grant McFarland as Ming Tzu
Daniel Sing as Ming T'ien
Daniel Lim as Ming T'ien (12 years)
Tai Hadfield as Chuang
Blair Fraser as Messenger
Peter Mason as Shopkeeper
William Kwan as Soldier

Xena receives a cryptic message from someone in her past, and as she heads to Chin to fulfill what has been asked of her, she begins to tell Gabrielle about the events in her life that took place after M'Lila was killed.

"The Debt" episodes are visually stunning, with breathtakingly beautiful scenes, and feature the best performances yet by both Reneé and Lucy. However, by being the most powerful they were also problematic, and were potentially the most dangerous for the producers of the show. Both Reneé and Lucy begged the audience at the Valley Forge convention not to hate them for making these episodes, and the week before they aired a representative from *X:WP*'s merchandising company wrote to various online mailing lists to tell fans to tape "The Debt" and watch it with "The Debt II," or else we could end up hating one of the characters for an entire week. Obviously some people were having second thoughts about being involved with this one!

Answering the requests of fans who asked for more information about Xena's past, the writers of this episode continue where "Destiny" left off, explaining what happened after M'Lila had been killed. Somehow Xena linked up with Borias and went to the kingdom of Chin (China), although we're never told how she met him. Borias — mentioned earlier as the father of Solan ("Orphan of War") — is played well by Marton Csokas, although the fact that we *just* saw him as Khrafstar in "The Deliverer" makes his first appearance a little disconcerting.

The episode opens with a great kung fu scene, although *enough* with the warrior spinning the two swords! It was hilarious in *Raiders of the Lost Ark*, but it must have been used at least three or four times on this show so far. The messenger brings Xena news from "the weak one, who is as soft as water, and as hard as the raging flood," whom we later discover as Lao Ma, wife of Lao Tzu, the author of the *Tao Te Ching* (see "The Debt II" for more information on Taoism).

As Xena begins to tell Gabrielle her story, she once again becomes cryptic. Gabrielle has expressed her annoyance at Xena's enigmatic methods of storytelling in the past, yet Xena continues to talk in circles, and this time her avoidance of the issue will land her in deep trouble. Xena's story begins with how she lashed out at the world after being betrayed by Caesar. As she places the heads of her victims on stakes and puts them into rows, she gruesomely mimics his practice of planting crucifixes in a row to send a message to the enemy.

The early Xena is not the shrewd, intelligent woman she will eventually become. She is a very different person, and throughout her story Gabrielle constantly interrupts to express her disbelief that Xena used to be this violent and evil. Xena tells Gabrielle to stay behind and not get involved, but she accompanies her, only to realize that she doesn't want to follow her all the way to Chin. Why does she accompany her to the boat? Does she plan on betraying Xena from the outset as some form of revenge? Or does she want to understand Xena and perhaps talk her out of what she's about to do? Why is Hope or what Gabrielle has just suffered through not mentioned at all? (These questions are eventually answered in a clip show later in the season called "Forget Me Not.")

Given the discrepancies of this episode, though, overall it was amazing to watch. Lao Ma is the freshest character on the show yet, and whenever the show was set in the "present" with Xena telling Gabrielle her story, I longed for an immediate return to Lao Ma. When Xena tries to kill Lao Ma early on, Lao Ma's graceful yet sharp movements stun the viewer with their simple complexities, setting us up for Xena's encounter with Taoism, a philosophy of paradoxes. The scenes with Xena and Lao Ma have a more serious lesbian innuendo than those with Gabrielle and Xena have ever had, for although Xena is the more powerful physically, Lao Ma is still in control and she makes Xena fall in love with her. Never have we seen Xena have this much respect for a single person, but Lao Ma earns every bit of it. Lao Ma tells Xena that she doesn't eat meat, which is in keeping with common Taoist practices but is also a euphemism for lesbianism. Jacqueline Kim delivers the line seriously and with dignity, the way the subtext should be handled on the show. When Lao Ma and Xena exchange breath in the underwater "kiss" scene, it is both surprising yet so tactfully handled. Notice that two of the doorways in Lao Ma's palace are ornamented exactly like the chakram.

Lao Ma tells Xena she is a woman capable of greatness, and she is probably the first person to have ever said that to Xena. She also makes comments that seem enigmatic to Xena, such as "Fill yourself with desire and see only illusion. Empty yourself of desire and understand the great mystery of things." Xena will later understand the meaning of her words, and so will we. Lucy is great in this episode, especially as she stumbles through the forest with Ming Tzu's hounds in hot pursuit. So, too, is the young actor who plays Ming Tien. This boy is wonderful as the precociously stern son of Ming Tzu, who scowls at Lao Ma yet keeps a completely solemn face throughout. The stand-out, though, is Jacqueline Kim as Lao Ma. Kim is known best for her work in *Star Trek Generations* as Demora Sulu, and she plays Lao Ma with such subtlety, beauty, and poise that she is perhaps the single best guest star on the show to date.

The final scene, where Gabrielle betrays Xena, is one of the most memorable scenes on *X:WP*, which will still be discussed in seasons to come. Xena rises from the water like some primordial creature, a scene directly copied from Francis Ford Coppolla's 1979 film, *Apocalypse Now*. Considering that the film was actually a retelling of Joseph Conrad's 1899 novella, *Heart of Darkness*, perhaps the writers are paying homage to this novella as their inspiration for this episode.

Only, the ending isn't what you'd expect. As Xena steadies the dagger, ready to plunge it into the chest of Ming Tien, what happens next probably caused every *X:WP* viewer to make an audible noise of some sort. The covers are thrown back to reveal Gabrielle, and the look on Lucy's face is one of stunned silence, as she struggles to comprehend what Gabrielle has done to her. Xena's been betrayed by Darphus, Borias, Caesar, and many others, but Gabrielle?! And as the viewers try to get their hearts out of their mouths, they are told it will be continued next week! "The horror, the horror," indeed.

TIME: 6th century BC, around the time that Lao Tzu wrote *Tao Te Ching*.

OOPS: In the kung fu scene at the beginning, Xena's chakram flies off her hip, but is back again in the next shot. Also, after the fight scene with Lao Ma, Borias leans down to tell Xena she must leave his camp. Watch the blood coming from her nose: shot from the side you can see it come down past her lips, yet straight on there's no trace of blood.

DISCLAIMER: "No Frock Tarts were killed during the production of this motion picture although they wish they had been." ["Frock tarts" is a Kiwi term for the costume designers.]

307 The Debt II

ORIGINAL AIR DATE: November 10, 1997
TELEPLAY BY: R.J. Stewart
STORY BY: Robert Tapert & R.J. Stewart
DIRECTED BY: Oley Sassone
GUEST CAST: Jacqueline Kim as Lao Ma
Marton Csokas as Borias
Grant McFarland as Ming Tzu
Daniel Sing as Ming T'ien
Daniel Lim as Ming T'ien (12 years)
Tai Hadfield as Chuang
Ric Chan as Jiu
Din Tran as Prison Guard

Gabrielle realizes that what she did was wrong and Xena finally understands everything that Lao Ma was trying to teach her.

After a gruelling week of wondering if Gabrielle's gone completely berserk, we realize that she deceived Xena because she'd gotten Ming Tien's word that Xena wouldn't be hurt. Regardless, she has betrayed Xena, who is thrown into a torturous prison. The prison scene itself is brilliant — prisoners are forced to wear what look like tables around their necks and walk around in filthy water up to their waists. The "lucky" few find rocks to sit on, but they shiver with cold as they perch atop them. Even Xena, who is rarely scared of anything, looks terrified right before she is thrown into the water (which, by the way, should have broken her legs and/or her neck as the board hit the water).

While in the prison, Xena has time to reflect on her past once again. Taking Xena under her wing, Lao Ma introduces her to her husband, Lao Tzu, an old man whom she keeps in a comatose state by using pressure points. Lao Tzu is the purported author of the *Tao Te Ching*, the testament of Taoism. Born in Ch'ü-jen, he was eventually appointed to the office of *shih* in the court of the Chou dynasty (1111–255 BC). The *shih* was a scholar who specialized in divination and astrology. Lao Tzu left the Chou dynasty when he realized it was sinking into spiritual decay along with the rest of the world. He decided he would go into the desert, but was stopped at Han-ku Pass by a gatekeeper who asked him to write a book. According to legend, Lao Tzu wrote the *Tao Te Ching*, which consisted of 5,000 characters and was divided into 81 sections, and he continued on his way. Little is known of his life after that, but Lao Tzu is still generally respected in China to this day, and he was worshipped by many succeeding dynasties. To suggest that it was written by his wife instead is not far-fetched, for many scholars have commented on how feminine some of the teachings seem to be.

The *Tao Te Ching* is a complicated yet simple text, and there is no way justice could be done to it here in a few paragraphs, so I will limit discussion of it to the passages that are relevant to *X:WP*. "Tao" is generally translated as the Path or the Way, the process by which one may achieve "enlightenment," and many philosophers suggest that Tao is, in essence, God. Taoism consists of numerous ideas that are essential to following that Path. It is interesting that the writers of *X:WP* decided to explore Taoism over every other philosophy, for the term Taoist is synonymous with the term, "Scholar Warrior," used to describe those who were following the way of Tao. Students of Tao are encouraged to spend a long time allowing its tenets to be absorbed. For most students, it takes a number of years to fully understand the Way; for Xena, it took over ten.

There are many aspects that must be understood. Although I'm forced to over-simplify them here, I encourage others to read more about it, for the way the writers of *X:WP* have used it on the show is wonderful and subtle. Learning about Tao offers a better understanding of the character of Lao Ma and what she teaches Xena. An important aspect is that of duality and opposites. Taoists believe that everything has an opposite, and that anything that displays extreme qualities will eventually display the opposite. Thus, Lao Ma takes Xena under her wing because she's convinced that Xena will eventually be a good warrior. Taoists believe in five elements: metal, fire, water, earth, and wood, of which water is the most important. Consider the initial description of Lao Ma: "soft as water; as hard as the raging flood." Water imagery is used, as is the Taoist idea of duality and paradox. If we look at some of the verses or chapters of the *Tao Te Ching*, we immediately find many elements that are mentioned in "The Debt" episodes. Verse 38 states that a truly good person doesn't know he is good, just as Xena doesn't realize she has the ability to do good. Verse 76 states, "The hard and strong will fall. / The soft and weak will overcome." Lao Ma overcomes Xena, and tries to convince her that she, too, must be weak. Verse 61 states that "The female overcomes the male with stillness." Ming Tien thought he overcame his mother when he killed her, but she is the one who ultimately won. When the people of the kingdom remember Lao Ma, they remember her goodness. They despise Ming Tien. Verse 78 seems to describe the character of Lao Ma, and the writers probably used it to inspire them: "Under heaven nothing is more soft and yielding than water. / Yet for attacking the solid and strong, nothing is better . . ." Verse 33 is where the writer got Lao Ma's credo, "To conquer others is to have power; to conquer yourself is to know the way."

Lucy is wonderful once again, although in the scene where Lao Ma shows her how she breaks bottles, Xena's character is completely inconsistent. She speaks, holds her face, and walks like Meg, not Xena. Where does that come from? Jacqueline Kim is amazing and if any one supporting character on the show is nominated for an Emmy it should be Kim. But the best acting goes to Reneé. When she explains to Xena how wrong she was as the two are standing in the water-deluged prison, her face looks like she's in deep pain. Her choking sob is like the one she uttered in "The Quest," and we all breathed a huge sigh of relief in that scene. Lucy and Reneé were phenomenal.

At the end of this episode Xena understands what Lao Ma means when she tells her to empty herself of hate, but does she follow her teachings? No. She uses them to destroy the palace and get herself out of the situation, and when Ming Tien mocks her she gives in to his taunts and kills him, letting on to Gabrielle that she didn't. Why did she lie? In killing Ming Tien, she has not made him small as Lao Ma suggested. Verse 31 of the *Tao Te Ching* reads, "If you rejoice in victory, then you delight in killing; / If you delight in killing, you cannot fulfill yourself." Xena will always turn to killing, and it is when we see this side of her that we understand why Gabrielle betrayed her. Xena's lie at the end of the episode is added to the pile of hatred that has been building up. "The Debt" and "The Debt II" were both amazing episodes, and possibly the bumpiest emotional roller coaster we've seen yet (only to be matched by the upcoming "Maternal Instincts" and "The Bitter Suite").

NITPICK: Why does Gabrielle hit Xena? The act was entirely out of character for Gabrielle, even if she were desperate, and it was just a contrived act to put a bigger chasm between the two. Also, she lost her blood innocence trying to save Khrafstar, yet here she makes *no* attempt to save Xena.

DISCLAIMER: "Xena and Gabrielle's relationship suffered another blow (although Gabrielle doesn't know it yet) during the production of this motion picture."

308 King of Assassins

ORIGINAL AIR DATE: November 17, 1997
WRITTEN BY: Adam Armus & Nora Kay Foster
DIRECTED BY: Bruce Campbell
GUEST CAST: Ted Raimi as Joxer
            Gina Torres as Cleopatra
            Bruce Campbell as Autolycus

Jonathon Hendry as Pontius
Larry Keating as Warlord
Christian Hodge as Prisoner
Benjamin Banse as Prison Guard
Russell Raethel as Guard #3
Nerida Nichols as Chambermaid
Jeremy Birchall as The Other Joxer/Jett

Gabrielle and Autolycus must try to save Cleopatra when they realize Joxer's twin brother, Jett, has been hired to assassinate her.

While "King of Assassins" was absolutely hilarious (largely due to Bruce Campbell), it was disturbing for two reasons. First, it interrupted the rift saga, and by airing after such solemn episodes, the actions of both Xena and Gabrielle seem completely out of character. Second, are the writers so mired in dark rift plot lines that the only way they can create humor is to show us yet another lookalike episode? First it was Lucy, now it's Ted. Those complaints aside, this was a very entertaining hour.

Cleopatra (69 BC–30 BC) was the daughter of King Ptolemy XII who died in 51 BC, leaving her and her brother, Ptolemy XIII, to rule Egypt. Her family wasn't actually Egyptian — they were of the Macedonian dynasty — yet Cleopatra learned Egyptian when she became ruler. Soon after becoming king, Ptolemy ousted Cleopatra from the throne through a civil war, and the kingdom was divided. Julius Caesar entered the scene when he chased Pompey into Egypt. Cleopatra seduced him, and it worked (if only Xena knew that Cleopatra would succeed where she had failed). She was a very ambitious woman, and assumed that if she could win over Caesar and become his bride, she'd be a very powerful woman. Caesar fought in the civil war and won, thereby restoring the brother-sister rule. Caesar returned to Rome after a brief affair with Cleopatra, and it is believed that he was the father of Cleopatra's first son, Caesarion.

In 45, Cleopatra and Ptolemy XIII went to Rome where Caesar had them honored, but when Caesar was assassinated in 44 BC, she returned to Egypt. In 42 Mark Antony became Caesar's heir-general, and Cleopatra realized that he was now the most powerful man in Rome. When he first saw her, Antony was immediately taken with her, and he followed her to Alexandria, where he vowed his undying love to her (despite already being married).

Meanwhile, a young Octavian, who was the real heir to Caesar's throne, started campaigns against Antony. In 40 BC, Antony returned to Italy, and in an attempt to appease Octavian, he married Octavian's sister, Octavia. Octavia was insulted, and Rome turned against Antony. In 34 both Antony and Cleopatra assumed the throne in Alexandria and Antony declared Caesarion to be Caesar's son, thus making Caesarion Caesar's legal heir. In 31, as Antony and Cleopatra were facing off against Octavian, Cleopatra suddenly took her ship and left the battle. Antony was defeated. He followed her, but she soon realized that she had nothing to gain from him now that he'd been defeated, and in a reversal of *Romeo and Juliet* she went to her mausoleum and sent messengers to tell Antony she was dead. When

Antony heard the news he fell on his sword out of grief. Octavian, now Augustus, heard that Cleopatra was vulnerable and decided to make an example of her and her children. Rather than be humiliated in front of her own people, she killed herself — probably with an asp — and she was buried with Antony. With their deaths, the Roman Republic was finished. Cleopatra was the last of the Macedonian queens.

"King of Assassins" appears to take place as Cleopatra is in the midst of the civil war with her brother. The choice of actresses was an intelligent one — Cleopatra probably resembled this actress more than she did Elizabeth Taylor. Reneé is very funny, and if the viewer can momentarily forget what has just happened in Britannia and Chin, they can enjoy this glimpse of the old Gabrielle: funny, intelligent, and chatty. Her "chakram" toss in the jail scene is particularly hysterical. Ted Raimi was also good, although Jett was not a convincing character. Raimi is a superb comic actor, but his dark side isn't particularly entertaining. The fact that after wearing his goofy armor all the time he just "happens" to go out and get an outfit that's exactly like his brother's is one of the most far-fetched things they've done on this show yet. All in all, this was amusing, but it had its problems.

TIME: 49–48 BC, the time of civil war between Cleopatra and Ptolemy.

GABRIELLE'S FIGHTING SKILLS: The scene at the end where Gabrielle takes on the two soldiers near the bath is her best fight scene yet.

NITPICKS: If Autolycus is the King of Thieves, why do we always see him getting caught? He set off the alarms in "The Royal Couple of Thieves," *H:TLJ*'s "Beanstalks and Bad Eggs," and at the beginning of this episode. He got caught trying to steal Xena's body and almost completely botched the dagger of Helios theft. Also, why would Xena have insisted that Gabrielle just go and tell Cleopatra that there was going to be an attempt on her life? Wouldn't Gabrielle be repeating what she'd just done in Chin?

OOPS: The double who plays Ted Raimi's back in the scenes with the twins looks nothing like him. He has sideburns (Raimi's hair doesn't even appear to be able to grow that way) and there are times when you see him straight on by accident. Not even close.

DISCLAIMER: "Due to the infliction of a severe wedgie, Joxer was slightly uncomfortable but not seriously harmed during the production of this motion picture."

309 Warrior . . . Priestess . . . Tramp

ORIGINAL AIR DATE: January 12, 1998
WRITTEN BY: Adam Armus and Nora Kay Foster
DIRECTED BY: Robert Ginty
GUEST CAST: Ted Raimi as Joxer
Macgregor Cameron as Bailius
Matty J. Ruys as Dexon

Ted Clarke as Thoracles

Tim Hosking as Blacksmith

Rob Sinkinson as Bystander/Drunk
Megan Nicol as Hestian Virgin #1
Jan Hellriegel as Hestian Virgin #2
Fred Morton as Bordello Girl #1
Jodie Dorday as Bordello Girl #2
Rachale Davies as Bordello Girl #3
Polly Baigent & Bobbie McKay as Xena/Leah/Meg
    Body Doubles

When Gabrielle finds a Hestian virgin who is identical to Xena, she and Xena must stop a plot against the temple of Hestia.

Well, folks, it's yet another lookalike episode. Once was funny, twice is silly (but still funny), but three times? (And they're not stopping there: watch next season for "Warrior . . . Poetess . . . Tramp.") This episode was *very* funny for the first half, but the second half of the show, where all the mix-ups and misunderstandings occur, was too much like last season's lookalike episode.

In this installment of the "coincidentally identical twin" gag, we are introduced to Leah, a virgin Hestian goddess with a speech impediment ("Allow me to intwoduce myself . . ."). Gabrielle finds Leah in a village (being sacrificed by a warlord) and she and Xena return to the temple with her, only to discover that Leah's being impersonated by Meg, whom we immediately recognize when she begins her sermon with a dirty joke. Throughout the episode, Leah's scorn and shock at considering any life involving sex is continuously funny, and her narrow view of what makes a woman pure is discredited. We discover that Meg works in a brothel, yet we never find out why. Last time we saw her she was King Lius's chef, yet there is no mention made of that, either. Meg had had a real cathartic experience in "Warrior . . . Princess . . . Tramp," and for that to be completely overlooked in this episode was not only disappointing, but very sloppy writing.

It's obvious they used a priestess because she'd be the direct opposite of Meg. It's disappointing that the titles of these episodes insist on referring to Meg as a tramp, which is a demeaning and sexist term. Luckily, the women in the brothel are made out to be fairly intelligent and independent. The best part of the episode is when Leah gets lost in the brothel, and as she opens door after door looking for Gabrielle, her look of shock at what she *does* find is priceless.

Joxer is a strange character in this one (and the 32 Variations on "Joxer the Mighty" is getting a little tired). We discover he frequents a brothel probably because only here is he made to feel like a true warrior, and Meg is still his favorite. Yet, he refers to Gabrielle as the woman he loves, then risks his life saving Meg, but only after insulting Meg to a woman whom he thought was Leah. It sounds like someone is a little confused. The dungeon, where he's eventually imprisoned, is the same one from "King of Assassins," and there's a very clever moment when he begins playing an ancient Greek version of Six Degrees of Separation with the guard.

"Warrior . . . Priestess . . . Tramp" is a funny episode, but you'd think Xena would start to question why so many women look like her. In my opinion, this plot is getting a little ridiculous.

NITPICK: Leah's lisp oscillates between sounding like Elmer Fudd and a New Zealander. Also, if Leah's the only woman who knows the ancient language of Hestian, as Bailius says, how do the other virgins understand her when she speaks the language?

DISCLAIMER: "Despite another Xena lookalike, the gene pool (or rather gene puddle) was not harmed during the production of this motion picture."

310 The Quill Is Mightier . . .

ORIGINAL AIR DATE: January 12, 1998
WRITTEN BY: Hilary J. Bader
DIRECTED BY: Andrew Merrifield
GUEST CAST: Ted Raimi as Joxer
              Alexandra Tydings as Aphrodite
              Kevin Smith as Ares
              Alison Wall as Minya
              Stephen Hall as Thelonius
              Ranald Hendriks as Munk
              John McKee as Scaberus
              Lawrence Makoare as Barbarian Leader
              Chris Auchinvole as Man
              Alvin Fitisemanu as Tavern Keeper
              Ann Baxter as Woman/Village Woman/Old Woman
              Jean Hyland as Priestess #1
              Beryl Te Wiata as Priestess #2
              Paul Norell as Peddler
              Peter Mason as Billius
              Andrew Glover as Man #2

When Aphrodite realizes that Xena is more popular than she is because of Gabrielle's stories, she puts a curse on Gabrielle's scrolls, making whatever Gabrielle writes come true.

I don't know who Hilary J. Bader is, but in writing only two very funny episodes of *X:WP*, she's become one of my favorites. Of course, "The Quill Is Mightier . . ." was just one more comic episode that delayed the end of the rift saga, but it was a welcome digression.

Ares and Aphrodite are at their funniest as they become squabbling siblings, and we get to see what happens to the goddess of love when she becomes a mortal, praying for the invention of hairspray and deodorant.

Joxer's presence in this Xena-lite episode doesn't become the focal point, as it did in "For Him The Bell Tolls" and "King of Assassins." Instead he stays off to one side, allowing the show's emphasis to be on Gabrielle while he remains a bumbling sidekick.

The tone of the episode is established in the opening, where two kids are spray-painting graffiti onto Aphrodite's temple walls, shouting, "Xena rules! Aphrodite blows!" as they run away. For the first time this season, the show returns to its origins — a campy show where 1990s language permeates ancient Greece. The opening fight scene with Gabrielle was the most over-the-top scene yet, but it was funny because we already know it's not supposed to be realistic.

As Gabrielle gets herself into one bad situation after another, each stumbling block is original and unpredictable. When she tries to end war, Ares loses his powers. When she calls upon the woman who owns Xena's whip, trying to bring Xena back to them, Minya appears (recall that Gabrielle had sold the whip to Minya for a frying pan in "A Day in the Life"). Joxer accidentally writes a limerick on the scrolls, causing three dancing, giggling, naked Gabrielles to appear.

One problematic scene is where Joxer sells his coveted scabbard to buy Gabrielle a necklace. After realizing he has just given up the only gift his father ever gave him, she grabs his nose, ties him up, yells at him, and refuses to allow him to help them out. Joxer didn't know the scrolls were in the scabbard, so couldn't she have been a little more forgiving? When's the Joxer/Gabrielle rift saga going to happen?

In the final scene, as Xena saves the day once again (where exactly had she been fishing?!), Ares actually seems to be *nice* to Gabrielle, behavior which, of course, is very fleeting. Joxer reports events like an ancient Howard Cosell, but the best line, when he and Ares are arguing over whether a creature is an octopus or a squid, is delivered by Ares: "I think I know a squid when I see one." This line is an inside joke about "The Lost Mariner," where Gabrielle is chewing on what is clearly an octopus, although everyone calls it squid.

As everything resolves itself in a very clever way, things seem to go back to normal. The only problem with this episode is when it aired. The next two episodes will take viewers on a roller coaster like this show has never seen, yet there is no sign here of any animosity between Xena and Gabrielle. Despite the timing, this was still an excellent episode. And now back to our regularly scheduled rift saga.

NITPICK: Ares' beard is at its all-time ugliest, and why doesn't he begin to smell, if Aphrodite does? Also, why does Gabrielle always chirp when she dances? (See "Hooves and Harlots"; "The Prodigal"; "Ulysses.")

OOPS: When the three naked Gabrielles first appear, it's clear they are three body doubles.

DISCLAIMER: "No naked Gabrielles were harmed during the production of this motion picture."

311 **Maternal Instincts**

ORIGINAL AIR DATE: January 26, 1998
WRITTEN BY: Chris Manheim
DIRECTED BY: Mark Beesley
GUEST CAST: Amy Morrison as Hope
David Taylor as Solan
Danielle Cormack as Ephiny
Jeff Boyd as Kaleipus
Hudson Leick as Callisto
Reece Rodewyk as Xenan
Chad Bennett as Sentry
Phil Adams as Centaur

Hope returns as a 10-year-old girl and when she frees Callisto, the two work together to try to destroy Xena once and for all.

After all the build-up, the rift has finally occurred, but once again, what makes the writing so exceptional is that both sides of the issue are made clear, and it's difficult to choose one side over the other. As Xena and Gabrielle return to the centaur village, Xena tells Gabrielle that it's been "one year, two months, and twelve days" since she's seen Solan, evoking genuine sympathy from Gabrielle. Why doesn't Xena realize that perhaps Gabrielle, too, is missing her child? When it comes to Hope, the aspect that is most disturbing is Xena's lack of understanding of what Gabrielle has actually gone through. Leaving your child to be raised by someone else is one thing; getting rid of it is something completely different.

Gabrielle confides in Ephiny, but not fully. She lets Ephiny think the baby died in its sleep, rather than be completely honest with her. Ephiny is probably Gabrielle's closest friend besides Xena, and when she stands up for Gabrielle later, we realize just how good a friend she really is. Why then, doesn't Gabrielle open up to her?

Hope is a strange-looking little girl, but the actress is wonderful. Gabrielle soon discovers that the girl is Hope, but it seems as if Xena has had her suspicions from the outset. After Hope tells everyone that Callisto is going to kill Solan, Gabrielle sits Hope in a chair and stands next to her. Xena looks at them and squints her eyes for a moment, as if she's realized that they do look alike.

Unfortunately, Gabrielle's guilt at having left Hope alone outweighs her reason and she never stops to consider that Hope could be evil. Even after Kaleipus dies, Gabrielle understandingly clings to the fact that Callisto could have done it. When Xena realizes that the child is Hope, she doesn't stop to consider Gabrielle's feelings. Instead she immediately begins planning how she can kill her. Gabrielle screams at Xena with such anger and vehemence in this scene that it seems like she's starting to equate Xena and Callisto in her mind.

Callisto the goddess is different from Callisto the angry warrioress that we've loved to hate for the last two seasons. Now she's immortal, and although in "Callisto" she seemed to long for death, she can no longer have that gift. Callisto is still callous and vengeful, and still speaks in her sing-song voice, but now she's ordered around by Hope. Callisto has never been ordered around, so this new element does alter her characterization (watching her throw Xena through the air with a flick of her finger was still a lot of fun, though).

This episode tested the dramatic range of all involved (and Lucy and Reneé's performances are topped only by what they achieve in "The Bitter Suite"). When Hope kills Solan, Xena's reduced to a meek, guilt-ridden mother rocking her son, while at the same time her anger is rising and she growls at Gabrielle like a demon possessed. The look on Gabrielle's face as she realizes what has happened moves among guilt, denial, and absolute horror. Hudson, too, is wonderful in this scene as she closes her eyes, listening to Xena's screams as if they were a beautiful aria. However, her face promptly falls, as she realizes her goal has been attained, but nothing has changed for her. All these years she has been hating Xena and working on destroying her, and now that her wishes have been fulfilled, Callisto no longer has her hatred which has kept her afloat for so long. As she and Xena face off in the cave, Xena somehow triumphs over her in combat. We know that Callisto could wave one hand and send Xena flying, so she's obviously given up — she's as destroyed as everyone else.

Meanwhile, Gabrielle quietly commits her second kill by poisoning Hope, and then almost attempts suicide. This scene is devastating because it is the portrait of a broken spirit. This season the writers have forced Gabrielle to accompany Xena to a foreign land where she is tricked into committing her first kill and subsequently loses her blood innocence; be violated on an altar and impregnated with a child of evil; give birth to that child while people are coming to kill it; have her best friend try to kill it and then abandon it in the hope that it might be saved; suffer a horrible guilt when she betrays Xena in Chin by thinking that she was helping her; find her child and have to hide its identity from people; suffer Xena's wrath when the child apparently kills Solan; kill that child; and give up. Gabrielle has been battered and bruised emotionally up to this point, and when Xena refuses her apology at the very end, we are left wondering if Gabrielle will ever regain her happiness and self-assurance. As Xena finds Gabrielle kneeling over her dead daughter, her eyes are cold and emotionless. She feels no sympathy for Gabrielle, only fury because Gabrielle had lied to her. The only nagging question is, is Hope really dead? Can pure evil be killed by poison? Hope did say to Callisto that the only way to hurt everyone is by hurting their children, and she is one of those children. We'll later find out that Hope isn't dead when she reappears on a *H:TLJ* episode.

This episode was a devastating one, altering all the major characters. Gabrielle, Xena, and Callisto have all given up in one way or another, leaving the viewer to hope that "The Bitter Suite" will somehow rectify this mess. This episode was beautifully acted, and cleverly written.

YAXI: Kaleipus is played by a different actor.

NITPICK: Why are there columns holding up the cave? Also, it it just me or is Xenan aging almost as quickly as Hope?

OOPS: When Gabrielle thinks Hope is an intruder, watch the camera angles as she holds up her staff. When we see Gabrielle from the front, her right elbow is up and the fuzzy white thing on her staff is behind her. Filmed from her back, her right arm is down and the white thing is on the front of the staff. Also, as Kaleipus dies, we can see that under the eye patch, his eye is fine.

DISCLAIMER: "Xena and Gabrielle's relationship was harmed during the production of this motion picture."

312 The Bitter Suite

ORIGINAL AIR DATE: February 2, 1998
WRITTEN BY: Steven L. Sears & Chris Manheim
LYRICS BY: Joseph LoDuca, Pamela Phillips Oland & Dennis Spiegel
DIRECTED BY: Oley Sassone
GUEST CAST: Ted Raimi as Joxer
Kevin Smith as Ares
Hudson Leick as Callisto
David Taylor as Solan
Daniel Sing as Ming T'ien
Marton Csokas as Khrafstar
Karl Urban as Caesar
Danielle Cormack as Ephiny
Willa O'Neill as Lila

Xena tries to kill Gabrielle and the hatred between the two whisks them off to Illusia, where they must try to resolve their differences through music.

What's that I hear? Handel's *Hallelujah Chorus*? Yes, the rift saga is over! "The Bitter Suite" is a lavish musical, featuring new sets, bright colors, song and dance, and wonderful direction. It'll be a long time before they can top this one.

However. . . the show opens with the single most horrific scene on *X:WP*. Ever. In my opinion, they've gone too far. The rift had reached its climax in the previous episode when Xena refused Gabrielle's apology and blamed her for Solan's death. But now, as if it wasn't enough to break Gabrielle's spirit, they must break her body, too. I won't go into gruesome detail about what happens, because the scene must be watched to be believed (and even then you might not believe your eyes). Suffice it to say it's a good thing to know that Argo would have nothing to do with the situation: notice how Xena ties Gabrielle to another horse. As Gabrielle escapes certain death at Xena's hands, we see a character who is more battered and bruised than any other character has ever been on this show. As she stands up in slow

Music composer Joseph LoDuca at Detroit, 1997

JENNIFER HALE

motion and turns a hate-filled eye to Xena, we realize that even Gabrielle can be pushed to murder, and she is. She pushes Xena over the falls and, in essence, kills both of them.

Apparently, Gabrielle and Xena are important not only to us, but to the gods as well. The Fates give them a second chance by allowing them to attempt to work out their differences in Illusia. We eventually discover that this world is created by Solan, who perhaps appealed to the Fates to give Xena and Gabrielle another chance. The first character Xena meets is Callisto, who sports a Dutch boy haircut and is singing! With the words, "Don't use words, sing a song / This is Illusia!" the musical begins. Callisto is dressed exactly like *The Fool* in the Rider-Waite Tarot deck, and as we move through the rest of the show, we realize that most of the outfits are based on various Tarot cards. The Fool is the most important card in a Tarot deck, for he moves through the other cards, making discoveries as he goes. The Fool card is sometimes the first card in the deck, sometimes the last, but corresponds with the first letter of the Hebrew alphabet, Aleph (there are 22 cards in the Tarot major arcana, and 22 Hebrew letters). Thus, as Xena floats through the water, we hear Callisto say, "Aleph am I," and she quotes verses from Paul Foster Case's *The Book of Tokens*. She is also accompanied by the white dog that appears on the card. What follows is an oversimplification of the Tarot, and I encourage anyone who was fascinated by this episode to read more about the Tarot and to look at a deck of cards with the Rider-Waite illustrations.

Each card of the Tarot deck has a divinatory meaning and a reversed meaning, and you determine which to use by how the card lands before you. The Fool represents the person who must move through life and make very important choices. He must make the right choice because he has the ability to accomplish great things. His reversed meaning, however, indicates that he will make the wrong choice. It is apt that Callisto should be the Fool, because she reminds Xena of the bad choices she has made in the past, and allows her to change her ways. Xena, in the long blue dress and sitting on the throne, is *The High Priestess*. Where The Fool represents potential, The High Priestess has the power to make things happen. If the card is turned over during a woman's reading, it can indicate that she can discover values in a friend, which is what will happen to Xena by the end of the episode. The wheel of the Fates that Callisto shows Xena is actually a combination of the *Wheel of Fortune* card and *The World* card. The Wheel of Fortune can raise peasants up and bring kings down. The card itself consists of the wheel in the centre, the jackal-headed soldier and serpent on either sides and the sphinx on top of the wheel. Its divinatory meaning prophesies success, while its reversed meaning indicates setbacks. Xena will encounter both of these in Illusia. The World card features a lion in the bottom righthand corner, a bull in the lower lefthand corner, an eagle in the top righthand corner, and a fair-haired individual in the top lefthand corner. It could mean attainment of one's goals, or it could indicate that a fear or other attachment will prevent the person from accomplishing their aims. The writers have used the cards brilliantly, and the sets and costumes are amazing in these scenes.

Gabrielle is pulled out of the water by Joxer, who hangs from a tree in the form of *The Hanged Man*. The Hanged Man indicates to the holder of the card that he/she must now take destiny into their own hands. Its divinatory meaning indicates wisdom and prophetic power, two qualities that Gabrielle has, and its reversed meaning connotes arrogance and someone who is ego-driven, attributes of, uh, Joxer. Joxer takes her to Poteidaia, where she is dressed like *The Empress*, a character usually surrounded by images from nature. The card can represent maternal or creative fertility, or it can mean destruction and psychological problems. Thus, Gabrielle's two choices are set up as well as Xena's. The Empress represents the power of activity that results from a suggestion: thus she listens to the other villagers and takes action against Xena.

Ares is dressed as *The Emperor*, whose forces are contrasted with those of The Empress (pretty clever writers, I must say!). The Emperor does not hold a sword in his hand, but he represents warlike power, a controlled sexual drive, and authority: the perfect description of Ares. His reversed meaning, however, is a loss of control and immaturity, attributes Ares has displayed in the past. He and Xena ride in *The Chariot*, which, like the card, is pulled by two sphinxes. It would appear the writers want us to have the reversed meaning here, which is an unethical victory, while its divinatory meaning indicates triumph and success. When Gabrielle is killed by Xena, Joxer enters as *The Hermit*. Here, too, the reversed meaning persists, as The Hermit can mean immaturity and foolish vices. His entrance indicates to Xena her refusal to listen to wisdom, another meaning of the card. Its divinatory meaning, that a journey is required to attain enlightenment, applies to both her and Gabrielle. Callisto now re-enters as *Justice*, who indicates to the holder of the card that they must use mercy and understanding with others, and could connote that justice will be had by all.

Xena and Gabrielle journey to *The Tower*, a dark card that means change or catastrophe, the perfect metaphor for the entire rift saga to this point. If one turns over The Tower card, they must change their ways to achieve enlightenment, which will occur after a disruption. When we first see The Tower in the show, there is a flash of lightning, which also appears on the card. The lightning reinforces purity and goodness and destroys what is evil. It was necessary for Gabrielle and Xena to go to The Tower before they could confront their pasts in Dahak's temple. What happens in the temple is closest to *The Judgement* card, where the angel Gabriel (how convenient!) blows a trumpet and releases people from their coffins. The card signifies a new awakening and rebirth, and here Xena and Gabrielle are able to conquer their hatred by traveling back in time to the places where hatred became a powerful part of their lives. The imagery in this scene, with Xena on the cross and Gabrielle on the altar, is spectacular. It is interesting to note that the picture on *The Devil* card looks remarkably like The Deliverer.

The next scene, with Solan appearing in a glowing garden, is most likely *The Sun* card. A naked fair-haired child rides a horse in a garden with the sun shining in the background, and he represents a spiritual triumph over material goods. He signifies success (the renewed friendship between Xena and Gabrielle) and happy reunions (Xena and Solan) and The Sun also corresponds with the word "Sol" in Solan, which was discussed in "Orphan of War." The final scene, with Xena and Gabrielle playing in the water à la *From Here To Eternity*, resembles *The Lovers* card, where a man and a woman stand near one another, signifying harmony in their relationship and love. The woman represents a combination of The High Priestess and The Empress, so if this scene was meant to imply The Lovers card, then the writers have taken the woman and split her in two, and removed the male from the equation. By using Tarot card imagery, the writers have indicated personal journeys for Xena and Gabrielle, where obstacles have been overcome and spiritual goals have been attained, and if we accept that the two women died when they fell over the cliff, they have been given a second chance at life through the gift of Solan.

The music in this episode is beautiful, and considering that none of these actors have appeared in a musical except for Lucy and Kevin, they all did a superb job. "Bitter Suite" was Kevin Smith's best work on this show yet, and the same can be said for both Lucy and Reneé. Even Joxer earns new respect as he races into the Amazon hut to save Gabrielle, and for the first time fights against a warrior without pausing to think of the consequences. Xena gets to tell Solan she loves him, and he calls her mother. And only now does Xena learn the true meaning of Lao Ma's words: by kneeling before Gabrielle, the one she thought she hated, she forces all of the pain and hatred out, and when she stops willing, Gabrielle reaches out and Ming Tien's hold over Xena is destroyed.

Although the first time I watched this I couldn't shake the opening image of Gabrielle being dragged by Xena, having listened closely to the words I believe the writers have succeeded in resolving the rift. Xena reaches out to Gabrielle and asks, "Forgive me my debt as only you could," and she's made an important observation. Gabrielle really does represent purity, and she can forgive Xena when no one else would. Although it is terrifying to think that Xena's dark side can still be pushed to such violence, this is the first time she has dropped to her knees begging for forgiveness of anyone. Sometimes it felt like they were going too far, but the conclusion to the rift was clever, inventive and satisfying (although, the effects of the rift will continue to linger in later episodes). Bravo!

YAXI: How did Xena get her whip back from Minya?

INTERESTING FACT: The singing voices for Reneé O'Connor and Hudson Leick were dubbed. Everyone else was actually singing. Also, when Gabrielle first enters Poteidaia, she is greeted by a villager played by Julie Moran from *Entertainment Tonight*, who was covering the making of the episode when she was asked to join in.

DISCLAIMER: "The musical genre was not harmed during the production of this motion picture. In fact, the Producers sincerely hope you were A-MUSE-D by this episode."

LIST OF WRITERS

WRITERS	EPISODES
Adam Armus & Nora Kay Foster	120: Ties That Bind
	204: Girls Just Wanna Have Fun
	216: For Him The Bell Tolls
	218: Blind Faith
	308: King of Assassins
	309: Warrior . . . Priestess . . . Tramp
Teleplay by Adam Armus & Nora Kay Foster	
Story by Josh Becker & Jack Perez	102: Chariots of War
Teleplay by Adam Armus & Nora Kay Foster	
Story by Babs Greyhosky, Adam Armus	
& Nora Kay Foster	109: Death in Chains
Teleplay by Adam Armus & Nora Kay Foster	
Story by Robert Sidney Mellette	210: The Xena Scrolls
Teleplay by Adam Armus & Nora Kay Foster	
Story by Roy Thomas & Janis Hendler	112: Beware Greeks Bearing Gifts
Hilary J. Bader	302: Been There, Done That
	310: The Quill Is Mightier . . .
Paul Robert Coyle	208: Ten Little Warlords
	214: A Necessary Evil
	217: The Execution
Peter Allan Fields	106: The Reckoning
	123: Death Mask
Alan Jay Glueckman	111: The Black Wolf
Brenda Lilly	115: Warrior . . . Princess
Chris Manheim	118: The Prodigal
	119: Altared States
	209: A Solstice Carol
	211: Here She Comes . . . Miss Amphipolis
	222: A Comedy of Eros
	311: Maternal Instincts
Teleplay by Chris Manheim	
Story by Chris Manheim & Steven L. Sears	202: Remember Nothing
Patricia Manney	124: Is There a Doctor in the House?
Teleplay by R.J. Stewart	
Story by Robert Tapert	101: Sins of the Past
Steven L. Sears	103: Dreamworker
	110: Hooves and Harlots
	117: The Royal Couple of Thieves
	121: The Greater Good
	201: Orphan of War
	207: Intimate Stranger
	220: The Price
	221: Lost Mariner
	303: The Dirty Half Dozen

Steven L. Sears & Chris Manheim
Teleplay by Steven L. Sears
Story by Chris Manheim, Steven L. Sears
    & R.J. Stewart
Julie Sherman
R.J. Stewart

304: The Deliverer
312: The Bitter Suite

213: The Quest
105: The Path Not Taken
107: The Titans
108: Prometheus
116: Mortal Beloved
122: Callisto
205: Return of Callisto
206: Warrior . . . Princess . . . Tramp
215: A Day in the Life
219: Ulysses
301: The Furies
305: Gabrielle's Hope

R.J. Stewart & Steven L. Sears

113: Athens City Academy of
        The Performing Bards
114: A Fistful of Dinars

Teleplay by R.J. Stewart & Steven L. Sears
Story by Robert Tapert
Teleplay by R.J. Stewart
Story by Robert Tapert & R.J. Stewart

Terence Winter

212: Destiny

306: The Debt
307: The Debt II
104: Cradle of Hope
203: The Giant Killer

LIST OF DIRECTORS

DIRECTOR	EPISODE
Jace Alexander	110: Hooves and Harlots
	113: Athens City Academy of The Performing Bards
Josh Becker	114: A Fistful of Dinars
	206: Warrior . . . Princess . . . Tramp
	216: For Him The Bell Tolls
	218: Blind Faith
Mark Beesley	214: A Necessary Evil
	311: Maternal Instincts
Eric Brevig	107: The Titans
John Cameron	117: A Royal Couple of Thieves
Bruce Campbell	308: King of Assassins
Harley Cokeliss	102: Chariots of War
Mario DiLeo	111: The Black Wolf
Robert Ginty	309: Warrior . . . Priestess . . . Tramp
Bruce Seth Green	103: Dreamworker
Charlie Haskell	210: The Xena Scrolls
Michael Hurst	215: A Day in the Life
Rick Jacobson	303: The Dirty Half Dozen
Gary Jones	121: The Greater Good
	203: The Giant Killer
	207: Intimate Stranger
John T. Kretchmer	118: The Prodigal
	209: A Solstice Carol
Doug Lefler	101: Sins of the Past
Michael Levine	104: Cradle of Hope
	115: Warrior . . . Princess
	119: Altared States
	213: The Quest
	219: Ulysses
Stewart Main	123: Death Mask
Garth Maxwell	116: Mortal Beloved
	217: The Execution
	221: Lost Mariner
Andrew Merrifield	302: Been There, Done That
	310: The Quill Is Mightier . . .
Stephen L. Posey	105: The Path Not Taken
	108: Prometheus
Marina Sargenti	211: Here She Comes . . . Miss Amphipolis
Oley Sassone	220: The Price
	304: The Deliverer
	306: The Debt
	307: The Debt II
	312: The Bitter Suite
T.J. Scott	112: Beware Greeks Bearing Gifts

344

D
I
R
E
C
T
O
R
S

TRIVIA ANSWERS

TRUE OR FALSE

1. False. The warlord Cortese attacked Xena's home.
2. True.
3. False. Hudson Leick's double appeared in "The Greater Good."
4. True.
5. False. M'Lila taught Xena pressure points.
6. False. Gabrielle named her daughter Hope.
7. True.
8. False. Meg calls Xena's chakram, "Shamrock."
9. True.
10. False. Xena's first encounter with a flying monster was in "Prometheus."
11. False. Gabrielle first rode Argo in "Sins of the Past."
12. True.
13. True.
14. False. Xena's descendant is Melinda "Mel" Pappas.
15. True.

THE CHARACTERS

1. Amphipolis
2. Jett
3. Poteidaia
4. Autolycus
5. Ephiny
6. Warlords
7. Gabrielle's younger sister
8. Lyceus
9. Elder brother
10. Cyrene and Atrius
11. Perdicus
12. To earn Gabrielle's love
13. Salmoneus
14. Warrior. Princess. Tramp
15. Tyldus
16. Aphrodite
17. Xenan

18. Ares
19. Argo
20. Callisto
21. Velasca
22. Cirra
23. Joxer. Callisto made her first appearance in "The Greater Good," although it wasn't Hudson.
24. Caesar, Julius Caesar
25. Bliss

EPISODE EVENTS

1. "The Reckoning"
2. "Surprise"
3. "The Warrior Princess"
4. "A Day in the Life"
5. "Death In Chains"
6. "Dreamworker"
7. "Sins of the Past"
8. "The Dirty Half Dozen"
9. "Unchained Heart"
10. "The Path Not Taken"
11. "Dreamworker"
12. "Cradle of Hope" and "Gabrielle's Hope"
13. "Been There, Done That" for Joxer and Gabrielle
14. "Ties That Bind," "The Debt II," and "A Day in the Life"
15. Gabrielle in "Altared States," on henbane and Xena in "The Furies," by the Furies
16. "The Black Wolf"
17. "Pathetic!" in "The Warrior Princess"
18. "Remember Nothing"
19. "Athens City Academy of The Performing Bards"
20. "The Deliverer"

LINES

1. "I've just cut off the flow of blood to your brain." — Xena
2. "A la la la la!" — Xena
3. "Life is an adventure to be explored, and without adventure, what's the point?" — Gabrielle
4. "Now I see why you ride the horse." — Ephiny
5. "Son of a bacchae!" — Xena
6. "I'm sorry sweetie, but that hurt me more than it hurt you." — Xena
7. "You can't hide from me, Gabrielle! You can't hide from a god!" — Velasca
8. "You don't want to make me mad, now do you?" — Xena
9. "You don't just kill me and walk away." — Callisto
10. "We played Truth or Dare, and she wasn't very good at it." — Callisto

11. "Gabrielle, you are a gift to me." — Xena
12. "Please don't let that light that shines out of her face go out. I couldn't stand the darkness that would follow." — Xena
13. "This world needs you. I need you." — Gabrielle
14. "Didn't your mother ever teach you it's rude to stare?" — Xena
15. "This is war! What did you expect, glamor?" — Xena
16. "Yeah, he got drunk and fell off the roof." — Meg
17. "I could always stop bathing and wear smelly wolf skin." — Xena
18. "Don't hate me because I'm beautiful." — Xena
19. "What do you know? You don't know anything!" — Xena
20. "Timing. We've got to work on timing." — Gabrielle

THE PEOPLE AND PLACES BEHIND XENA

1. New Xenaland
2. a soap opera actor on television
3. March 29
4. February 15
5. *Hercules* co-star Michael Hurst
6. Robert Tapert and John Schulian
7. *Hercules and the Amazon Women*
8. *Hercules and the Lost Kingdom*
9. *Darkman II*
10. Porky Pig
11. *Funny Business*
12. *Peach*
13. R.J. Stewart
14. T.J. Scott
15. Tyldus

SUBTEXT

1. "Return of Callisto"
2. "Altared States"
3. "A Day in the Life"
4. Lao Ma
5. Cleopatra

SOURCES

Barwick, Scott. "The Power of Myth." *TotalTV* Online. 5 May 1997.

Blincow, Neil. "Big Bonus for Xena." *New Zealand Woman's Weekly* 10 February 1997.

Bonko, Larry. "Hero Worship." *Virginian Pilot* 10 March 1997: E1.

Calkins, Laurel Brubaker. "Warrior Princess 'Xena's' Renee O'Connor returns to home and fans in Austin." *People Online* Online. 6 June 1997.

Carter, Carmen. "All Warrior Woman." *Dreamwatch* April 1997: 48–51.

Castro, Peter. "Double Jeopardy." *People Online* Online. 28 July 1997.

Davey, Garry. Personal interview. 27 November 1997.

Flaherty, Mike. "Xenaphilia." *Entertainment Weekly* 7 March 1997: 38–42.

Fraser, Antonia. *The Warrior Queens*. New York: Alfred A. Knopf, 1989.

Gaar, Gillian G. "50 Foot Queenie." *The Rocket* 12–26 March 1997.

___. "Lucy Lawless Interview." *Mr. Showbiz* Online. 28 January 1997.

Gayley, Charles Mills. *The Classic Myths in English Literature and Art*. New York: Blaisdell Publishing Co., 1963.

Geairns, Alex J. "Feminist Warrior." *Satellite Times*. March 1997.

Glanton, Eileen. "Lucy Lawless Lays Down the Law as 'Xena'." *Associated Press* 17 Sept. 1996.

Gonzalez, Desiree. "Renée O'Connor." *Sci-Fi Universe* September 1997: 48.

Good News Bible. Toronto: Canadian Bible Society, 1976.

Gordon, Stuart. *The Encyclopedia of Myths and Legends*. London: Headline Book Publishing, 1994.

Graham, Jefferson. "The fall and rise of Xena." *USA Today* 15 January 1997.

___. " 'Xena' makes Lawless an accidental action star." *USA Today* 15 February 1996: D3.

Grant, Michael and John Hazel. *Gods and Mortals in Classical Mythology*. Springfield, Massachusetts: G&C Merriam and Co., 1973.

Gray, Eden. *A Complete Guide to the Tarot* New York: Bantam, 1970.

"Grease's Warrior Princess Survives Another Close Call." *New York Times* 23 July 1997.

Grimal, Pierre. *The Dictionary of Classical Mythology*. Trans. A.R. Maxwell. Hyslop Oxford: Blackwell Publishers Ltd., 1996.

Hathorn, Richmond Y. *Greek Mythology*. Lebanon: American U of Beirut, 1977.

Holloway, Diane. "Xena's Sidekick Gabrielle Kicks Back at Threadgill's." *The Austin-American Statesman* 5 September 1996.

Hotier, Malaurie. "ROC Interview." *The Spur* 12 May 1997.

Johnson, Allan. "Xena Usually Has Fight on Her Hands." *Chicago Tribune* 11 March 1997: C1.

Kay, Laura Smith. "Lucy Lawless: Down Under on Top." *People Online* Online. 1 June 1997.

Knutzen, Eirik. "Followers Can't Fault TV Heroine." *NZ TV Guide* February 1997.

____. "Wild at Heart." *Cleo* January 1997.

Lao Tsu. *Tao Te Ching*. Trans. Gia-Fu Feng and Jane English. New York: Vintage, 1989.

Lawless, Lucy. Radio Interview. *National Radio NZ*. 25 April 1997.

Lawless, Lucy. Interview. *TV Hits* March 1997.

Littlefield, Kinney. "Lucy Lawless dishes the new season of 'Xena: Warrior Princess'." *Knight-Ridder* 3 October 1996.

Littleton, Cynthia. "Universal TV Renews Top Syndies." *Variety* 1–7 September 1997: 22.

Magnusson, Magnus. General Editor. *Larousse Biographical Dictionary*. New York: Larousse, 1994.

Matthews, Philip. "Badass, kickass gal." *Listener* 17 August 1996: 26–27.

McDaniel, Mike. "Houstonian revels as 'Xena' Sidekick." *The Houston Chronicle* 9 November 1995: 1.

Minkowitz, Donna. "Xena: She's Big, Tall, Strong and Popular." *Ms.* July/August 1996: 74–77.

Nazarro, Joe. "Hip or Myth?" *SFX* 19. December 1996.

____. "Story-Telling Sidekick." *Starburst* 228. August 1997.

____. "Warrior Sidekick." *Starlog* 236. March 1997.

____. "Xena: Warrior Princess." *Starlog* 237. April 1997.

"New Interview with Lucy!" *Jetthead's Xena Page* Online. 5 February 1997.

Norton, Peter B. et al, eds. *The New Encyclopedia Britannica*. Vol. 28. 15th ed. Chicago: Encyclopedia Britannica, Inc., 1995. 29 vols.

O'Connor, Reneé. Radio interview. KYSM Mankato, MN. 24 April 1997.

____. Interview with Toni Yates. *WB17 News at Ten* 6 October 1997.

Ostrow, Joanne. "It's no wonder this woman has become Xena: Worldwide Cult Queen." *Denver Post* 20 November 1996: 1.

Pringle, Gill. "My Mum's Got Real Girl Power." *TV Times Star Story* 12–18 July 1997.

Propps, Jacquie. "Interview with Sandra Wilson." *Whoosh!* 5. Online. February 1997.

Rensin, David. "Playboy's 20 Questions: Lucy Lawless."*Playboy* May 1997.

"ROC's AOL Chat." Online. 23 April 1997.

Rose, H.J. *A Handbook of Greek Mythology*. London: Methuen and Co., 1965.

Ruffell, Julie. "Brave Women Warriors of Greek Myth: An Amazon Roster." *Whoosh!* 12. Online. September 1997.

Schaefer, Stephen. " 'Xena' takes on Broadway." *USA Today* 26 August 1997.

Schneider, Karen S. "Xena-Phile." *People* 8 April 1996.

Schulz, Ronny. "10 Questions to Sandra Wilson." *Xenafan's Page* Online. 7 August 1997.

Shales, Tom. "Sweeps Showdown; Fan Fare for the Common Man: TV to Make You Laugh, Cry, or Tremble in Terror: 'The Rockford Files.' " *Washington Post* 14 May 1995.

Sharp, Keith. "Xena Close to Reality for Star." *TV Guide* 16 August 1996.

Smyntek, John. "Xena Gets It Off Her Chest." *Detroit Free Press* 8 May 1997.

Sowerby, Robin. *The Greeks: An Introduction to their Culture*. London and New York: Routledge, 1995.

"Stars of Television's #1 Action Shows 'Hercules Legendary Journeys' and 'Xena

Warrior Princess' Arrive Via Chariots Unveil Colossal Two-Story Sword." *PR Newswire* 10 July 1997.

Taborn, Kym Masera. "Mysteries Surrounding the Creation of the Syndicated Television Show, Xena: Warrior Princess." *Whoosh!* 3. Online. November 1996.

Wakefield, Rowan. "Lucy Was Always Popular with the Boys!" *NZ Woman's Weekly* October 1996.

Wedlan, Canadace A. "Guest Workout: Not Even a Horse Can Throw Xena For a Loop." *LA Times* 26 March 1997.

Weiner, Jennifer. "She's a Kick: Xena, Warrior Princess, is TV's toughest sister." *Knight-Ridder* 31 January 1996.

Werksman, Harry and Gabrielle Stanton. "The Universe Interview: Lucy Lawless." *Sci-Fi Universe* September 1997: 18–22.

"What a (Side)Kick! For Xena's Warrior Pal, Staying Out of Trouble Is Half the Battle." *Chicago Tribune* 28 May 1996: 7.

Wiltshire, Megan. "Lucy Flawless!" *Woman's Day (NZ)* February 1997.

Zekas, Rita. "To-dye-for Movie Roles and Klingons Unglued." *Toronto Star* 8 May 1994: E2.